The Life Course

Also by Stephen Hunt:

Anyone for Alpha? Evangelism in a Post Christian Society
Christian Millenarianism
Religion in Western Society
Alternative Religion: A Sociological Introduction

The Life Course

A Sociological Introduction

Stephen Hunt

First published 2005 by
PALGRAVE MACMILLAN
Houndmills, Basingstoke, Hampshire RG21 6XS and
175 Fifth Avenue, New York, N.Y. 10010
Companies and representatives throughout the world.

PALGRAVE MACMILLAN is the global academic imprint of the Palgrave
Macmillan division of St. Martin's Press, LLC and of Palgrave Macmillan Ltd.
Macmillan® is a registered trademark in the United States, United Kingdom
and other countries. Palgrave is a registered trademark in the European
Union and other countries.

ISBN-13: 978 1–4039–1469–9 hardback
ISBN-10: 1–4039–1469–9 hardback
ISBN-13: 978 1–4039–1470–5 paperback
ISBN-10: 1–4039–1470–2 paperback

This book is printed on paper suitable for recycling and made from fully
managed and sustained forest sources.

A catalogue record for this book is available from the British Library.

A catalog record for this book is available from the Library of Congress.

Library of Congress Catalog Card Number: 2004051404

10 9 8 7 6 5 4
14 13 12 11 10 09 08 07

Printed in China

Contents

Acknowledgements

The author and publishers wish to thank the following for granting permission to reproduce copyright material:

Age Concern for the inclusion of material in Table 9.1 (Age Concern, 1998).

The controller of Her Majesty's Stationery Office, for Crown Copyright material.

Every effort has been made to trace all the copyright-holders, but if any have been inadvertently overlooked the publishers will be pleased to make the necessary arrangements at the first opportunity.

Introduction

Today, specialized sociological textbooks abound in some number. It is perhaps all the more surprizing then, that at a time when the contemporary life course is increasingly researched and theorized, and accordingly taught widely in institutions of higher education and as part of the training of the 'caring professions', that sociological volumes on the topic are few and far between. This book seeks to rectify this discrepancy by 'filling the gap' and in doing so has a number of broad objectives. These objectives will inform the discussion and analysis throughout the various chapters to come in, I hope, an informative and accessible way, but one which also does justice to recent research across a number of themes broadly related to the subject of the life course.

Another paramount reason for producing a book on the life course is to develop a particular orientation and approach that is concerned with what is a renewed and indeed growing interest within sociology – experiences of human life from its beginning to end, at least within contemporary Western societies. Hence, the volume overviews life course changes and continuities at the commencement of the twenty-first century through an analysis which is both topical and relevant, alongside an appraisal of developing theoretical frameworks.

What amounts to a fresh interest in the life course over recent years is not easy to account for. Perhaps the most obvious explanation, however, is a particularly notable development: the repercussions of an increasing life span which, in turn, would seem to impact so many other areas of social life. The twentieth century witnessed a remarkable proliferation in life expectancy. Scarcely half of the 20-year olds living in 1900 could have expected to live to 65 years of age; women born at this time, on average, lived only for approximately 48 years, while the life expectancy of men was around two years fewer. By contrast, in the UK most women born in the mid-1990s can look forward to an average of 79 years of life; and men to just over 74 years (*Social Trends* 1997, 122). This represents an increase in excess of 60 per cent over the last 100 years. Some scientists anticipate that within 40 years the average life span in the West will be in the region of 110 years. Another indication of increasing life longevity is that in 1951 there were only 271 centurions, while according to the 1991 UK census, 4400 people had reached their century. By the year 2030, there may well be 30,000 people living beyond their hundredth birthday.

1

There is some debate as to the underlying reasons behind this striking gain in life span, although broadly speaking they are undeniably related to improved environmental conditions and to a lesser extent (although it is not the sociological vogue to acknowledge it) medical advances which have virtually eliminated infectious diseases in contemporary Western societies. What is also beyond doubt are the consequences of a longer life span. One is that we may be forced to radically restructure the life course and reconsider the familiar 'stages' of life, raising such profound questions as what exactly will constitute 'old age'. Will it be 65, 75, or 85 years old?

At the same time as life expectancy increases, the age categories which once formed a primary basis for social order and stratification are clearly breaking down, with those such as childhood and youth, youth and adulthood, becoming confused. Moreover, some of these categories are increasingly shortened, others lengthened. Hence, we can raise such questions as, when does childhood end? When does mid-life begin? Is old age a meaningful construct in contemporary societies?

The recent sociological tendency has been to practically abandon concepts related to the 'stages' of life in favour of a social constructionist approach which is more concerned with discovering how such concepts as 'stages' have come to be put together in the first place. Nonetheless, it would probably be wrong to entirely discard these age categories, even if those like childhood and mid-life no longer comprehensively provide guides as to how we should behave and think. In short, they have lost their more deterministic qualities and provide only broad markers in life experiences and expectations. Perhaps they are better designated as 'phases' of life; lacking coherence, direction, and open to considerable negotiation and discontinuity. Some aspects of these 'phases' of life have changed, others have endured. Thus, both change and continuity will be explored in this volume in relation to the intricacies regarding the on-going debates about the life course in Western societies. These debates are of more than sociological interest, since they forge current political and moral discourse on the topics of the ageing population, sexualities, and the ethics surrounding some emergent technologies. It is such discourse which, if a generalization can be made, now informs the life course literally from (if not before) the cradle to the grave. Together then, sociological enquiry, political and moral discourse, and the very real changes in contemporary life, make a consideration of the life course not only relevant but imperative.

Yet, while the so-called 'stages' of life might be transformed, how we envisage and negotiate the years ahead may influence our reflexive thinking in the present. In short, what is unique about Western culture is not just individualism and individuality, but the way in which many people plan ahead and engage and negotiate their future years. In this sense the life course may have become more meaningful, more subjective, and exposed to biographical accounts and projection than ever before. At the same time, the life course now seems less predictable and determined, more subject to risk and discontinuity.

If such reflexive thinking and experience for quite a significant part of the population marks a profound shift in how the life course is appraised and comprehended, then this tilt has been accompanied by some notable socio-cultural transformations, particularly over the last few decades. These transformations have been rapid and far-reaching, and are largely due to a vast number of economic, technological, and cultural variables associated with what has come to be alternatively known as late- or postmodernity. The emergence of the so-called 'new' technologies, and the move to an economy of consumption rather than production – one accompanied by a distinct culture of choice, have all forged a fresh mode of social experience. It is an experience which is also synonymous with the ambiguous moralities which surround some of the key areas of life such as reproduction, sexualities, family life, and the medicalization of ageing and death.

A related observation is that those developing the theoretical perspectives now in vogue have clearly built upon the increasing distinction between the 'life-cycle' and the 'life course', the latter being the preferred operational framework. This shift in theoretical underpinnings in the sociological endeavour reflects some of the changes now observable in social life. More succinctly, it may be argued that to a large degree notions of the 'life-cycle' are now redundant outside of medical circles and make little sense in this changing world where, as we have tentatively noted above, the once assumed 'stages' of life such as 'childhood' and 'adulthood', and what they entailed for life chances, are no longer so 'fixed' and predictable.

Accompanying the broader concept of the life course are new sociological theories, largely forged to make sense of life in late- or postmodernity. These highlight the impact of globalization, consumerism and choice, identity and constructs of self, and the consequences of ever-advancing technologies. A consideration of all these hallmarks of contemporary society is given scope in the chapters to come, as are the developing sociological paradigms. Yet, it is probably true to say that sociological theory is now betwixt 'n' between. New theories have not quite been universally accepted, while the old are by no means entirely redundant. To be sure, the evolving theories are not just fads but mark earnest attempts to analyse important socio-cultural developments. There is still room, nonetheless, to apply conventional sociological theories. Many of these are concerned with such issues as structured social inequalities – class, gender, ethnicity and, of course, age – topics not yet made superfluous by the profound changes observable at the end of the twentieth century and the beginning of a new millennium.

If it can be claimed that contemporary societies are undergoing rapid transformation, what precisely may they be compared to? Although this is far from its principal aim, another concern of this book is to present a historical and cross-cultural approach to the life course since an understanding of its major characteristics today can only be fully grasped with a measure of comparison with non-Western societies – past and present. A comparative dimension permits an appreciation of how much of the life course is socially constructed in any given social context. In this respect there are clearly marked cultural similarities between societies, not only observable through the so-called 'stages' of life, but also the way that biological and psychological processes, and not least of all the process of ageing, are perceived. Just as importantly, are the differences in the life course to be found in contrasting types of society – a variation generated by economic, political, and cultural variables. By taking a comparative approach which straddles, to put it broadly, 'traditional', 'modern', and 'postmodern' societies, we may come to understand how radically different Western societies are from those gone before and others to be found in the world today. This is despite the significant globalizing forces which make the world a smaller place in that we may achieve a greater awareness (if not understanding) of the cultures of other societies.

Finally, this volume is concerned with current and possibly future 'trends', although such notions of 'trends' are now radically challenged by postmodern theorizing in particular – suggesting that little, be it economic or cultural, can be viewed as long term or predicted with any certainty. Nonetheless, there are observable important demographic developments, most notably the increasing size of those of retirement age compared to younger age categories. Profound consequences for the generations to come cannot be doubted. Later on in the twenty-first century there will be grave problems related to the dependency ratio. In short, there will be more and more dependents and fewer and fewer people of working age to economically support them. This is a dilemma that must be tackled by new social agendas, however unpopular they may prove to be. Sociology may be of help here. If sociology is a discipline that examines and accounts for social trends, then it has a predictive element. For instance, it can anticipate future developments that may aid government and welfare agencies in their policies regarding the elderly in the decades to come. This is sociology's practical side.

The difficulty is that sociology has a mixed track record in predicting the future. Sometimes its exponents have been impressively accurate and, at other times, disastrously wrong. With the onset of modernity, or in some cases when it was well under way, the early sociologists such as Herbert Spencer, Emile Durkheim, and Max Weber outlined, accounted for, and anticipated future possibilities. Not all the predictions came true. Perhaps in the present day, however, sociologists may be permitted to set down their excuses well in advance since forecasts are perhaps more difficult now than ever before.

Uncertainty and lack of predictability, so late- or postmodernist sociologists would maintain, are the hallmarks of the contemporary world. What is also lost, they frequently argue, is the declining faith in progress as an inevitable evolutionary process. Thus, the optimism of the founding fathers of the discipline appears to have receded, suggesting that any notion of 'progress' should be jettisoned. The postmodernists may or not be right. What is clearly evident, nonetheless, is *uncertainty* about what the future holds. Partly this uncertainty is associated with potential disasters, which might well occur: economic depression or environmental catastrophe remain strong possibilities. The world is one of risk and, as individuals, we face a future of uncertainty throughout the life course: the possibility of unemployment, family breakdown, and the relentless challenge of having to adapt to rapid technological transformations.

The unpredictability of the future is supplemented by the matter of choice. As never before, there are more and more choices offered to us and we are at greater liberty than ever to chart our way through the life course. Many of us not only prepare for tomorrow and next year but later on in life – as if we project ourselves into the future, anticipating opportunities and pitfalls. Nonetheless, much remains uncertain. The West is now increasingly characterized, to use Ulrich Beck's phase, as the 'risk society' (Beck 1992). Risks come in many forms and some cannot be anticipated. Planning for the future is a hazardous enterprize. The world is changing and changing rapidly. Social trends seem short term and cultural fads come and go with increasing regularity. There is not just 'fast food' but fast everything, from fast changing fashions, to music, to interior decor.

Discontinuity is also a fact of life for many individuals. It is economic developments that are largely, but not wholly, responsible for this. Few people believe that their job is guaranteed for life, while global recession can lead to large-scale unemployment. Indeed, globalization is perhaps the 'buzz' word. Because of advances in technology and communication human life must now be studied within a global perspective. The experiences of communities and the existence led by individuals have to be seen in the context of the world at large. Yet, much remains uncertain, and it is the uncertainty, which will make life in the twenty-first century so different.

If much indeed appears uncertain, it is also the case that we do not know whether anticipated social change will be for the better. There are good and bad aspects of the emerging social order. Presently, we may make only subjective judgments as to the merits of a world where long-established structures appear to be disintegrating. Such structures are not just those related to communities, the family, or systems of morality. They also include class, ethnicity, and gender. All have previously impacted on the life course. If they are disappearing then they are arguably being replaced by pluralism, cultural fragmentation, pick 'n' mix' lifestyles, and a society that is finely fragmented by people's ability to participate in the consumer society. At the same time, the decline of these social structures will have implications for our concept of 'self'. After all, it was class, gender, ethnicity, family, and community that once gave individuals, for better or for worse, a sense of belonging and identity. Now we are faced with the prospect of creating our own identity in a largely consumerist society, while at the same time finding it increasingly difficult to forge a sense of belonging.

Given all these above variables associated with the life course, some subject to change and others to continuity, a fresh look would seem to be warranted. The approach taken in this volume is largely sociological, but it is one also supplemented by a consideration of the political and moral debates surrounding some of the changes in the life course (and indeed is concerned with how these debates are constructed). This is not any easy task. Perhaps the most obvious difficulty is related to how the chapters could plausibly be organized. Given the flexibility and unpredictability associated with the 'phases' of life, it might be unjustifiable to use them as chapter headings. Yet, even developments within late- or postmodernity have not yet rendered them entirely invalid and they at least present starting points from which to begin a broad analysis. There also remains a certain logic in commencing with the beginning of life and ending with its close; from birth to death. Hence, the chapters loosely follow the phases of biological growth, while acutely aware that they are subject to social construction and elaboration. Indeed, the significance of social constructs, alongside other determinants of the life course, is the subject of the first two chapters that seek to explore theoretical frameworks. These frameworks are brought to bear on subsequent chapters related to infanthood, childhood, youth, adulthood, mid-life, and old age. Organizing the volume in this way has hopefully contributed to both its accessibility and relevance.

1

Theoretical Accounts of the Life Course

The Sociological Enterprise and the Life Course

It is evident today that the discipline of sociology finds itself in a state of flux. Undoubtedly, this is at least partly due to the rapidly changing nature of that which it seeks to describe and analyse – the human experience in a collective setting. Clearly, contemporary societies, whether the complex post-industrial societies of the West or the vast varieties of cultures which may be placed somewhat awkwardly under the rubric of 'industrializing', 'emerging economies', or 'Third World countries', are undergoing considerable transformations in a rising global order. The sociological endeavour, despite changing conceptualizations and contextualizations, continues its erstwhile project in attempting to comprehend the human experience in terms of the institutional context or, as frequently preferred in the case of late- or postmodernity, the 'processes' which forge the lives of individuals, and the life chances and opportunities of particular social constituencies.

These institutions or processes be they economic, technological, cultural, or political, continue to shape our lives in many different respects, and for all of our lives. Considering these changes in terms of the life course is an attractive one. There is so much about the life course that is indicative of the nature of contemporary society, at least within the Western setting. Once it would have been appealing to discuss the experiences of the life course, or the 'life-cycle' as once preferred, in terms of the impact of social institutions at particular stages of life. This was particularly so by way of those which appeared to be universal and enduring. The family seemed to be the most obvious institution in this respect. Whether through the nurturing or early socialization of the child or the institution of marriage and parenting that seemed to provide a marker of adult maturity and social responsibility for both genders, kinship structures were central. Much no longer holds however. The so-called 'decline' of the family and increasing rates of marital breakdown, coupled with the emergence of

7

variations in family life, typified by the single parent and reconstituted family, ensure that generalizations and predictions regarding experiences of the family during the life course are impossible or at least problematic.

The transformations of the family, to which we can add the rapid changes also evident in institutions such as those of education and the workplace, have also flagged up the relevance of a social constructionist approach as an essential part of the sociological enterprize. Above all, the emergence of the post-industrial society has reminded us that, sociologically speaking, nothing is inevitable and the once taken-for-granted social institutions or processes are by no means universal or enviable. There are patent and palpable implications here for the life course, suggesting that the key 'markers' of life may always have been subject to cultural variation, if not change.

Comparative sociological and anthropological works have long underlined the richness and variety in social life and the organization (a term itself perhaps now redundant) of the life course. Research, whether comparative or historical, proved that many of the experiences that we may encounter in life are imposed upon us by social convention. For instance, it is a typically romantic Western view that we should find a mate of the opposite sex, fall in love, marry, and have children. Marriage in some societies is, however, 'arranged'. In a number of Muslim countries, for instance, a young girl (not infrequently as young as eight years old) will be betrothed for a dowry and know well in advance whom it is she will marry. Through such marriages families of relatively equal wealth and status will come together to advance their common interests. Between these two poles, marriage arrangements are numerous alternatives where, to some degree or another, relatives will have a say on who marries whom. Human experience of mate-selection as with many other aspects of social life is, therefore, infinitely varied, even if some widespread patterns are clearly observable.

Recent sociological writings have pointed out that such conventions as marriage, once so central to the life course, are increasingly superfluous in the late- or postmodern age. The social compulsion to marry seems to have declined. It is now more a matter of choice and lifestyle preference. This exemplifies, at least in Western societies, how many of the once assumed certainties of life no longer seem so certain. There are an increasing number of alternatives to the conventional marriage: there exists the freedom to choose the single life, to cohabitate, and now the legal liberty to live in union with a member of the same sex.

Perhaps, above all, current research has shown how in late- or postmodernity the 'inevitability' of the so-called 'stages' of life, irrespective of their diversity, is increasingly challenged. In doing so, sociology verifies that contemporary society with its relativism, pluralism, and inherent reflexivity, points to the social construction of such 'stages', whether child-hood, youth, or old age. The latter provides a more than adequate exam-ple. In this regard sociological accounts of popular perceptions of ageing, such as that of Andrew Blakie, show that 'old age' has had varying conno-tations according to historical periods, and differs between cultures (Blakie 1999). Much is as true today as it ever was. The postmodern society, however, has broadened options for older people. This is not to suggest that other considerations, most notably, marginalization and medicaliza-tion, no longer help shape age classifications. Nonetheless, choice and lifestyles continue to break down the distinction between 'old age' and other phases of life.

Sociology has sought to understand the implications of recent socio-cultural change, not least of all in terms of the life course. Attempts to do so have not always subtracted from sociology's often negative reputation. This was one frequently earned by disagreements within the discipline and, particularly in the case of Western Europe, its radical and critical image. As in the case of rival disciplines, disagreements within sociology are reflected in competing theories and an often undisguised ideological discourse as to how the subject should be approached, what methods should be utilized and how, and subjective recommendations for social enhancement. Theoretical diversity had always stimulated debate. At the same time, however, diversity suggested a lack of rigour and focus. Today, sociology can perhaps be forgiven for its theoretical and analytical multiplic-ity. Social change, its speed, and trajectories, are ever more undermining sociological 'certainties' and long-cherished paradigms. This has proved to be so for the sociological account of the life course.

As is evident in the short discussion above, that changing theoretical perspectives need a measure of primary exploration in the context of the life course. In the first two chapters of this book we are largely concerned with developing some of the theoretical remits for a study of the life course, raising some key issues, and developing a broad framework by which we can achieve an understanding of both change and continuity. In Chapter 2 we will consider the importance of social differentiation and what can be broadly termed 'inequalities' in forging the life course and the degree to which they are relevant in late- or postmodernity. The impact of the vari-ables of social class, gender, ethnicity, and indeed age categories, now appear to be less certain than they once were. Nonetheless, they still con-tinue to inform sociological literature as well as government report find-ings in terms of 'hard facts'. They are not as yet, then, entirely redundant. However, late- or postmodernity has brought a challenge to the broad way in which life course studies have been approached. The central themes fre-quently considered in this respect will inform the rest of this chapter. Before overviewing some of the more recent theoretical developments it would nonetheless be pertinent to briefly explore a few of the common themes long associated with the life course noting, in particular, the continuities and changes which have led to a preference for a life course rather than life-cycle approach. Only then can contemporary theorizing be placed within its true context.

The Life-Cycle: Biological and Psychological Approaches

Biological Dimensions – Changing Perceptions

So far we have referred to the 'life-cycle' as if it is now a redundant concept. This needs substantiation. For many decades the life-cycle approach to human existence dominated sociological and anthropological thinking and grounded research studies. Much appeared to be associated with observations concerning biological and psychological processes. This was perhaps understandable. For human beings there are perhaps few things that are certain in this world. Some events are nonetheless fairly predictable. In this sense, the 'biological cycle' of life would seem to be an inevitable one. Human beings are living organisms with observable biological patterns which are dictated by their physiological constitution. There are inevitable, if uneven, biological processes which take the individual from infanthood into adult maturity and old age: growth and physical decline, and eventually death. All these are universal human experiences, unchanging processes which are shared with other animal species. Variations are, of course, to be discerned since historically speaking high rates of infant mortality have been common and living one's three score years and ten has proved to be by no means a forgone conclusion in many previous societies and for the majority of people in the Third World today. The ageing process can therefore be impacted, for good or for bad, by a range of social and environmental variables that interact with the range of biological factors responsible for differing rates of morbidity and mortality.

In simple terms, the 'life-cycle' can be reduced to a developmental model or models which outline the social and psychological change encountered as a person passes through the major 'stages' of life: childhood, adolescence, mid-life, old age, and eventually death. Much of the early literature on the subject seemed to reflect an underlying commonsense conviction which reduced behaviour and outlooks associated with these stages to the 'biological clock' in that ageing was seen as merely a biological process. Although focusing upon inevitable biological development as the principal bedrock to the life-cycle, these changes were, and frequently still are, associated with psychological repercussions.

In considering biological factors, there is the also the importance of the human reproductive system. In the case of females, there will be the commencement of menstruation, the years when a woman is fertile, and the time when her capacity to reproduce comes to an end. Yet even these biological 'stages' have long been subject to social construction. In Western society this is perhaps most evident through the medicalization of natural processes which has frequently framed them into so-called inevitable 'stages of life'. In many instances the feminist critique has identified this as a reflection of patriarchy – one which associates the end of the female reproductive capacity with the inevitable onslaught of menopause and all of its perceived accompanying ills.

Biological processes are also subject to attendant moralities and value appraisals and many would seem to accompany the different 'stages' of the life-cycle, particularly through adult maturity and restrictions related to sexualities. Another set of values may be linked to age-related behaviour. For example, society largely dictates how the young are expected to conduct themselves given that they have not yet reached adult maturity and the responsibilities that this is believed to entail.

In industrial society there may appear to be more confusion around a number of core moral values. Such change has frequently been engendered by the economic, technological, and cultural transformations of the society in which we live. Hence, it is possible to explain this moral hiatus in terms of 'classical' sociological theorizing to which the work of Emile Durkheim would seem to readily lend itself. According to Durkheim, the breakdown of communities and their moral cohesion, along with the speed of social change, rendered modernity particularly susceptible to moral confusion, an 'anomic' state that could be rectified once society 'settled down' (Durkheim 1970).

It may be argued that in the contemporary West, and particularly within a globalized order, culture is changing so rapidly that it is now increasingly difficult for individuals, and indeed collectives, to be sure of what their values are: what can be regarded as good or bad, desirable or undesirable norms of behaviour. For example, in Western societies – and this is evident in legislation regarding so-called 'permissive' issues such as the age of consent for young people – the boundaries as to what sexual behaviour is tolerable are increasingly being pushed back. Thus the age of consent for gay sexuality in many Western societies is 16 years old. Merely 40 years ago homosexuality in practically all Western societies was regarded a serious offence and moral digression punishable by a long prison sentence. Much has changed but debates over what is permissible continues. Public discourse surrounding the lowering of the age of consent, for both heterosexuals and gays, is frequently based on notions of 'respon-sibility'; whether young people can make informed choices given that they may not be sufficiently mature, physically, emotionally, and socially. Here, we may note that, since 'responsibility' is often assumed to be a mark of adulthood, the lowering of the age of consent may be interpreted as indi-cating the earlier onset of adulthood.

As far as technology is concerned, recent developments have proved to have considerable impact on many different aspects of life, including biological processes. This may suggest negative consequences as we have noted above through the impact of medicalization and this theme will be considered again in the chapters to come in this volume. On the 'plus' side medical science, along with a better diet (in many respects at least) and environmental conditions, has aided the lengthening of the life-span through new technologies of scientific advance so that a relatively long life is now practically guaranteed given that life expectancy is twice it was a century ago. Indeed, perhaps the most noteworthy aspect of adulthood in Western societies is that today people can look forward to living through several decades stretching right through to 'deep' old age, per-haps with the aid of a heart 'pace-maker' or 'spare-part' surgery. In pre-modern times, few could confront such a future with much confidence. Death through sickness and disease was far more common than it is at present, while women in particular were at greater risk because of the high rate of mortality at childbirth.

Psychological Dimensions

It was once common in sociology and anthropology to speak loosely of a psychological impact on the 'life-cycle'. Some anthropologist had seen a psychological dimension most clearly at work in the rites of passage of tribal societies. Psychologically speaking, such rituals were interpreted as expressing the ambivalent attitudes of adults towards the generation mak-ing the transition from the stages of childhood to adulthood. The members of the younger generation were emerging to some degree as status rivals to the older age cohorts. One day they would replace their elders in positions of authority and the relationship of dependence reversed as their parents aged. Such was Beidelman's explanation for the emergence of rites of pas-sage which often involve the humiliation, the infliction of pain upon, and not infrequently the mutilation of the initiates by their elders (Beidelman 1966). Initiation rituals could also be viewed as having educational func-tions based upon psychological manipulation. Initiates for adulthood may be taught to think and act as adults and to know what it is to take on an adult role in the community. Thus, the infliction of pain could be interpreted as a kind of shock tactic designed to induce a psychological disposition to behave in an adult way in the years ahead (Whiting et al. 1958).

Aspects of the rites of passage of pre-industrial cultures are just one of the psychological dimensions observable in the life-cycle approach. In Western society, however, psychological aspects may be more pronounced and explicit. Medical science, and a fair few sociologists, may still refer to the psychological upheaval of adolescence which can have a profound impact upon the behaviour of the young. Similarly, so-called 'mid-life' is often identified with a 'crisis' brought on by negative psychological responses to loosing the vigour of youth and which, in turn, exacerbate physiological changes, most notably among women. Then, it is frequently asserted that as individuals age they find it psychologically more difficult to adapt to change, in short, older people grow into a conservative frame of mind.

Understanding the dynamics of social constructionism allows us to discern a strong cultural component in all of these supposed psychological upheavals. It brings a recognition that society shapes our perception of human biology and its supposed psychological implications, say, the female reproductive system of pregnancy and childbirth. While young people pass through puberty and grow into adults, notions of 'youth' and 'adolescence' and their accompanying traumas are largely Western social constructs. As much can be said about 'mid-life' and the 'crisis' that is supposed to accompany it. Similarly, perceptions of the elderly are frequently forged by stereotypical images of inevitable mental and physical decline – images exemplified by various explicit or implicit expressions of discrimination against the elderly or what is more commonly known as 'ageism'.

Sociology and the Life-Cycle Approach

Until relatively recently (as we shall explore in detail below), notions of a life-cycle were practically synonymous with *modernity*. Its roots are however deeper since the life-cycle was frequently discussed within sociological frameworks by way of another increasingly redundant term, that of the 'traditional' society which is a loose, catch-all typology, one incorporating a vast range of societies; tribal to settled agricultural communities, to large-scale feudal orders.

Compared to 'modern' industrial societies, pre-industrial societies had a less complex and relatively undifferentiated 'cycle-of-life' and typically involved merely pre-adult and adult 'stages' – a simple distinction that endured over the generations. This basic differentiation was marked out by the near-universal phenomenon of rites of passage. Writings emerging from the Structural Functionalist school of sociology and anthropology had a noteworthy influence on the study of pre-industrial, tribal societies – one which accounted for such rites in social rather than psychological terms. Thus, Radcliffe-Browne (1939) focused on what he called the 'ritual prohibition' of rites of passage. Such prohibition centred around behaviour concerning things that must be avoided and subject to taboo and social boundaries, including people, places, objects, words, or names, at times of crucial life transformation and stages. For Radcliffe-Browne, these rituals emphasized social values and helped bind people together in a sense of community. Typical were rites surrounding marriage since the institution allowed social continuity and amplified social values. Other rites dealt with natural processes associated with danger. Thus, among the Andaman Islanders there was ritual avoidance surrounding childbirth. Here, at this precarious time, parents were forbidden to eat certain foods, while friends of the parents were prohibited from using the name of the parents.

Each stage of the life-cycle in pre-industrial societies seem to present characteristic problems and transitions that involve learning something new and unlearning familiar roles and routines. Anthropological studies of these societies, including such works of Gluckman (1963), Douglas (1966), and Van Gennep (1908), proved particularly influential in providing insights into a fairly structured life-cycle. They indicated how these rites of passage often related to biological changes and their social implications, as well as psychological adaptation to socially constructed institutions such as marriage. Religious significance and taboo status were frequently attached to these transitions especially when they connected to what amounted to a 'life crisis'. These 'crises' were precipitated by a significant individual and collective feeling of uncertainty that resulted from experiences like pregnancy and childbirth – events which required psychological and social adjustment. They have also been perceived as inherently dangerous as Van Gennep showed in his *The Rites of Passage* (1908), where rites were associated with boundaries, ambiguities, and anomalies – in other words, things which were at the margins of established categories, the transitions from one category to another, or things which did not quite fit into established classifications.

Anthropological studies of pre-modern, indigenous societies showed that in many of these communities there was no transitional youth stage. People progress directly from childhood to adulthood and this transition was usually marked by one form or another of rites of passage which celebrated this sudden and fundamental change of status. For example, when a child reached the age when s/he was ready to be recognized as an adult there was typically an initiation ceremony, after which they were 'reborn' as an 'adult'. In some circumstances this could have been a highly traumatic ordeal for the young person whose initiation varied from circumcision for males, to having their head shaved, to being temporarily excluded from the community. Much depends on the culture and tradition. For example, among the Mbuti people in North Zaire today boys around the age of 13 are put through 'Nkumbi', a ritual that symbolically represents the 'death' of the child. The boys are then 'reborn' socially as men, and thereafter expected to behave as adults. Such rites typically involve permanent marking of the body. These can appear quite brutal acts such as scarification or tattoos, or the more subtle registration of status including painted decoration, wearing jewellery, ear piercing, and tattoos.

Seemingly justifying a life-cycle approach to pre-industrial societies was the observation that for a good part of human so-called 'civilized' history clearly defined stages of life and age categories have proved to be an important form of social stratification or at least the basis of expected norms of behaviour. Works such as Eisenstadt's *From Generation to Generation* (1956) insisted that common to most societies are the different culturally defined expressions of how people of a particular age are supposed to behave. In the past at least, as a person grows older, s/he was expected to progress through a series of statuses, roles, and relationships according to particular cultural markers and perceptions of the biological changes which come with ageing. In pre-industrial or 'traditional' societies the fact that as people get older they pass through socially acknowledged status is usually of much greater structural significance than in the West today. This is because getting older in this kind of community environment is not just a question of securing certain basic legal rights, but with acquiring social prestige. A particularly crucial stage of status acquisition occurs when an individual enters social adulthood and is allowed to do things that only an adult is permitted to, such as marry or conduct warfare against neighbouring tribes.

In dealing with the relevance of age categories sociologists and anthropologists have developed specific terms such as *age group* or *age-set* which refer to a group of people differentiated from others according to the stage of life reached. The related term *age grade* is commonly used to describe age groups which are clearly and formally established, especially in relation to so-called 'tribal' societies that rigorously stratify people according to age. Within the concept of a life-cycle, the importance of age categories seemed central and indispensable. For example, male aborigines in Australia traditionally graduate through the age grades of the hunter, warrior, and eventually they become the elders of the tribe. Here, age is best conceptualized in terms of the life-cycle if we mean those stages through which all who survive a full life-span pass. Furthermore, age-sets can be seen as a form of stratification based on an ascribed status which allows no or only limited social mobility and which is essentially linked to stages of physical development. Such pre-industrial societies allocate status (and

sometimes wealth) not according to merit or achievement (as is supposedly the case in Western societies), but to one's age category.

In age-set societies, the change in status involved in getting older may
not have a legal foundation but is frequently institutionalized to such a
degree that it often constitutes the very basis of political organization. Age
represents a form of social structure which impacts practically every
aspect of life – stipulating what an individual can or cannot do. For
instance, in such societies, those males who are ritually initiated together
constitute an age set if they are of the same age – perhaps 13–18 years old –
and members of each set together pass through a series of age grades.
Different sets perform different political tasks. For example, a set of elders
will be largely responsible for internal political and legal matters and may
have a religious priestly role to perform.

Unlike Western societies, social structures and culture in pre-industrial
societies are usually static or change very slowly. The generations that pass
through the age categories will invariably be subject to similar experiences. This is far less the case in the contemporary West where the notion
of *age cohort* is more relevant. This contrast serves to highlight the fact that
traditional societies built on age are slow to change which, in turn, allows a
degree of predictability. One knows with assurance what age set one will
be in years to come and what this will entail by way of expected modes
of behaviour.

The importance of age-sets can be seen in the example of the black
Galla-speaking tribal peoples of North East Africa (the largest ethnic
grouping in the region). Males, in particular, traditionally progress
through the age-linked roles in life in an orderly and predictable way: as
bachelors, warriors, married family men, political leaders and judges, and
religious ritual officials. Age-sets are formalized into 'grades' – arranged
on five point cycles of eight years each. Sons are initiated into their generational set when their fathers are in the reigning grade, five stages and
40 years further on in the system. In seeing how their fathers behave, the
young are presented with the acquired model of behaviour when they
reach that age, while certain aspects of the life-cycle (such as marriage) for
the younger generation has to be initiated at the right time – sometimes in
the form of 'mass' weddings.

Life-Cycle Models

In sociological terms, there has never been a complete agreement on the
precise length and nature of the life-cycle in human society. Although the
sociological endeavour has identified patterns and processes common to
most societies, different and contrasting models of the life-cycle have been

constructed. Among the most well-known (but now often widely criticized) frameworks is the eight-stage model of the life-cycle presented by Erik Erikson (1963). It was one which epitomized much of the thinking about the life-cycle. Erikson's model was typical in that it was a developmental one which attempted to present the maturational relationship between the biological, chronological, psychological, and social aspects of human progress through the life-cycle as a fairly universal phenomenon. For Erikson, the basic biological processes are probably more or less similar in all human societies, although crucially the rate and quality of biological change is subject to wide individual variation in terms of both genetic and environmental variables which, in turn, are supplemented by social arrangements.

Erikson identified a central 'crisis' for the individual in every stage of the life-cycle. For instance, the period of adolescence he regarded as one such stage which brings its own 'crisis' as the child slowly becomes an adult. In doing so, adolescence engenders specific and vital social relationships and wider implications for the community, as well as demanding psychological personal adjustments. The most important aspect of Erikson's model was, nonetheless, the emphasis placed on the social context by way of significant relationships and institutions in which individual development occurs at a given stage. For example, in the first year of life the potential 'crisis' is whether the infant forges a bond of trust with its mother. In the next stage of life, the child must develop a level of self-control and obviously this is important in the wider process of socialization. Also, by way of example, as part of the crisis associated with the fifth stage of life, adolescence, the young person must establish a sense of individual and communal identity. These stages of life were, for Erikson, very general and allowed for significant cultural variations.

Erikson's model was always open to the charge of ethnocentricity since it seemed to venerate the alleged virtues of monogamy and the nuclear family which are Western values and institutions respectively, rather than truly universal social arrangements, while his assertions regarding the 'crisis' in early life made generalized assumptions about mother–infant bonding as a 'natural' arrangement. Another charge was that the model took for granted the completion of the life-cycle which at the time was the dominant view and largely reflected experiences in Western societies. In short, it might be thought that models such as Erikson's are more or less standard and constitute a supposedly universal historical framework. However, history indicates that such models were more applicable to developments of the life course largely synonymous with *modernity*.

In terms of culture, politics, and economics, modernity radically departed from pre-industrial or what was often abstractly referred to as 'traditional society'. Modernity, in the view of 'classical' sociology typified by Durkheim and Weber, suggested a radical contrast to the traditional order and implied the progressive economic and administrative rationalization and differentiation of the social world. The developments which began first in the West included the emergence of capitalism which was given generally to refer to a system of commodity production involving both a competitive products market and the commodification of labour power: processes which brought into being new social formations such as social class.

More broadly, 'modernization' denoted a reference to the stages of social development which were signified by the growth of science and technology, differentiation, and urbanization. Also characterizing modernity was the emergence of the nation state which ushered in new forms of social control and itself contributed to the industrialized society by educational and welfare reforms, and by extending the rights of its citizens (although in different countries to various degrees) through democratic processes and institutions. In this way the state, as well as the onset of the industrial-capitalist order, brought the growth of bureaucracies which were identified not only by, as Max Weber (1978) noted, certain 'internal' arrangements such as a pervading rationalism, hierarchy, and division of labour, but also by the regularized control of social relations of time and space – implementing a regularity and regimentation epitomized by the factory system.

These changes identified with modernity profoundly impacted life experiences and brought a restructuring of the life course in discernible and sometimes in less discernible ways. Changes were perceived as establishing what could be called the 'modern life-cycle' of childhood, youth, young and later adulthood, mid-life, and old age. Under the impact of industrialization and the demographic changes of the nineteenth century a gradual differentiation in age groups and a greater specialization in age-related functions began to emerge, although it was by no means complete by the end of the century. Many such age groups structured social roles and at least some of them came to be discerned as 'natural' – that of childhood and adolescence providing prime examples. This cycle seemed static as long as the processes which forged them remained relatively stable. Moreover, for Kohli this structuring of the life course of modernity through institutions and chronological age proved to be an effective form of social control. Educated in schools as children, career stages in the labour market and retirement – legitimated by deferred gratification – meant that individuals passed in an orderly and calculable way through life. Rather than individual life patterns being ascribed according to positions in family and community as in pre-industrial times, status and identity were increasingly achieved by successfully negotiating expectations of each stage of life (Kohli 1988).

We may be more precise in identifying the link between modernity and the life-cycle approach. In Western societies such models as that developed by Erikson which outlines the stages of childhood, school, work, marriage, retirement, and old age, are ones that are largely applicable only after the 1930s and became well-established as late as the 1970s for the bulk of the population. Erikson's model contrasted very markedly with life in the mid-eighteenth century. At that time some 60 per cent of the male population died between 25 and 65 years old. The child-bearing period for females lasted until about 40 years of age as a result of almost continuous pregnancies and childbirth. Working life began in childhood and continued throughout the adult years. Then, slowly the life-cycle, as often described in sociological models, truly emerged; first among the middle-classes at the end of the nineteenth century and eventually filtering down to the working-classes. Increased life-expectancy meant that the significance of the 'generations' grew as three family generations (children, parents, grandparents) coexisting at the same time became more established.

In the West more events also began to occur in the early years of the individual's development and new 'slots' in the life-cycle were created such as 'adolescence'. This had the effect of marking a reduction in the span over which life transitions took place and, up to fairly recently at least, brought a greater orderliness in the life course. In industrial society, adolescence emerged as a buffer between childhood and adulthood. Corresponding roughly to the teenage years, this is the stage of life when young people are expected to establish some independence and learn the responsibilities and specialized skills required for adult life.

The age categories firmly established in the mid-twentieth century have by no means been extinguished. One legacy of modernity is that, culturally speaking, we may still be inclined to see childhood, ideally at least, as a clear, distinct, and 'natural' stage of life, perhaps broadly as the first 12 years of life before puberty, free from the burdens of the adult world. In retrospect, this construct of childhood might however prove to be a short-lived one. Right up to the beginning of the twentieth century, in most Western countries, children were expected to work at a very early age and for long hours and in many other respects not regarded as significantly different from adults. Factory legislation and laws concerning the child's welfare and education became important in constructing a clear period that came to constitute childhood. The same economic and political changes also helped forge the categories of 'youth' or 'teenager'. They have few parallel in non-industrialized societies.

Three quarters of the way into the twentieth century, life-cycle models had developed into something of a finely tuned art. Some very elaborate models were contrived in order to outline developments in the contemporary Western world. One such model was that developed by Levinson et al. (1978) which depicted the life-span as a series of critical transitions (at least for a small sample of middle-class males) in some detail. Here, the period of childhood, adolescence, and adulthood were sub-divided into 'early' periods, stages of transition, and consolidation. For example, 'early adulthood' included early adult transition (12–22); entering the adult world (22–28); mature adult transition (28–33); and a 'settling down' period (33–40). In this model adulthood was viewed as that period where most of life's accomplishments typically began. For many people this meant leaving the family home, getting married, setting up their own home, moving house, becoming a parent, and maintaining a household and career.

This kind of model had parallels in common-sense life-cycle percep-tions held by the population at large. Even up to fairly recently the daily lives of people in Western societies were circumscribed by relatively clear age-related norms. Some distinctions were once fairly finely grained. Once it would have been expected that children aged five would act very differ-ently from those aged seven. It might have been thought that the age of 18 years was too young to marry, while it was envisaged that both males and females should be married by the age of 30. Empirical evidence of such cultural expectations were to be found in a study published in 1965 by Neugarten et al. in the USA which indicated a high percentage of adults who accepted certain age-related characteristics. The correlation for both men and women was high. For example, some 85 per cent of the popula-tion surveyed regarded a 'young man' or 'young woman' as someone between the age of 18 and 22; around the same per cent believed that the 'best age for a woman to marry' was between 19 and 24; 75 per cent that most men should be settled on a career between the age of 24 and 26; and just over 80 per cent maintained most people should become grandpar-ents. Other evidence of socially prescribed views of age norms are offered by Hockey and James who suggest that indications of chronological age was often more subtle in the twentieth century than ever before. For exam-ple, in the inter-war UK, age status was discernible by dress: young boys under 14 wore short trousers, while females of this age were not permitted to use make-up. In such ways 'children' were clearly separated from the adult world (Hockey and James 1993, 50).

Notions of a coherent series of 'transitions' particularly related to becoming a mature adult – marriage, retirement, and death – were fairly popular in sociological literature up until at least the 1970s and seemed to be applicable to a modern life-cycle approach. Sociological frameworks, however, appeared to become more intricate; allowing for complexities of various kinds. Much seemed exemplified by the work of Glasner and Strauss. Building on the idea of rites of passage, Glasner and Strauss pre-ferred the term 'life course', one which denoted a series of transitions from one social state to the next. Each status passage consisted of a negotiated process in which both the properties of the passage and the awareness of each participant would vary. Among the properties explored were those of desirability, inevitability, reversibility, whether or not the passage occurs alone, whether it is voluntary, the degree of control over the process, legitimation by others, centrality of importance of events for persons involved, and the duration of passage. Each passage had a 'trajectory' – a managed period featuring the chronological sequence of events and a sequence of shifts in self image in which the individual combines a number of roles to establish their own career paths or role career (Glanser and Strauss 1965, 1–13).

It was clear that at the end of the twentieth century the notion of a life-cycle became almost impossible to sustain, despite recognition of the complexities and variations involved in historical and cross-cultural analysis. Partly this was due to a greater acceptance that the models produced were biased towards experiences in Western societies and even then were increasingly less easy to conceptually and practically apply. Secondly, life-cycle models appeared to put far too much emphasis on age as a form of social stratification. Other social variables, especially in contemporary society, also had a considerable impact, forging different experiences and variation in the life-cycle. This included structured inequalities such as social class, ethnicity, and gender.

Next, in rejecting the life-cycle model sociologists began to display a greater acknowledgement that although each stage of life is linked to the biological process of ageing, the life course is largely a social construction and that earlier models were often forged by enculturated views of the world. For this reason, people in one society may experience a stage of life quite differently from another, or not at all. This acceptance allowed for a greater cross-cultural approach and an enhanced appreciation of the similarities and differences between societies. Finally, further differentiation was recognized in Western societies by the increasing chance of discontinuities in life and the complex variety of experiences of being an adult. In relationships there might be the possible experience of divorce, remarriage, or cohabitation. Changes in the labour market structure including redundancy, job retraining, and early retirement, similarly complicated the picture. This meant that transitions and status passages were not simply linear but became ever more characterized by synchronicity (the coincidence of events) and even reversibility (Du Bois-Reymond 1998). Given the evidence, then, the notion of life-cycle appeared increasingly redundant. In contrast, that of the 'life course' had the attraction of being more flexible, more workable. The term 'life course' does not, unlike that of 'life-cycle', assume a stable social system but one that is constantly changing. It recognized that in Western societies in particular, constant change and variation is to be expected. More widely, however, the term life course allowed for a greater historical and cross-cultural comparison, and this seemed important given the changing nature of contemporary society and, indeed, a changing global order.

The Life Course: Developing Approaches

There was always more to the radical transformation of sociological theorizing than the need to account for the life course in a period of social change. Important developments *within* the sociological discipline itself were also discernible. From the 1950s until the 1980s, according to Gielle and Elder, the life course approach arose out of the confluence of several major theoretical streams of research concerned with integrating schools emphasizing social structure on the one hand and individual agency on the other. The developing life course perspective was therefore one which sought to take into account *both* the 'social surroundings' of the individual and a dynamic approach which traced the stories of people's lives over time in an ever-changing society (Gielle and Elder 1998). The former was concerned with social relations either impacted by social institutions or the significance of small groups and face-to-face interaction. The latter – tracing people's life experiences – was closer to the life history tradition advanced by the Chicago school of sociology, including the utilization of the work of Herbert Mead 1931 on socialization and the growth of the self resulting from social interaction and internalization (Mead 1931).

The difficulty was in merging the two approaches. Gielle and Elder, nonetheless, identified various ways in which this could be attempted. One was Gielle's model of role and life course change as bidirectional. For example, societal values and institutions and informal groups transmit influences to a woman that affected her life pattern. The woman as a social actor may, in turn, conform to past standards or attempt to change norms, institutional rules, and social values related to her reproductive capacity. By adopting such an approach, along with comparing the timing and occurrence of retrospective life histories across different birth cohorts, Gielle discovered a clear shift in multiple roles over the generations (Gielle 1988).

Second, Gielle and Elder added to this dimension the importance of 'time and place'. Thus, the general and unique aspects of individual location impact personal experience and can thus be understood as being socially and culturally *patterned* in ways that carry through time (Gielle and Elder 1998, 9–10). Such an approach promised to bring a greater recognition that people's life experiences varied depending on when precisely in the history of that society they were born. Hence, a *cohort* is a category of people with common characteristics, usually their age. Age cohorts are likely to have been influenced by the same economic and cultural trends so that members typically display comparable attitudes and values and can claim similar experiences. The lives of women and men born early in the twentieth century, for instance, were framed by an economic depression and two world wars. Another example, pertinent today, is that younger people are entering adulthood during a period of economic uncertainty that has dampened the optimism that characterized, by way of contrast, the generation that came out of the 1960s.

This cohort affect, according to Gielle and Elder (1998, 9–12), was also likely to be influenced by other variables. First, 'linked social lives' (social integration with others through cultures and institutions) may show discontinuity and disruption through experiences in the world of the family, education, or work. Second, there was the matter of 'human agency' which denotes the 'actor's' attempt to fulfil goals such as being economically secure, seeking satisfaction, or avoiding pain. Third, there is the 'timing of lives' which involves a strategic adaptation to external events and the resources available to an individual. Hence, how and when a person accumulates or deploys his/her resources such as wealth or education, takes a job, or starts a family are instances of various possible strategies. To conclude, for Gielle and Elder the way in which all these elements come together is through the funnel of timing. Whatever a person's social location and cultural heritage, friendship and networks, or personal motivation, all come together and are experienced through the individual's adaptation to concrete situations and events.

Gielle and Elder (1998, 13–25) maintained that this integrated approach to the life course lent itself to various styles of research. First, historical demography through such means as family reconstruction, official records, and other evidence of the significant economic and political factors of the time could throw light upon the key demographic events which shaped everyday life. Second, the sociology of ageing moved from an interest in ageing as primarily concerned with the end of life, to show variations over time and place. For example, Uhlenberg-Mauve's article (1969), divulged evidence of life patterns of women before 1900 and, discovered that only a fraction ever lived to marry or have children. Third, the life history approach proved attractive from the early 1950s and was typified by Erikson's model mentioned above – one which focused on maturation and development. Of particular importance here was the impact of biological and psychological dimensions on 'identity formation'. Finally, sociological work could take the form of panel studies and longitudinal surveys. Such an approach had the potential to show the impact of social structure and human agency over a period of time. To this end survey data of age cohorts could be used.

The integrated approach advanced by Gielle and Elder would seem to produce a more precise picture of how the individual's life is mutually shaped by personal characteristics and social environment; by structure and agency. It was an approach which clearly had merit and many of the methods advanced continue to be constructively utilized. The problem, however, is that in the last decades of the twentieth century socio-cultural change had proved so rapid that new theoretical paradigms were needed to analyse society at large, and this included frameworks related to the life course. It was here that writings on late- or postmodernity began to prove increasingly significant.

Late- or Postmodernity

Although notions of 'modernity' permeated sociological writings for generations as a clear and unchanging typology, it could not be sustained across the broad discipline by the end of the twentieth century. It became abundantly clear that Western society was changing rapidly in terms of the economy, technology, and culture, and that all these have impacted on the life course. Thus, there has proved to be radical implications for how the study of the life course was approached and theorized.

Profound social and economic changes, some of which have been comparably as far-reaching as the arrival of the industrial order of the nineteenth century, have reshaped the individual's experiences of the life course. This subsequently raised questions, or at least brought reconsideration, of rather taken-for granted theories. In short, the theoretical frameworks no longer adequately fitted and even the term 'modernity' seemed to be an unsatisfactory one. New terminology began to arise and enjoy widespread use. Those of 'late' or 'high-modernity', 'post-industrial', or 'postmodernity' were not always precise but at least indicated that the present state of 'development' (again an increasingly uncertain term) was radically different from the initial emergence of modernity.

If 'modernity' was once a contested concept, then this is certainly so with that of postmodernity, although it undoubtedly implies a somewhat different view of social change and its implication for the life course. While it is possible to identify a number of important streams of social theory leading into the contemporary fascination with the postmodern, there is little agreement about the meaning of the related concepts involved. Hence, rather different approaches, or at least emphasis, may be observed in current theorizing.

Featherstone has explored the broad framework of postmodernity, along with other terms such as 'postmodernism' and 'postmodernization' in contemporary writings (Featherstone 1991, 195–214). 'Postmodernization' in much of the sociological literature, he suggests, implies a process with degrees of implementation, rather than a fully fledged social order or totality.

In one sense it is in the form of 'becoming', a socio-cultural order which has not fully arrived. Alternatively, in other usages it amounts to trends and identifiable processes and does not (although he acknowledges that there is disagreement) point to a new stage of society. Featherstone writes that if 'the modern' and 'the postmodern' are generic terms it is immediately apparent that the prefix 'post' signifies that which comes after, a break or rupture with the modern defined in counter-distinction to it (Featherstone 1991, 197). Yet, he argues, the term 'postmodernism' is more strongly based on a negation of the modern, a perceived, abandonment with or shift away from the definitive features of modernity. This would make the postmodern a relatively ill-defined term as contemporary society is only on the threshold of the alleged shift, rather than planted firmly in it as an economic-cultural phenomenon.

Featherstone recognizes that in most of the sociological literature there is the inherent assumption that postmodernity constitutes an epochal transformation or break from modernity involving the emergence of a new social totality with its own distinct organizing principles. For many commentators the principal debate is, however, whether that new epoch has yet arrived. At the same time there are less radical interpretations. For instance, David Lyon states that the advent of postmodernity should not be understood to imply that modernity has somehow ground to a halt. Rather, postmodernity is a kind of interim situation where some of the characteristics of modernity have been inflated to such an extent that it becomes scarcely recognizable. At the same time, Lyon insists that what exactly the new situation amounts to, or even whether it can become 'settled', is unclear (Lyon 2000, 7).

For Lyon, the 'inflated characteristics of modernity' which give rise to postmodern premonitions, relate above all to communication and information technologies (CITs) and the shift towards consumerism. Both are bound up with the restructuring of capitalism that has been underway for at least the last quarter of a century. This is not to suggest parallel transformations are not observable. Certainly, there are many features of postmodernity which include the reorganization of cities, the deregulation of financial markets and public utilities, the bypassing of nation-state power, global travel and tourism and, importantly, experimentation with traditional life courses. Nonetheless, the preponderance of writings on postmodernity places an emphasis on the economic and technological changes which have profoundly impacted the cultural sphere.

To be sure, the post-industrialized society has become transformed by the development of sophisticated technologies. These have impacted in different ways. The postmodern form of production would appear to be virtually synonymous with post-Fordism, the production of goods for niche-marketing – a development only allowed by sophisticated technologies. At the same time, emerging new technologies have radically changed the nature of health care and brought controversies related to such areas as human reproduction. For the postmodernists, however, the greatest impact of new technology is frequently said to be in the sphere of culture, especially those related to mass communication.

Baudrillard, for one, stresses new forms of technology and information as being central to a shift from a productive to reproductive social order in which simulations and models increasingly constitute the world so that the distinction between the real and appearance become erased. For Baudrillard, with the spread of a modern mass technology of communications, it is not only a great expansion of services and a leisure industry that is discernible, but a growing simulation of reality. In short, the implosion of 'signs' eventually undermines our sense of reality (Baudrillard 1983). The result is that, in our media-dominated world, the concept of meaning itself (which depends on stable boundaries, fixed structures, and shared consensus) dissolves. The media reconstructs an image of reality, which not only reacts with it, but attempts to re-establish an imaginary and nostalgic world.

Another contribution is that of Castell who links technology more clearly with economic developments. In essence, he sees the emerging postmodern order resting upon the dual pillars of consumerism and information technologies (Castells 1989). For Castells, the proliferation of such technology and new forms of media in the 'information age' accentuates the power of the image which, in turn, enhances the cultural significance of consumption and lifestyles.

While such developments as the emergence of the information media serve to overlap the link between technology and economics, Bauman focuses more on the latter and the tilt towards consumer capitalism. The developing economic system is not just about consumption per se but a cultural transformation that emphasizes choice (Bauman 1992). Consumer choice has, in turn, become the criteria for much more than shopping. The skills acquired for consumer choice are called upon in different spheres of life including education, health, and the family. The slogan of 'free to choose' is relevant in so many areas and in this respect market culture displaces citizenship with consumerism. There are many important implications here and, as we shall see in the chapters to come, the cultural notion of 'choice' has also impacted the life course in many important respects, as indeed have changes in technology.

Postmodernity can also be associated with other aspects of cultural change. Thus, Lyotard argues that post-industrial society and postmodern culture began to develop in the mid-twentieth century, although the rate of development and the stage reached varies between and within countries. These transformations are essentially related to technology, science, and a number of distinct social developments, but most importantly they are connected with changes in language and meta-narratives. In short, simple, and singular ways of seeing the world, Lyotard talks about the postmodern society, or postmodern age, which is premised on the move to a post-industrial order. His specific interest is in the repercussions of the 'computerization of society' that has brought a restructuring of knowledge that erodes traditional forms and brings the loss of meaning (Lyotard 1984).

Theories of postmodernity, such as that of Lyotard, hold that today the decline in mega-narratives includes a universal disenchantment with the notion of 'progress'. There is less confidence about what the future holds and, in fact, that life chances are getting worse, not better. Second, there is the growing belief that science no longer holds all the answers to human problems. The defining trait of the modern era was a scientific outlook and a confident belief that technology would make life better. It is at least implicit in a good number of postmodernist writings which suggest contemporary society has created more problems than it has solved. They also observe there is a widespread criticism of the very foundation of science, above all, a questioning that objective reality and truth exist in any meaningful sense. In short, a culture has developed in which all 'truths' are relative, as are all values and systems of morality. It is not so much a matter of risk but the uncertainty and lack of guidelines that postmodernity brings in terms of once-cherished moralities that informed the life course; for example, the notion that sex should be limited to marriage – a value construct enforced by the cultural and social power of the Christian church – is increasingly hard to sustain in the relativistic post-Christian society.

Late Industrial Society

It is undoubtedly indicative of contemporary sociology that other commentators use a number of alternative terms to describe the current nature of contemporary society. For instance, Anthony Giddens, uses a variety of terms such as 'high' or 'reflexive' modernity (Giddens 1991). Yet, he is discussing phenomena which might equally well be considered as 'postmodern' and suggest an outgrowth of those features that forged modernity. It is the key characteristics of late modernity which have shaped our expectations and perceptions of life and the life course. While writings such as that of Giddens may appear to be a less radical version of postmodernist theorizing, there is a variance with postmodernist works in the discussion of the relevance of the advancement of science, rationalism, instrumentalism and, to some extent at least, the significance and trajectories of individualism.

Many of the theories related to late modernity seem to have notions of the life course as a central concern and this is largely derived from a recognition that individualism as a cultural value and general orientation has come to the fore. Individualism, however, merges with other recent developments. Giddens points out that today we are practically guaranteed of living our life-span. This allows us as individuals to predict the future, calculate risks, and plan ahead with a view to future possibilities and with alternatives in mind. We can negotiate optional courses of action through making present decisions from a number of choices presented to us. Thus, we chart our way through the life course with a great deal of assurance that we will reach old age. The increasing tendency for people to have a pension scheme and prepare for retirement is indicative of this. Underlying such a change is the fact that in the Western world we are able to control various aspects of the environment through scientific progress including the overcoming of some of the 'killer diseases' of the past which frequently limited life-expectancy.

Giddens provides a detailed account of what he calls the 'contours' of late- or high-modernity. He commences with 'the question of modernity' in which he concludes that developments at the turn of the twenty-first century are currently proving problematic to the sociological enquiry and, moreover, that an analysis of current transformations requires a reworking of the major basic assumptions and premises regarding what precisely constitutes modernity (Giddens 1991, 1). What is unique about contemporary institutions and processes, according to Giddens, is the way they undercut traditional habits and customs. To be sure, in terms of globalizing processes, there is an erosion of experiences of day-to-day life – profoundly impacting the individual and his/her perceptions of self. Hence, the emergence of high modernity with its identifying features including the reorganization of time and space, globalization, and the radicalization of pre-established institutional traits of modernity, transform the content and nature of day-to-day social life (Giddens 1991, 2).

Globalization and Its Consequences

Globalization constitutes a vast field of sociological study. Indeed, it is one where theories of late- and postmodernity frequently converge. Through the relevant literature it is perceived as having various consequences, not least of all for the life course and the wider cultural backdrop in which it is experienced.

Waters has traced the inter-related developments of globalization that inform sociological works. First, there is an emerging global culture or consciousness. This is arguably currently the most rapid phase of development. Second, globalization involves the systematic relationship of all individual social ties. In a fully globalized context, no given relationship or set of relationships can remain isolated or bounded. In this way globalization increases the inclusiveness and unification of human society. Third, the phenomenon of globalization is reflexive. The inhabitants of different societies orient themselves to the world market as a whole by way of economic consumption and counter-cultures. Globalization, fourth, involves a collapse of universalism and particularism. This differentiation is registered in the distinction between life chances and lifestyle. Each person in any relationship is simultaneously an individual and a member of the human species. Fifth, globalization brings, paradoxically, elements of risk and trust. Individuals trust unknown persons, impersonal forces and norms in technological communication and economic exchange – but each involves an element of risk as in the case of disclosing personal banking details to commercial firms through the worldwide net (Waters 1995, 62–64).

Globalization features in Gidden's account of contemporary society. The world of high modernity stretches out well beyond the milieu of individual activities and personal engagements: it is a society which brings its own risks and dangers and one which intrudes deeply into the heart of self-identity and human emotions. For Giddens, globalizing processes have accentuated aspects of risk; whether it is economic forces or political events in the world, there will be far-reaching consequences for the lives of many by way of undercutting reflexive life projects (Giddens 1991, chapter 4). There may be considerable implications. For example, the global economy means that recession in one part of the world may have substantial impact on another. Thousands of people may be made redundant as a result of the collapse of an international company – their life prospects severely undermined and life opportunities placed outside of their control.

Globalization has also been an integral part of postmodernists' theorizing. For one thing globalization is seen as impacting localized culture in which life courses may be well established. Long before the twenty-first century, globalization amounted to the beginning of a new epoch in human affairs. There is now what is often referred to as the 'global village'. In recent decades even the furthest reaches of the earth have become more easily accessible through advances in technology and communication in a world that grows increasingly 'smaller'. Although the process of globalization has a long history, it is today genuinely different both in scale from what has gone before. The sheer impact, speed, and intensity of global cultural communications are now unprecedented. The increasing diffusion of radio, television, the Internet, satellite, digital technologies, and other forms of mass media have made instant communication possible. Via such media people throughout the world are exposed to the dynamics of other cultures as never before. It follows that human life must now be studied within a global perspective. Communities and the individuals that comprise them have to be seen in the context of a shrinking international arena. This is one where the societies of the world are increasingly interconnected.

Globalization disturbs the way that 'culture' is conceptualized, one which has long had connotations tying it to the idea of a fixed locality. Indeed, 'culture' paralleled the notion of 'a society' as a bounded entity occupying a physical territory mapped by way of a political territory (the nation state wrought by *modernity*) and binding individual meaning constructs into this circumscribed social and political space. There are various implications which globalization brings. One is that the collapse of a modernist way of seeing the world suggests that postmodernity also includes a desire to combine cultural symbols from very varied codes or frameworks of meaning, perhaps from different parts of the globe, even at the cost of disjunction and eclecticism. It follows that for postmodernist theorists, culture in contemporary societies has very many syncretic elements – a tendency brought about by the collapse of the boundaries between 'high' and 'popular' forms of culture. Especially through new technology and modes of communication, people all over the world now share many tastes in music, clothes and food, and often the same choices of lifestyles (Tomlinson 1999, 28).

Late- or Postmodernity and the Life Course

There are various direct or indirect ways by which late- or postmodernist writers have approached the subject of the life course and some of their speculations have been implicit in the above discussions, not least of all that of globalization. Yet, perhaps most obviously, postmodernist theorists argue that it is arduous to suggest that people go through such clearly demarcated stages of life as in previous decades. For instance, it is now difficult to stipulate where childhood ends and adolescence begins and whether age norms still hold, although it is apparent that to one degree or another some expectations remain. What is clearly lacking is the rigidity. Writers such as Featherstone and Hepworth (1991) and Bauman (1992) see the postmodern life course as characterized by a number of overlapping, often disparate conditions associated with the blurring of traditional chronological boundaries and the integration of formally segregated periods of life. Fixed definitions of childhood, middle age, and old age are eroding under pressure from two cultural directions that have accompanied the profound shifts in the political economy of labour, retirement, and traditionally structured forms of inequality such as social class. This has various repercussions. One is that in late- or postmodern culture, the prospect of an endless life has been revived through images of perpetual youth and a blurring of traditional life course boundaries. Now life in Western societies is reduced to a series of individual choices and projected plans for the future that have little community significance. It follows that rites of passage in Western societies are mostly optional, not compulsory aspects of social life and are likely to disappear with the rise of individualism and the decline of the community setting where they were once an integral part of life and helped establish social identity.

In Western societies we are now inclined to anticipate risks and future possibilities at least partly by choice. However, the stance taken by late- or postmodernist writers differs in this respect. Giddens argues that choice implies an underlying denial of inevitability which comes with a rational mode of thinking, nothing is inevitable. At the same time, late-modern society is void of communal obligations, and fixed social status and roles. Today, we regard ourselves as highly individualistic. This means that individualism and individual choice are key values (Giddens 1991, 5–6, 147–8). It follows that we may not necessarily pass through stringent and clearly marked out stages of the life course but make choices and negotiate risks surrounding such matters as whether to marry or have children, or at what age we wish to retire – a more or less previously assumed inevitable life event.

Postmodernist writers are less likely to talk in terms of life course 'risks' as emphasized by Giddens, and more in terms of the uncertainty and unpredictability in the life course. One of the key uncertainties comes from the fragmentation of 'self'. There is now a search for 'self', personal identity, and meaning. Postmodernity confronts people with pluralism and choice, but also with an absence of tradition which means that there is very little help provided by society in establishing identities and in selecting moral guides to living.

Postmodernity has also brought something different for the life-span. There is increasing demographic evidence that life-expectancy is drawing closer to life-span potential. Hence, Westerners ideally anticipate long, active, and healthy lives. However, the features of postmodern ageing also derive from cultural industries that distribute pleasure and leisure across an unrestricted range of objects, identities, styles, and expectations. In doing so, claims Katz, 'such industries recast the life-span in "fantastic ways", in particular, "the masking of ageing and the fantasy of timelessness" ' (Katz 1995, 69). Whether the contemporary approach to the life-span is quite as radical as Katz suggests is open to debate. What is clear, however, is that its restructuring does have weighty consequences for various aspects of the life course.

Summary

Profound changes in the contemporary life course bring observable departures from 'traditional' and 'modern' societies with their distinctive forms of social organization more synonymous with a structured 'life-cycle'.

The implications of current changes accompanying late- or postmodernity, as we have only briefly overviewed so far, are indeed considerable. All stages of life, if it makes sense to speak of 'stages' in any meaningful sense, have been impacted by numerous transformations whether structural, related to institutions such as family life, or impacted by cultural and economic trends including developments within childhood and youth. In the chapters to come we shall explore some of these transformations, as well as the continuities, in far more detail. In the next chapter, however, we will consider the importance of age and age categories in greater depth – categories which, historically speaking, have been among the most important variable in shaping life experiences and social relationships. Other important variables which have long formulated aspects of the life course, namely class, gender, and ethnicity, will also be overviewed. This will allow us to appreciate that many of the current changes in Western societies which impact on the life course, are supplemented by structures of social inequality which have by no means been eclipsed.

Further Reading

Allat,P., Bryman,A. and Bytheway,B. (1987) (eds) *Women and the Life Cycle: Transitions and Turning Points*, Basingstoke: McMillan.
Becker,H. (ed.) (1991) *Life Histories and Generation*, Utrecht: Isor.
Blakie,A. (1999) *Ageing and Popular Culture*, Cambridge: Cambridge University Press.
Bryman,A. Bytheway,B., Allat,P., and Keil,T. (eds) (1987) *Rethinking the Life-Cycle*, London: Methuen.
Featherstone,M. (1995) *Undoing Culture: Globalization, Postmodernism and Identity*, London: Sage.
Hockey,J. and James,A. (1993) *Growing Up and Growing Old: Ageing and Dependency in the Life Course*, London: Sage.
Jones,G. and Bell,R. (2000) *Balancing Acts: Youth, Parenting and Public Policy*, York: York Publishing Services for Joseph Rowntree Foundation.
Kotre,J. (1990) *Seasons of Life: The Dramatic Journey from Birth to Death*, Ann Arbour: University of Michigan Press.
Pilcher,J. (1995) *Age and Generation in Modern Britain*, Oxford: Oxford University Press.
Riley,M. (ed.) *Sociological Lives. Social Change and the Life Course*, Newbury Park: Sage.

2

Social Differentiation and Determinants of the Life Course

To refer to social differentiation and determinants of the life course may seem at odds with many of the principal themes developed in the literature on late- or postmodernity. Indeed, in this respect Harriet Bradley speaks of 'a crisis of stratification theory' (Bradley 1996, 1–3). Bradley suggests that the approach of postmodernist writing, in particular, would seem to undermine traditional sociological accounts of structured inequalities. First, that its emphasis on fragmentation would appear to play down notions of coherent and structured formation of inequality such as social class. From this perspective, the demise of class has largely been replaced by an emphasis on cross-cutting forms of social disadvantage and the degrees of opportunity open to make choices of lifestyle preference. Second, class, and gender for that matter, have been approached by postmodernists more in terms of how such social categories came to be classified as such in the first place. In short, the sociological task becomes one of deconstructing the building of social categories that force people, perhaps with negative consequences, into generalized identities. The latter approach, suggests Bradley, fits uneasily with material factors related to equality and deprivation (Bradley 1996, 3).

The apparent decline or at least fragmentation of traditionalized institutions such as the family or the disintegration of rigidly structured social divisions synonymous with *modernity*, perhaps most obviously class, would seem to render a discussion of 'determinants' somewhat redundant. Yet, the emphasis upon identity, consumption, globalization, and even reflexivity, does not necessarily denote the complete demise of variables that at least influence the life course and life chances. These are most clearly evident in sociological interests in life 'discontinuities' and the emergence of the risk society explored by Giddens (1991) and Beck (1992). There remains, however, a certain ambiguity in how early concerns,

33

especially with the stringent inequalities derived from class, gender, age, and ethnicity are negotiated and utilized. In this sense, the uncertainty of sociology in discussing such issues reflects a cultural uncertainty. This possibility is explored by Bauman in an article entitled *Is There a Postmodern Sociology?* Bauman identifies an evolving new self-awareness in sociological discourse that seeks to account for the drastic changes observable in the contemporary world including developing technology, the plurality of cultures, relativism, many 'life-worlds', the apparent reversal of rationalism, and the effects of consumerism. The result is the development of contrasting theories and complex debates, some of which relate to the interface between established and developing theories and their applicability to the emerging socio-cultural order.

One of the underlying concerns of current sociological debates, and this is not always evident in the literature, is the recognition that society continues to shape and limit life experiences and life chances throughout the life course. The way in which this is manifest in postmodernity may not always be obvious or discerned by way of long-term trends, nonetheless, largely through aspects of consumption and technological development, as well as varying levels of status associated with gender and ethnicity, society continues to impact throughout the life course. This is certainly observable through experiences of childhood and youth, experiences which can have profound repercussion in later life. Given that such determinants still prevail and that others are growing in significance, this chapter considers a number of the important developments within late- and postmodernity and overviews some of the broad implications for the life course.

The Perseverance of Social Categories and Inequalities: Age

Pilcher has noted that like class, ethnicity, and gender, age is a social category through which people define and identify individuals and groups as part of their social experience. In contemporary Western societies age categories continue to create differential access to power, status, material resources, and citizenship (Pilcher 1995, 1). The fact remains, however, that age differentiation may not now be so important largely because of the flexibility of the different phases of life and perhaps attendant discontinuities, as well as broader structural changes in contemporary society. At the very least, its relevance and meaning seem to have changed.

Among the important variations between pre-industrial and modern societies are that in the former older people tend to have higher status, more power, and do not retire merely because they are old. This is a reminder that societies attach different meanings to a particular time of life. Margaret Mead (1928), comparing the old in the early twentieth century with those in tribal society, believed that 'the wisdom of the aged' was fast disappearing. Universally 'old age' is a separate social category in all societies and provides one of the most obvious socially constructed phases of life. In many pre-industrial societies, however, older people are integrated into dimensions of social life and regularly continue to act as political, judicial, and civil leaders and, indeed, their status would seem to increase with age. Not uncommonly, in such societies a great sense of mutual responsibility between the old and their adult children exist.

In Western societies, by contrast, rapid change and value orientation combine to define the experiences of older people as unimportant or even obsolete. Rapid change may mean that younger people frequently dismiss the elderly because they seem unaware of new trends and fashions and important developments in the contemporary world. At the same time, at least in *modernity*, the rigorous structuring of the life course, especially through retirement, means social and economic disengagement and the loss of status.

The opening chapter of this volume explored how the significance of age categories is changing and declining in the late- or postmodern West. This is not to suggest that they do not continue to inform aspects of social inequality. Western societies put a cultural emphasis on being young and the socially constructed advantages of 'youth' in terms of fitness and vitality, as well as adapting to the challenges of the workplace. At the same time, nonetheless, a lack of status is also marked in the years of youth and early adulthood which are circumscribed by legal proscription outlining what young people can or cannot do. Thus, in UK law, and this obviously varies elsewhere, 16 is the age of consent and 18 is the age at which one can vote and purchase alcohol.

To be sure, people in Western societies continue to define themselves in terms of their membership of particular age categories. Self-perceptions are closely bound up with how the young or the old see themselves and this, in turn, often depends on how others see them. Identification with age, however, has been found to carry different weight throughout the life course. In the 1960s, Kuhn (1960), in a study of the USA, found that only 25 per cent of nine-year-olds identified themselves by age. Yet, 75 per cent of thirteen-year-olds identified themselves in this way. Thus, age awareness seemed to be of increasing significance in the teenage years at a time that youth cultures were emerging as a new social phenomenon.

It is not just a matter of how those of a similar age see themselves but how others see them. Clearly, what is regarded as 'old' in one community is not in another. Much depends largely on the life-expectancy of any given society. In the West, for instance, old age comprises the later years of adulthood and the final stage of life itself. This arguably begins from about the mid-1960s. Moreover, age is given specific meaning in different contexts. In all different types of society individuals move through and participate in many varied social circles during their day-to-day lives. People respond to others in terms of different age categories. As they move from one context to another they are defined differently by those with which they interact depending on the nature of proscribed relationship norms and conventions surrounding age. At work colleagues may consider others 'young' or 'old' according to their own age. Parents will regard their sons and daughters as 'children', perhaps 'the kids', even into their adult years. This is certainly true in more 'traditional' societies where this may be expressed in terms of status and authority. A rather exaggerated version of this authoritative association with the younger generation is to be found in Haiti where parents are expected to strike their child if it is troublesome – even if s/he is 50 years old.

Modernity appeared to bring highly structured norms to accompany clearly established stages of life and in some contexts, age required the adoption of a subordinate position, in others a dominant position. The way age was perceived carried different expectations concerning how individuals were meant to behave and respond to others. However, much of this may be changing in late- or postmodernity where there is a greater ambiguity related to the way people should behave according to their age and how they relate to other generations. To a great degree this is because clearly defined age categories are beginning to breakdown, along with strict norms as to how people of a certain age are expected to behave. Thus Bradley (1996, 7) prefers to talk in terms of social relationships and the way we categorize them rather than stringent age demarcations. Moreover, he argues that the relationships between different generations could be best understood in terms of 'dynamics' – various locations of age which may be impacted by aspects of gender and ethnic inequalities and occupational reward. Such distinctions are a social reality with very real consequences, but these distinctions are sometimes fixed and sometimes fluid. Furthermore, aspects of age status may not hold if chronological age is not in keeping with particular social responsibilities. For example, an unemployed and homeless young adult may not be afforded the same status as a peer who is more integrated into the adult world through the spheres of employment and family responsibilities.

Demographic Change and Intergenerational Conflict

Conflict between generations may constitute an important determinant in life experiences. Such conflict may have various origins. To some extent potential generational conflict could be generated by demographic changes and Western societies may be facing such potential conflicts. As we have already noted. the twentieth century witnessed a remarkable increase in life-expectancy. Improved standards of living over the decades have promoted the health of people of all ages, while more recent medical strides have been made in fending off cancer and heart disease, afflictions common to the elderly. This increase in life-expectancy will prove to have significant consequences for the size of the elderly as a segment of the population in many Western societies. By 2020, one in five people are likely to be over the age of 65 (Walker and Maltby 1997, 1). In 1951, out of a population of 50.3 million people in the UK, 1.8 million were aged 75 years and over. By 1981, whilst the total population had only increased to 56.4 million, those aged over 75 years numbered 3.3 million (*Social Trends* 1988). The figure is likely to rise to 6.8 million people by 2020 (*Social Trends* 1997, 17). This considerable increase will occur as the 'baby boomers' of the immediate post-war years reach their sixties before 2010. A similar pattern is emerging in Europe, although there are differences across countries with Ireland having the youngest population of the EU nations and Sweden the oldest.

In Western societies there are several major implications of this projected rise of the elderly as a section of the population. Typically, rich nations have low birth-rates, and the long-term repercussion of this trend is frequently referred to as the 'demographic time bomb'. This highlights the dependency ratio – the number of dependent children and retired persons relative to productive age groups. Recently, because of falling fertility and the decline in family size, the dependency ratio has been declining. While this is not a problem at the moment, the changes predicted for the twenty-first century suggest an underlying dilemma in the dependency ratio – there will be fewer and fewer people of working age, while more and more will be dependents.

The ratio of elderly people to working age adults will almost double in the next 50 years – rising from 20 to 37 of the elderly per 100 people aged 18 to 64 years. As elderly people steadily retire from the labour force, the proportion of non-working adults will generate ever-greater demands for social resources and welfare programmes. One key concern is health care, since the elderly today account for a quarter of all medical expenditure. This will place an unprecedented demand on health-care systems in advanced societies. It is not surprizing, therefore, that anxiety over the elderly tends to be intermingled with an uncomfortable awareness that care of the elderly is very costly. Inevitably, the old will be allocated a growing proportion of public expenditure, despite the claims of other needy groups, and this may add to the stigma of old age.

One important aspect of age stratification in *modernity* was the emergence of a distinct form of generational conflict. Since the 1960s the notion of intergeneration conflict in Western societies largely centred on the opposed values of youth and adults. As Attias-Donfurt and Arber note, however, the new conflict is not so much about politics and culture but economics derived from the demographic trends sketched above. Thus, the issues may no longer be the refutation of generational, or for that matter gender hierarchies, inside the family or public sphere, but instead will increasingly focus upon the sharing of public resources between separate cohorts before, during, and after working life. Therefore, the risk of conflict now largely comes from generational inequality in welfare contributions, as well as in the distribution of benefits (Attias-Donfurt and Arber 2000).

Age Disadvantages

Age disadvantages may come in various forms. One is material wealth. In some respects the economic position of the elderly has improved. This is not to suggest that high levels of poverty do not still exist among some older people. A generation ago, the elderly were at the greatest risk of poverty. They still remain at risk, but studies now conclude that a 'new poverty' has emerged among children. At the same time, the numbers of elderly needing assistance declined in the UK from 1.8 million in 1974 to 1.4 million in 1991. Today, the burden of poverty inflicts hardship on children in particular. The numbers of children under 16 needing assistance in the UK rose from 800,000 in 1974 to 2.3 million in 1991. In the mid-1990s, 10 per cent of children were designated as living below the poverty line (Funken and Cooper 1995, 12).

Despite the apparent improvement of the economic position of elderly people, one enhanced by opportunities to partake of the consumer society, a high level of discrimination or ageism would still seem to be evident in Western societies. Much like 'racism' and 'sexism', ageism can be blatant (when the elderly are denied a job because of their age) or subtle forms of infantilization (as when people speak to the elderly with a condescending tone, as if they were children) (Kalish 1979). Within Western culture language is used as a social signifier to denote power relationships within society. Terms such as 'the elderly', 'the old' or 'OAPs' (old age pensioners) both depersonalize and stigmatize the people to whom they refer.

Few countries have legislated against discrimination, those that do include the USA, Spain, France, Canada, New Zealand, and Australia. Discrimination against the elderly can be identified in different spheres of social life. Employment is an important area. The UK's Age Discrimination in Employment Act (1967) barred employers from denying job opportunities or dismissing employees between the ages of 40–65 solely on the basis of age. In 1978, the law was amended to include persons up to the age of 70, and in 1986, it was amended again to remove the upper limit of 70 for most workers. Thus the law is now meant to protect all workers over the age of 40. In the workplace there is frequently less chance of promotion – employers may wish to find employees who will be in positions for a long time without retiring, will accept lower salaries, and are presumed to be more flexible when it comes to new technologies. It is assumed that older people cannot perform certain jobs effectively, for example, heavy lifting in factories or adapting to changing administrative procedures. Evidence of discrimination includes a survey carried out by the Institute of Employment Rights (1999) which found that 12 per cent of employers thought that people were too old to employ at 30 years old, while 25 per cent thought that they were too old at 50.

Ageism is also based on stereotypes: in the case of the elderly, people consider greying hair and wrinkled skin, helplessness, confusion, and a conservative view of the world opposed to change, as practically synonymous with ageing. These images tend to gloss over people's individuality and the vast biological and psychological differences between older individuals. Statistically speaking, older people are more likely than the young to be mentally and physically impaired. However, ageism comes with unwarranted negative generalizations about an entire category of people.

Friedan (1993), surveying the mass media, concludes that elderly people are still conspicuous by their absence, for example, only a small percentage are featured on television shows. They are, then, socially invisible, while the gender stereotyping of older people add to levels of stigmatization, for example, that ageing women may be frequently perceived as having little personal or sexual appeal. Yet, the situation is perhaps improving. Issues related to the impact of ageing and the social and psychological problems associated with it are increasingly discussed in the media and this is bound to be the case given the fact that older people are growing as a distinct section of the population. Such films as *On Golden Pond* (1981) have directly featured older people in central roles, and through them have engaged with issues of ageing, redundancy, illness, and death. Older people also have spending power in the consumer society and have become the subject of niche-marketing which, in turn, highlights the more positive aspects of being older. Blakie notes, by way of illustration, that the American Association for Retired Person *Modern Maturity* has overtaken Reader's Digest as the US magazine with the largest circulation. It is a publication that carries positive images of older people and targets them as consumers (Blakie 1999, 103). Since they are a growing section of the population the elderly are also likely to have increasing political power by way of voting and influencing social policy.

Although older people may find it difficult to mobilize their interests, few politicians are likely to ignore their demands.

On the other hand, a good number of older people have few means of gaining resources, be they financial or of status. They find it hard to organize as an interest group, unlike trade unions and professional bodies, and are unable to withdraw labour or offer any other significant sanction to advance their cause. Townsend and Walker (1983) have highlighted this tendency with the links between old age, dependency, divisions of labour, and structures of inequality, hence developing the idea of 'structured dependency' – the process by which some people in society receive an unequal share in the 'results of social production'. Essentially, this refers to material dependency and focuses upon the ways in which the elderly are structured out of work and into low incomes and poverty and how this is reflected in welfare and health care policies generally.

A crucial factor in material disadvantage is retirement since it means a loss of income for most: the average income for families in which at least one member is 65 or older is only half the average wage for the UK as a whole. The decline in the value of savings and pensions means the worst-off are often the very old (Vincent 1996, 23–4). Indeed, there is a systematic curve which shows that income starts low in early life, increases until middle age and then declines through later years. *The General Household Survey* (2000) found that the income of the majority of men and women over 74 years old in the UK to be less than half of what it was when they were working. At the same time, more of the income of both sexes has to be spent on the basics of life such as food, fuel, and housing. Finally, despite claims made regarding the increasing wealth of retired people, the elderly in the UK are still less likely to be homeowners than the rest of the population. In 1991, 47 per cent of the over 80s lived in rented accommodation compared to only 25 per cent of those aged 45–50. This fact highlights the cohort effects of earlier generations, of experiences of economic booms and depressions, which may impact inequalities and restrict meaningful choice in lifestyle preferences in later years.

Social Class

Part of the ongoing sociological enterprize has been concerned with attempting to understand how society shapes life experiences and life opportunities from the cradle to the grave. Evidence suggests that life chances may be discernible even earlier. It is clear that various factors can impact on human development before birth. This can include the mother's diet, her living environment, whether or not she smokes, and levels of pre-natal care. Such environmental factors continue to be important throughout the life course: where people live, the kind of work undertaken, and formal and informal relationship, are all evident in positive or negative ways.

These factors are frequently linked to economic concerns and, in particular, social class differences. In *modernity*, differences of class, alongside gender and ethnicity, seem to supplement and even surpass age as the most important social divisions. In terms of class, the 'classical' Marxist analysis identified social inequalities as part of ongoing dialectical processes related to the ownership or non-ownership of the means of production. In Marx's defence, it may be acknowledged that at the very least, economic well-being, or failure to realize it, is obviously a major determinant of experiences and chances throughout the life course. The reality, however, is that Marx's assessment of class is difficult to uphold today despite revisions of his theory. Works such as that of Ohlin Wright (1987) retain notions of the polarization of wealth and a monopoly of the ownership and control of the means of production, while recognizing that class structures have undoubtedly been transformed. The problem is, nonetheless, that in bolstering part of Marx's theory, other important foundations of his class analysis are compromised.

The tendency over recent decades is to conceptualize class not so much in terms of the ownership of production but occupational reward by way of income and status and its link to consumer power in relation to lifestyles and opportunities. This approach has been forced to recognize that the Western economy has moved from an emphasis on production to that of consumption. Moreover, that class classifications, as traditionally defined, do not conform to the Marxist interpretation. At the end of the twentieth century less than a third of the economically active population was engaged in industrial labour, marking the shrinking size of the working-class population. The middle-class, by which is generally meant the non-manual occupations that Marx had more or less ignored, now accounts for around 45–50 per cent of the workforce and has grown as traditional manual occupations have steadily declined (Eyde and Lintner 1996, 108). Such class divisions seem to account for differences in life experiences and the degrees to which people can encounter negative events in their lives. Evidence in the 1990s pointed to the fact that infant mortality in the first year of life was three times higher in manual occupation families; manual workers were three times more likely to have a serious long-term illness; unskilled manual worker would die around seven years earlier than a counterpart born to professional parents; divorce levels were four times higher among manual workers than professionals; and unemployment rates appeared to have more than 10 per cent difference between these occupational groupings (Macionis and Plummer 1997, 275).

This division of society into manual and non-manual has, however, proved to be increasingly misleading. While it is convenient to call manual workers 'working-class' and non-manual workers 'middle-class', much disguises the vast differences *within* social classes. As far as the latter is concerned, there is a great deal of variation between well-paid profes- sional people in stable careers and white-collar clerical workers with salaries and employment opportunities that do not compare favourably even with those of many skilled manual workers. There are other reasons too for paying less attention to 'classical' class differentiation. For Pahl, social mobility in industrial class systems has been most pronounced near the middle, where people's social position is most likely to alter. This mobility has subsequently blurred the lines between classes, suggesting that they have all fragmented to the extent that class is no longer a mean- ingful concept (Pahl 1984). At the same time, according to Pahl, it appears that there has occurred a general 'levelling up', with traditional working- class communities largely vanishing and the lives of manual workers considerably forged by home ownership and a reasonable level of afflu- ence and consumerism. Today, the overall standard of living in the societies of the West (along with Japan) is the highest in the world. Relative to most regions of the globe, fewer people face the most severe forms of life threatening inequalities that Marx once wrote about.

There is, nonetheless, more to the equation. Research over the past few years has suggested that, although a larger middle class may have gradu- ally emerged, the gap between the wealthy and the poor in Europe and North America have been growing and part of this development is that the number of poor in the population has increased in relative terms (Funken and Cooper 1995). Moreover, in the last two decades there has also arisen what has come to be known as the 'underclass' comprized of those people 'under' the class structure who are economically, politically, and socially marginalized and excluded. This has been recognized in some works related to late- or postmodernity. Giddens, for instance, identifies an underclass comprised of a heterogeneous group of people including, the unemployed, many members of ethnic communities, the disabled, the homeless, and one-parent families who appear to be outside of the increasing prosperity of contemporary society (Giddens 1991, 85–6). This suggests that while class structures have radically changed, the repercussions of a society in which there remains a considerable gulf between the 'haves' and 'have nots' continue to influence life chances.

Gender

Gender is another basis of social stratification evident in the great majority of historical communities – those ranging from 'primitive' to complex industrialized societies – shaping life chances and opportunities through economics, family and work structures, and patriarchal ideologies. Until the 1970s, with the rise of a new wave of feminism, the sociological preoccupation with social class tended to obscure the significance of major gender divisions and inequalities in Western societies. Indeed, the conventional ways of defining class until very recently focused on male heads of households. Women were excluded. Including women in the picture complicates the issue of social class and forges new controversies such as how child-bearing and child-raising fit into the labour structure.

While overt discrimination is illegal in most Western countries, women remain more likely to be concentrated into lower paid occupations like social work, nursing, childcare, primary school teaching, and secretarial roles. Moreover, women as a group earn less than men – even if they can claim the same qualifications, expertise, and experience. Although chances of promotion in various occupations are improving for women, the existence of what has come to be known as the 'glass ceiling' indicates that hidden aspects of discrimination in terms of career advancement exist despite legislation regarding equal opportunities. All these aspects of work may severely restrict life experiences and life chances.

Women are also over-represented in the poverty statistics. In this regard, the term 'feminization of poverty' describes the trend by which women represent an increasing proportion of the poor. Townsend (1987) has identified four groups of women that make up the 'female poor': single (including divorced) women with children, elderly women pensioners, 'carers' who look after children or other dependants, and women with low earnings. The feminization of poverty is, in turn, part of a larger change: the rapidly increasing number of households – at all class levels – headed by single women. This trend, coupled with the fact that households run exclusively by women are at high risk of poverty, explains why women (and their children) represent an increasing share of the poor in Western societies.

Dimension of material deprivation are very general restrictions that women may face during the life course. In more specific terms there are particular junctures in the life course where women may face disadvantages. In this respect, the volume edited by Allat et al., *Women and the Life Cycle*, provides useful insights into the particular difficulties faced by women through such areas as relationships in the teenage years, the restricted opportunities at school-leaving age, inequalities in late marital life, leisure opportunities, trade union activities, and discontinuities throughout the life course. All these aspects compare poorly with the experiences of many men, who either do not confront these difficulties or find themselves at a greater advantage.

While acknowledging different aspects of gender inequality, one of the principal questions for feminists at the present time is in theorizing the extent and nature of the ubiquity of patriarchy through which male domination and differentiated social roles are expressed in late- or post-modernity. Almost certainly many would take exception to Giddens' brief account which strikes an over-positive and optimistic tone regarding women in the emerging socio-cultural order of late modernity. Giddens sees women becoming the equal of men in many areas of public life. There have also been major advances for women in the realm of self-identity, the body, identity, and contentious areas such as abortion. Giddens courts controversy, however, by claiming that women's attitudes to the world are radically different compared to men and that this is largely determined by their reproductive system (Giddens 1991, 219–20).

For at least some feminists the postmodernist paradigm is more attractive and this is so in relation to aspects of the life course. Traditional feminist sociology and some aspects of postmodern theory overlap in their display of a critical content in the interpretation of contemporary society. The common ground is evident in social constructionist approaches. This is unmistakable, for example, in feminists' accounts of medicalization. Much is exemplified by the notion of 'biology as ideology' – a term derived from R.C. Lewontin's work (1992). Lewontin argued that the biological determinism advanced by the medical profession is a philosophical, scientific, and political theory which, from a feminist perspective, is set within the social and economic differences between the sexes – the goal being to legitimize inequality, to make it appear a natural and inevitable outcome. The discourse surrounding biological determinism would seem to focus on information which supports the theory and ignores that which contradicts it (Albee 1982).

The deconstructionist element in the more long-standing feminist writing has also provided fertile ground for comparative study, not least of all in relation to the life course. More recent feminist work continues to stress that women's biological, psychological, and social development across the life course is compromised by cultural, political, and economic factors which forge lifestyles, habits, expectations, and roles which place women at a disadvantage. We may take, for example, perceptions of the process of ageing. Thus, Linda Gannon, in *Women and Ageing* (1996), considers the social forces that shape such issues as psychological well-being, menopause, and sexuality. Gannon suggests that these issues can only be addressed in a feminist context – one which challenges the traditional assumptions that ageing is necessarily associated with intellectual deterioration, depression, physical disability, and social disengagement. Here, social skills and support, the woman's control over her life, and social and economic roles are cited as major determinants of well-being. Gannon argues that with age, biology becomes relatively less important as the combined influences of pollution, trauma, sexism, ageism, poverty, and access to quality care accumulate over a lifetime. She contends that such deconstruction is not incompatible with the postmodernist mode of thinking and its emphasis on the social deconstruction of discourse and categorization (Gannon 1996, 1). This view is shared by Yeatman who suggests that both feminist and postmodernist theorizing contest the foundationist pre-suppositions of modernist discursive formations, in short, assumptions which ground the validity of knowledge claims with reference to taken-for-granted truths or meta-narratives. In that way, all knowledge becomes historically and culturally produced. Therefore, all discourse, commonsense assumptions about gender, and medicalized concepts, can be deconstructed to reveal patriarchal ideologies (Yeatman 1994).

Not all feminist writers have been wholly happy with the challenges of postmodernist theories. Assiter, for example, goes against the grain of current orthodoxies to challenge some of the postmodern assumptions and has defended many of the tenets of more traditional expressions of feminism. Assiter makes a powerful argument for the continuing reality of gender inequality, the reality of the distinction between sex and gender, and insists that universal claims about the disadvantages experienced by women can be justified. This leads here to advocate a partial return to feminist modernist values. In doing so, she brings a defence of modernist realism and Enlightenment philosophy (Assiter 1996).

'Race' and Ethnicity

Postmodernist writers face a number of difficulties, or at least challenges, in the area of 'race' and ethnicity. To some extent this is because they have inherited problems of conceptualization and classification which have plagued sociology generally for a number of years. Nonetheless, it has long been recognized that how people define 'race' is frequently determined by the dominant belief system of a given society, in particular, the attitude of acceptance or hostility by particular social groups in various historical contexts. The term 'ethnicity' is usually seen as defining communities by way of cultural characteristics rather than their supposed biological differences and most sociologists see ethnicity as a more valid way of classifying people than 'race' which may be interpreted as a social construct: it has no biological basis and is more to do with how people classify physical differences.

A number of sociological approaches to 'race' and ethnicity have concentrated on their relationship with other forms of social stratification. Those who take this position have long argued that class and status often coincide with racial and ethnic inequalities. 'Race' and skin colour simply make minorities more visible and more vulnerable to economic and class exploitation. On the other hand, sociologists such as Rex (1970), maintain that this fails to give recognition to the unique problems raised by 'race' and ethnicity. In fact, both can dissect class lines, although certain perceptions related to distinct ethnic groups are built into Western culture and appear to have no connection to class. Often these connotations are used to justify discrimination directed towards a specific 'race' including its supposed biological inferiority, while unequal power balances are likely to have negative consequences for the self-image of racial groups. Being working-class and of low status as immigrants can make them perhaps the most underprivileged groups in society and complicate simple assumptions concerning experiences and opportunities throughout the life course.

The postmodernist enterprize is one which would also seek to deconstruct categories of 'race' and 'ethnicity', even to the point of playing down the more obvious aspects of social and economic inequalities. One growing emphasis has tended to be on ethnicity and identity especially in relation to culture in the global context. In this respect, some commentators recognize that the process of globalization both negates and enhances ethnic identity. Once, in the pre-modern world, ethnicity was a taken-for-granted component of identity associated with tribalism and regionalism. The increasing integration of economic processes and the growing interconnectedness of political practices, along with the emergence of a common global lifestyle rapidly mediated by electronic communication and personal mobility, has established what has been referred to as 'Cosmopolitania'. In other words, it is increasingly difficult for ethnic communities to retain a distinct culture and sense of identity, a challenge to which they may respond to in various ways (Smith 1991).

The important point in terms of the life course, from a postmodernist approach, is that global culture is created through the increasing interconnectedness of varied local cultures. They are all becoming subcultures within the wider whole. But to this global interrelated diversity people can respond in different ways. There are, according to Smith, 'cosmopolitans', and there are 'locals'. The former are a plurality of cultures and includes a positive stance towards diversity itself – an openness and search for contrasts. Others try to localize themselves. For example, ethnic minorities, taken away from their territorial base of local culture, might encapsulate themselves within a reproduction of it (Smith 1991). Hence, there may be a greater sense of cohesion brought by the very threats presented by these tendencies – its relativism and a search for identities of the past in a postmodern world where identity is associated with lifestyle and taste, and is therefore constantly shifting and changeable. From one perspective this may lead to a revalorization of the past and the construct of mythological values and narratives.

In postmodern Western societies, which are practically synonymous with pluralism, relativism, and multi-ethnic communities, a search for cultural and moral certainties through embracing traditional values and other attributes of ethnic identity, such as religion, is increasingly complex. At the same time, responses to racism and discrimination on the one hand, and the forces of cultural assimilation on the other, make identity formation particularly problematic. Moreover, while an ethnic cultural foundationism is perhaps evident in the postmodern world, some expressions of ethnicity may result in something more contrived, inconsequential, and somewhat more superficial. In this way, Waters suggests, the search for tradition can contribute to the postmodern ambiance by mixing the symbolic content of the past and the present to the extent that everyday life becomes an 'historical and ethnic Disneyland' (Waters 1995, 137).

It is clear that postmodernist writers, as with so many other themes, have developed different approaches to ethnicity. This should not be too surprising given that they are describing the emergence of a radically new social order which has profound global dimensions. As with the approach to gender issues, the growing body of literature still has a long way to go in forging a distinct postmodern approach to ethnicity, especially one which can comprehensively account for the continuation of inequalities and discrimination throughout the life course.

The reality is that very profound inequalities do exist between ethnic groupings, although the picture is increasingly complicated. To be sure, over the generations growing numbers of members in most ethnic communities have begun to filter through to the better-paid professional occupations in Western societies. However, since the 1970s the most important changes in the overall position of ethnic and racial minorities of people is, in the case of the UK, very high unemployment rates among Asians and West Indians. The Joseph Rowntree Foundation's (1995) study of poverty in the UK continued to pay testimony to the problems facing ethnic groups since it was 'particularly concerned … at what is happening to the non-white population'. It found that one in three of the non-white population was in the poorest fifth of the overall population. Most significant here were alarming rates of unemployment (worst of all among people of Pakistani origin) and, above all, the plight of Afro-Caribbean single-parent families. There is also a gender dimension in that black women appear in all categories related to the feminization of poverty, especially where they are single and elderly (Glendinning and Millar 1987).

Just as there are different patterns of employment for men and women, so there are variations among ethnic groups. The Fourth Policy Studies Institute survey, *Ethnic Minorities in Britain: Diversity and Disadvantage* (1997), offered the following summary of the employment position of different ethnic groups: African Asians are as likely as whites to be in professional and managerial jobs; Chinese men are half as likely again to be in this position and Chinese women are twice as likely as white women to be in top jobs; and Indians and Caribbeans are situated in a central position. Caribbean male employees average just over 90 per cent of the earnings of white men and Indians 85 per cent; Pakistanis and Bangladeshis are twice as liable to be in manual work as in non-manual work, whereas white males are evenly split between these types of employment. Pakistanis and Bangladeshis experience severe and wide-spread poverty since 80 per cent of their households have incomes below half the national average compared to 20 per cent of white homes. Given such evidence, inequalities clearly impact a number of ethnic groups differentially and this is bound to forge the experiences of many individuals who belong to them throughout the duration of the life course.

Late- or Postmodernity: Life Chances, Lifestyles, and the Consumer Society

In accounting for those variables that may impact upon the life course, its opportunities, experiences, and limitations, the dimensions of social differentiation traditionally addressed in earlier sociological accounts by way of class, gender, ethnicity, and age, tend to be played down by theories of late- or postmodernity. At the very least, they are interpreted more in terms of social constructs or identified as structures that are rapidly disintegrating as sources of community and identity.

This re-orientation does not mean that in contemporary Western society individuals and communities fail to be impacted by processes that can have positive and negative repercussions for the life course and are bound up with life chances and experiences. The starting point, however, is radically different. Theorists place less stress on 'determinants' and structures such as 'class' in favour of notions of 'self' and 'identity' and the related concerns of the significance of consumption and the opportunity or lack of opportunity in realizing enriching and meaningful lifestyles. At the same time, in late- and postmodernist theorizing, contemporary experiences of the life course are given greater emphasis by way of the dynamics of globalizing forces which may bring discontinuities in economic and cultural terms.

Less constrained by social structures such as class, according to late- or postmodernist accounts, choice becomes a fundamental component of daily activity at the level of the self and identity. The emerging order confronts the individual with a complex diversity of choices primarily in terms of lifestyle preferences The world thus becomes full of potential ways of being and acting, as part of a lifestyle and thus, according to Giddens, individuals see the life course as a series of 'passages' to be nego-tiated in terms of opportunities and risks (Giddens 1991, 78–9). But such passages are not institutionalized, or accompanied by formalized rituals. Life passages give particular cogency to the interaction of risk and oppor-tunities especially when they are to a substantial degree initiated by the individual – perhaps negotiating significant transitions of life, leaving home, changing job, forming a new relationship, and confronting illness and a range of other discontinuities.

An important dimension of choice, to situate things succinctly, is in constructing a meaningful lifestyle. The relationship of lifestyle to the self is in forging a more or less integrated set of practices and life orientations, not because they fulfil utilitarian needs, but because they give material form to a particular narrative of self-identity throughout the life course.

This link between identity and lifestyle must be put in broader perspec-tive. Weeks (1990) differentiates between social and personal identity. The social identity constitutes lived relationships with others; the personal are reflections of experience – highly complex and individualized in terms of social significance. In late- or postmodernity social identity is eroded, stripped from an anchorage in community belonging or at least subject to fleeting social interaction. The personal becomes more important since identity is open to choice, transformation, and negotiation. While identity is 'handed down' in pre-industrial societies, in the contemporary world with its lack of tradition and generational roots, identity is subject to choice as an integral part of the construct of self.

In today's society people are still obliged to construct and maintain a coherent self-identity or face a 'crisis' of meaning or, to perhaps put it rather misleadingly, may be subject to an 'identity crisis'. The process of late- or postmodernity, its pluralism, fragmentation, and rootlessness, is behind such a development. At the same time, however, contemporary society also provides the means for a purposeful construction of self, largely through lifestyle preferences. Thus in a great deal of sociological literature post-modernity is increasingly associated with lifestyle choices, life-planning, and the values of consumption. At the same time, the disintegration of traditional processes of socialization, means that the formation of self takes place in the context of the individual sense of self, rather than community contexts and void of references to well-established values, moralities, and tradition. The consumer culture thus becomes the site in which identity construction largely takes place. Now, we are what we consume: selfhood becomes a matter of lifestyle choice and the construction of an 'off-the-shelf' image which may change quite dramatically throughout our lives. It follows that there is a choice, or potential choice of lifestyles associated with the different phases of life as part of a reflexive process.

The link between self, identity, and consumption comes across strongly in the extant sociological literature. Under a consumer culture, consumption becomes the main form of self-expression and the chief source of individual identity (Waters 1995, 140–1). This implies that both material and non-material items including kinship, affection, art, and intellect, become commodified. That is, their value is assessed by the context of their exchange, rather than the context of their production or use. Commodification is intimately bound up with consumption, and it is evident that the extension and development of the consumer culture in the twentieth century has depended upon the creation of new markets not least of all through the production of images and advice on lifestyles (Featherstone 1991).

At this point, a little more needs to be said regarding the nature of the dynamics of the consumer economy and its accompanying culture. Perhaps the most important observation in respect of economic developments is that a late- or postmodernized consumer culture may be said to experience hypercommodification in which minute differences between products or minute improvements in them can determine variations in demand, and in which consumption is differentiated on the basis of the signifiers known as 'brand names' (Crooks et al. 1992) Here consumption, or more precisely a capacity to consume, is itself a matter of reflexivity. This tendency is captured in such terms as 'taste', 'fashion', and 'lifestyle' which become key sources of social differentiation, displacing class and political affiliation since they may say a great deal about income, status, and the opportunity to realize choices.

The consumer culture is created through the advertizing and simulatory effects of the mass media. In its original form consumerism was probably a deliberate creation but under postmodernized conditions, according to Baudrillard, it is 'hypersimulated': having a life of its own that is beyond the control of any particular group, a commodification occurs where all things can be bought and sold (Baudrillard 1983). Moreover, consumerism means more than simple consumption since in postmodernity it also generates a distinct culture which, in many respects, brings a radical departure from *modernity*, although there are obvious traits of continuity. In the consumer culture of postmodernity the items consumed take on a symbolic and not merely a material value.

There are two broad views of the way in which consumer culture influences the individual. The most common explanation is one in which individual identity is conflated to culture. Capitalism transforms people into consumers by altering their self-images, their structure of wants, in directions that serve capitalist accumulation. This arises in societies where powerful groups, usually those seeking to accumulate capital, encourage consumers to 'want' more than they 'need'. At the same time, for critics of the emerging economic order, commodification represents a distinct narrowing and convergence of cultural experience rather than an expanding experience of the world. This is succinctly put by Baudrillard who argues that in the postmodern society 'there is nowhere to go but to the shops' (Baudrillard 1983).

An alternative, more liberating interpretation, is that the new consumer society ushers in meaningful choices of lifestyle (Featherstone 1991). It is also liberating in that consumer culture is symbolically and globally mediated, freeing values and preferences from particular social and geographical locations. This it does by declassifying or dedifferentiating culture, by mixing high and low culture – important structures once found in modernity since they were closely associated with social class and class tastes. What is regarded as 'good' culture is now a matter of opinion and can be accepted or rejected at will under the relativizing influences of postmodernity.

Globalizing influences enhance commodification and visa versa. In the globalized context there may be the influence by other cultures which can be prepackaged for a new environment – whether African style clothes or Peruvian music, or a whole variety of food genres from around the world. It may well be that interaction with these goods is a meaningful way by which we construct identity and lifestyles and make sense of our lives. Especially through new technology and modes of communication, people all over the world now share many tastes in music, clothes, and food, and often the same choices of lifestyles.

The 'Problem' of Identity and the Construction of Self

As briefly noted above, discussions related to late or postmodernity frequently focus on the theme of the 'self' and identity as problematic, although the subject is often approached in very different ways. What is central to both perspectives, however, is a greater emphasis on the problem faced by individuals, rather than the group, in relation to identity. Hence, the disadvantages encountered on the life course are not so much derived from social structures such as class, but the ability to deal with challenges to the self and identity – central concerns which are impacted by uncertainty, aspects of risk, and restrictions in realizing life potentials. These are a new and challenging range of problems which beset late- or postmodernity.

Giddens talks about 'dilemmas of the self' (Giddens 1991, 187–8). In conditions of late modernity in a way very different from that experienced in pre-modern and early modernity, globalizing processes in particular bring the danger of the fragmentation of self. The problem of uniting the self concerns protecting and reconstructing the self in the face of massive intentional and extensional changes. For Giddens, high modernity brings a new sense of identity which involves 'finding oneself' and this will inevitably entail biographical construction and reconstruction of the life course (Giddens 1991, 12). While postmodernist commentators are preoccupied with the prevailing pessimism of postmodernity that comes through relativizing impulses, Giddens is more concerned with the uncertainty brought by the breakdown of community and tradition on the one hand, and globalizing forces on the other. At the same time, there has emerged the threat of personal meaninglessness – potentially disturbing existential questions that are not answered by the social order (Giddens 1991, 121–2).

In Gidden's account, late modernity finds a way by which individuals can create an integrated sense of self. In the pre-modern context, the fragmentation of experience was not a prime source of anxiety. Trust relations were localized and focused through personal ties. Today, a range of possibilities present themselves, not just in terms of options of behaviour, but by way of 'openness of the world' to the individual. Quoting Goffman (1967), Giddens argues (1991, 191–2) that the individual can leave one encounter and enter another and in doing so adjusts him/herself to different contexts. For Gidden, the life course has become a reflexive project of self and one where individuals have become apt at adapting the self to different environments: thus the late modernity that fragments and creates problems in terms of identity, also unites at different levels of social experience.

Gidden's overriding concern in *Modernity and Self-Identity* is to examine the emergence of new mechanisms of self-identity which are shaped by the institutions of high modernity and a society where kinship and community structures continue to be eroded. While the problems that these generate may be overcome, globalizing processes put much beyond the control of the individual – undermining coherent and structured aspects of the life course (Giddens 1991, 2). This is a theme also taken up by Beck. Global variables, as well as localized context, can profoundly impact on the individual's life experiences. While the cultural emphasis on the self and identity carries notions of individual responsibility, there are aspects of realization which are out of the control of the individual. Nonetheless, according to Beck (1992), many of the hurdles that confront the individual from day to day are now perceived as a consequence of individual actions rather than resulting from social background such as class position or processes beyond his/her influence.

According to Beck, industrial society, based on the rational application of science, is being replaced by the risk society. Whereas industrial society was seen as an ordered and predictable social structure, late modernity is perceived as a more dangerous and unpredictable place in which we are constantly confronted with risk. Such risks not only include the threat of nuclear war or environmental disasters but a range of more localized risks which have to be negotiated in our daily lives. Importantly, with the decline of the social networks associated with the old generations, people are forced to negotiate these fresh dangers as individuals rather than as members of a community.

The Body in Late- or Postmodernity

According to Giddens, it is clear that self-identity, as a coherent phenomenon, presumes a narrative of the self. The reflexivity of the self extends to the body, where the body is part of the action system rather than merely a passive object and includes a constant observation of bodily processes often linked to levels of health, exercise, and diet. Self-actualization is understood in terms of a balance between opportunity and risk. Letting go of the past, through the various techniques of becoming free from oppressive emotional habits, generates a multiplicity of opportunities for self-development. Through his own distinct approach Giddens suggests that the reflexivity of the self pervasively affects the body as well as psychic processes. The body is less and less an extrinsic 'given', functioning outside the internally referential systems of modernity, but itself becomes reflexively mobilized (Giddens 1991, 7).

The emphasis by Giddens on the body is in line with a growing volume of literature on the theme of the body, including its significance for the life course. A wealth of anthropological material reveals the body being used in many societies to make statements about social status (Polhemus 1978). In Western culture forms of body alteration predominate the medicalization of life – from breast enlargement through to dieting, to spare-part surgery. The medicalization of the body also impacts ageing throughout the life course through techniques applied to staying and looking young – techniques perhaps exemplified by 'face lifts'. In this sense the body marks the site of the quest to obtain the status of youth and beauty.

As Featherstone argues, the body is taking on increasing social significance in postmodernity. Through the conjoining of the inner and outer body, appearance has now come to signify the self, to the extent that 'the penalties of bodily neglect are a lowering of one's acceptability as a person' (Featherstone 1982, 26). This has a consequence for how we see ageing as 'old age'. With a 'self preservationist conception of the body', imaged in the youthful bodies of contemporary Western popular culture, the social consequences of this shift in emphasis are considerable.

An old, fat, or disfigured body implies an undesirable self and a correspondingly reduced social status. As Featherstone and Wernick point out in their Introduction to *Images of Ageing* (1995, 3) the capacity to give significance to ageing, old age, and death is itself subject to change, not merely through alternations in modes of cultural classification, but also via the way a particular form of knowledge, through biomedical and information technology, has increasingly developed the capacity to alter not just the meaning, but the very material structure of the body. While it is increasingly the site of self-improvement and status, the body is also the centre of debate, discourse, and controversy. While issues related to such areas as the reproductive system are exposed to political and moral debate, the body is also a contested area of medicalized interest – of medical control and the resistance to it throughout the various phases of the life course.

Summary

We may have come a long way from our initial discussion of structured inequalities such as class, gender, age, and ethnicity, but necessarily so. The late- or postmodernist reduction of the life course is radically different from earlier sociological accounts locked within the framework of modernity where many of these structures and attendant inequalities seemed to forge a more predicable life course. Late- or postmodernity would seem to negate these structures and some of their more deterministic or predictable impacts, but not entirely. The implications of such inequalities continue to leave an impression on the life course, its experiences, and opportunities.

Within the consumer culture practically synonymous with late-postmodernity, one tendency is the fragmentation and differentiation of markets. In its most extreme formulation this is seen as entailing the end of the significance of social class and the increase in the consumption of an endless series of signs and images which do not cohere and cannot be used to formulate a structured lifestyle and set of tastes throughout the life course. In a more moderate view, however, patterns of consumption, largely influenced by inequality of income and wealth, set up a homologous relationship between the consumer's identity, notions of self, the body, and the product (Sawcuch 1995, 174). These patterns of consumption can impact on life experiences, status and material qualities from infancy to old age.

Culturally speaking, there is a link between late- or postmodern society and the power and symbols of consumption which directly influence the different 'phases' of life. Mass marketing has been replaced by ever-more sophisticated techniques of market segmentation in which consumer markets are identified and targeted. Thus, the commodification of such phases begins with childhood – often linked not to the product but the brand identity. While this may help reflect age groupings it plausibly reinforces it by creating age identities. But at the same time such markets may blur age categories, for example, make-up for female children or the discussion of sex in magazines for young 'teens.

Where does this all leave the significance of occupational groupings marked by differing income rewards (if notions of class are jettisoned) or age, gender, and ethnicity as determinants in the life course? For one thing, the world of consumption is not available to all and thus becomes itself a major marker of inequality. This may be put succinctly. Consumption patterns may lead to various ways of excluding people. Many people simply do not have sufficient money to purchase all the latest foods or holidays on offer, and suffer economic exclusion as a result; other people may be excluded spatially; they live without a car or good public transport and hence are not able to make trips to shopping malls and places of consumption to make meaningful choices. They become, in essence, second-class citizens. Not being part of the consumer world is therefore a form of social exclusion that may differentially affect individuals by way of age, gender, and ethnic background.

To conclude, the evidence suggests that such social categories as 'working-class' no longer hold the clear distinctions they once did. The divides now appear to occur around consumption and lifestyles which cut across old class lines. Indeed, some sociologists would argue that class is being replaced by 'lifestyle differences' and all sorts of complex inequalities. At the same time, new feminist approaches seek to move away from the stereotyping of women and have stressed diversity such as ethnicity which may cut across class – marking the life chances of women in some ethnic communities as the poorest. For such women the postmodern world may be one of potential and possible self-actualization but their experience of it is one of risk, restriction, and disadvantage.

The significance of late- or postmodernity in forging inequalities, then, is that in a society of choice and lifestyles, economic factors, and status may enhance and hinder the realization of those things which are regarded as culturally desirable. This may not only be in terms of consumer durables by which to forge meaningful and healthy lifestyles, but by way of making significant choices in respect of the different phases of life. At the same time, contemporary society is bounded by risks. This ensures that the life course is not only prejudiced by degrees of opportunities for realization, but risks and discontinuities which continue to undermine life experiences and life chances. Ironically, and this is a point emphasized by Beck in his account, in the 'risk society' inequalities continue to exert a powerful hold over people's lives, but they increasingly do so at the level of individual experiences rather than the social group or community. Yet, those inequalities are deemed to be related to individual actions and responsibility rather than to structural factors like social class, gender, or ethnicity (Beck 1992).

Further Reading

Allat,P., Keil,T., Bryman,A. and Bythenay,B. (eds) (1987) *Women and the Life Cycle*: *Transitions and Turning Points. Explorations in Sociology*, Basingstoke: McMillan.

Arber,S. and Ginn, J. (eds) (1995) *Connecting Gender and Ageing*: *A Sociological Approach*, Buckingham: University Press.

Attias-Donfurt,C. and Arber,S. (2000) 'Equity and Solidarity across the Generations', in Attias-Donfurt and Arber (eds), *The Myth of Generational Conflict*, London: Routledge.

Bauman,Z. (1992) 'Is There a Postmodern Sociology?', *Theory and Society*, 4(1): 2–3.

Beck,U. (1992) *Risk Society*: *Towards a New Modernity*, London: Sage.

Featherstone,M. and Hepworth,M. (1991) 'The Mask of Ageing and the Postmodern Life Course', in M.Featherstone, M.Hepworth, and B.Turner. (eds) *The Body Process and Cultural Theory*, London: Sage.

Fraser,N. and Nicolson,L. (1985) 'Social Criticism Without Philosophy: An Encounter Between Feminism and Post-Modernism', in A.Ross (ed.) *Universal Abandon? The Politics of Postmodernism*, Minneapolis: University of Minneapolis Press.

Kellner,D. (1988) 'Postmodernism as Social Theory: Some Challenges and Problems', *Theory and Society*, 4(1): 239–69.

3

Reproduction, Infancy, and Parenting

This and the following chapter focus on the early phases of life through conception, infancy, and childhood. Both chapters will consider a number of the recent developments and accompanying debates surrounding these areas and explore the tendency for current moral and political discourse to accompany the early years – problemitizing the first phases of the life course. This problematizing is partly a result of medicalizing influences and partly because of the way that cultural, economic, and technological changes have been brought to bear on infancy and parenting in late- or postmodernity.

In this chapter we will also discuss the overlapping themes of contemporary parenthood – the changing role of motherhood and fatherhood, parent–child relations, and child-raising practices. Although concerned primarily with recent developments in late- or postmodern Western society, scope is also given to historical and cross-cultural perspectives which will provide a comparative means of exploring the social construct of the first years of the life course and the enduring impact of patriarchy and other expressions of inequality particularly those pertinent to aspects of gender. In this respect, it will be become evident that while many fresh changes are wrought in last/postmodernity, underpinning aspects of inequality remain even if their expressions have been transformed.

Pregnancy and Childbirth

The beginning of human life is of course conception, followed then by maturity in the womb, and finally birth into the physical and social world. In various ways human societies have control over these biological processes as they do with other stages of life, whether it is through the rites of passage associated with pregnancy more common in pre-industrial societies, or the dominion over childbirth exercised by the medical profession in the contemporary world. These facts mark a recognition that every society concerns itself with the human reproductive capacity and, as we shall see again in a number of subsequent chapters, the related area of sexuality and systems of morality associated with it.

Motherhood, commencing with pregnancy, is interpreted in feminist writings as a biological process that has been subject to ideological constructs. Frequently identified are cultural notions of incapacitation which infer that biology limits women's social functions through pregnancy and care of the infant, whereas, in the words of Oakley, 'reproduction is not a handicap, but an achievement of women' (Oakley 1980, 49). It is the feminist approach which most of all brings an appreciation that the experience of being a mother is influenced by a variety of social institutions and the parenting which the woman herself quite possibly received and whereby engendered perceptions of parenting are passed through the generations. Even before conception, however, there is evidence of patriarchal control of the female reproductive system and this is clear in taboos surrounding menstruation.

There are many historical examples. For instance, among the Sioux Indian tribe of North America a number of prohibitions surrounding female menstruation was evident. At the time of her period a woman was believed to be 'unclean' and in a state of taboo. She was thus expected to observe a number of ritual practices and be removed from contact with the community. It was the tradition to remove menstruating women to separate communal lodges where they were brought food and water and otherwise 'cared' for by female friends. There they remained until menstruation ceased. This segregation occurred because Sioux men believed that sacred objects and war paraphernalia were subject to contamination from a woman in this condition. Women, even when not menstruating, were considered a sufficiently corrupting influence that to touch a man's food, medicine, or weapons was to defile them. Accompanying this set of taboos there prevailed the belief that having intercourse with a woman up to four days before a religious ceremony or going to war could be detrimental to future outcomes.

Various explanations as to why women are regarded as being in a state of taboo at the time of menstruation have been advanced; the most celebrated perhaps being that forwarded by Mary Douglas (1966). Douglas interprets the regulations relating to menstruation and menstrual blood, which she sees as very widespread, as often essentially manipulative devices by which men dominate and control women. By the use of taboos the former are able to assert male superiority by contrasting females as unclean and polluting, as opposed to male purity. This entails the designation of separate male and female social spheres which exclude women from male areas of life in order to control strategic resources such as food and tools, and to blame women for sickness and misfortune caused by breach of taboo regulations, possibly extracting compensation for them.

Historically and cross-culturally speaking, pregnancy and birth have been a precarious and uncertain time. This is in stark contrast to experiences in Western society where infant mortality during the early stages after birth is extremely low. Potential danger to mother and child in pre-industrial societies means that these natural processes are circumscribed by religious beliefs and rites of passage which are assumed to provide supernatural help for both mother and child. Fruzzetti's study (1982) of Islamic rituals in Bengali culture provides a fine example where particular rites seek supernatural help but at the same time display patriarchal overtones. Following the birth the mother and child are secluded for a period from family and friends – a time that is related to beliefs bound up with impurity and where boundaries become important. Fruzzetti's account gives scope to feminist appraisals of such rites of passage. Patriarchy would seem to be evident in that at the time of birth the midwife (usually a low-caste Hindu woman) is an important figure during what constitutes an impure period that is surrounded by taboo and social restrictions. As an 'outcast' it is she who is responsible for performing this lowly social task. Although such social exclusion for the mother may seem curious to Westerners, it is not dissimilar from the now largely superfluous tradition known as 'Churching' where the female was not permitted to rejoin her church congregation for a month after giving birth on the grounds that she was in a defiled state.

The Medicalization of Motherhood

Social control of the female reproductive system is by no means limited to pre-industrial societies. In 1975, Ivan Illich published his famous critique of modern medicine and the medical profession, *Medical Nemesis*. In this volume he put forward his arguments for what he saw as the negative and damaging repercussions of medicine. Illich also attempted to show how the profession had increasingly come to control many areas of life, including its natural processes such as birth and death. The themes developed by Illich have subsequently been extended by other commentators. From the last decades of the twentieth century much research has been conducted into motherhood as increasingly a medicalized domain. Moreover, control by the medical profession over motherhood is now regarded as so extensive that it has become a feminist issue since the profession is dominated by men who have come to oversee the female natural process of childbirth as part of the wider cultural control of the female body.

The medicalization of childbirth is evident in the dramatic increase in the proportion of babies born in hospital (from 15 per cent in 1927, to 98 per cent in 1980 in the UK), alongside the proliferation of medical techniques for monitoring pregnancy, intervening in childbirth, and for the care of new-born infants. All this involves the use of a medical frame of reference to make sense of and shape expectations, experiences, and aspects of risk during pregnancy and childbirth. It is the medical world which tends to sees pregnant women as 'patients', pregnancy as an 'illness', and successful childbearing in terms which downplays its social and emotional aspects.

As the management of pregnancy and childbirth has passed into the control of the medical domain, many women may be left with a sense of being mere onlookers in the essential process of giving birth – reducing another sphere of women's power over their lives. The need felt by some women to circumvent the medicalization of motherhood has frequently led them to opt for one variety or another of 'natural' childbirth techniques. The latter would appear to open up choices for mothers who, through a natural process, are weighing up various risks involved in either the medicalization of childbirth or the various 'alternatives' now on offer.

A vast amount of feminist literature has explored themes related to the medicalization of motherhood. Those such as Oakley, in her aptly named *Captured Womb* (1984), focus on upon the medial patriarchal control of the development of the foetus. A different approach is to consider male hegemony through professional–patient relationship and female reproduction, one which is essentially a power relationship hedged around by a dominant patriarchal discourse (Tew 1990). Others still, such as Duelli-Klein (1989), have considered the harmful effects on the self brought by medical insemination, while Stanworth (1987) and Rowland (1993) have detailed the negative implications of reproductive technologies. While such works are largely focused upon modern medical contexts, historical and comparative studies are able to show that medicalization is merely one of a number of means by which males exercise domination over the female reproductive system (Oakley 1990).

A subject for much of the feminist literature is related to the health risks which medicalization brings. Late- or postmodernity may usher in choice, but that choice is not without its dangers. A common-sense view is that medical and scientific advances have allowed women to limit their fertility and, by making childbirth safer, furnished them with more freedom in influencing their own natural processes. There are various shortcomings however. First, the contraceptive pill and the (Intra uterine device) IUD – heralded in the 1960s as instruments of women's liberation – appear to now carry significant health risks, and a range of unwanted side-effects. The widespread use of the pill means that it is generally accepted that women, not men, are responsible for contraception. Second, the technical possibility of fertility control coexists with dominant ideas about motherhood – the belief that motherhood is the natural, desired, and ultimate goal of all 'normal' women, and that there is something wrong with women who deny their so-called 'maternal instincts'.

Ethical Issues and New Reproductive Technology

In late- or postmodernity many of the emergent new technologies have brought with them far-reaching ethical debates. This is highlighted in technologies related to reproduction. The rapid growth of medical science and technology generally in advanced Western societies has impacted upon the sphere of health and medicine and, in turn, biological processes such as human reproduction. In doing so, this has raised numerous ethical debates related to just what should be permitted in a civilized society. Embryo research, sperm banks, ovary and egg donation, cloning, surrogacy, and 'artificial wombs' are all issues that are well established and will continue to generate controversy into the future. The key theme related to all these issues is that when it comes to manipulating life, what is technically possible may not always be morally desirable.

At times the state has found it necessary to intervene and occasionally offer guidelines or set limitations to reproductive technology. Typical of this was the UK government's establishment, in 1982, of the Warnock Committee. Its remit was to consider the ethical implications of new reproductive technology. In its final report the Committee recommended very close regulation of such developments mentioned above through a new body, the Human Fertilization and Embryology Authority, which had the power to license (in vitro fertilization) IVF clinics. It also banned, in contrast to the USA, the commercialization of such practices – where wombs could be 'sold' or 'rented'. Ethical decisions are also related to perhaps less controversial issues. For instance, it is doctors and hospitals that restrict IVF to women under 40 years of age who have male partners, while single women, older women, and lesbian couples are only slowly gaining access to this technology.

These new technological developments in reproduction also raise ethical issues ranging from laboratory fertilization to surrogate motherhood – in which one woman bears a child for another – all of which create problems with traditional definitions of the family. In this instance, the question might be asked: who is the real mother? In 1991, Arlette Schweitzer, a 42-year-old woman in the USA became the first woman on record to give birth to her own grandchildren (in this case twins). Because her daughter was unable to see a pregnancy to full term, she agreed to have her daughter's fertilized embryos surgically implanted in her own womb. Such a case obviously raises complex ethical questions about the creation and manipulation of life itself. At the same time, it illustrates how new reproductive technologies have created fresh choices for women but, in the eyes of critics, further undermined the family as a core social institution.

Another emerging controversy is in regard to anonymous sperm donors. Hitherto, men who have donated sperm for childless couples have enjoyed the legal right to be anonymous. However, a generation of children is growing up wishing to know who their biological fathers are. In Holland and Sweden they now have that right. Other Western countries are debating the issue. The discourse related to this particular debate is surrounded by the issue of 'rights'. Children demanding information as to who their fathers are, speak of the right to know. The fathers who donated their sperm have frequently argued for the right to privacy. The biological mother and her infertile husband may have different thoughts on the issue. Should the debate fall to the advantage of the child then, ironically, men considering donating sperm for altruistic reasons may think twice about doing so.

Contraception has also brought profound social consequences. The family has, in various respects, been radically shaped by the choices offered by contraception. One repercussion is that the average number of children per family is declining and now stands at 1.8 and is falling. This includes those children adopted – the rate of which has also fallen sharply, for example, 6000 in England and Wales in 1994, compared with 21,000 in 1971. The rapid decline in the birth rate, and consequently a trend towards smaller families, was a pattern started by professional and middle-class couples but followed later by manual occupational groups. Rising consumerist and career aspirations, declining infant mortality and, more recently, the widespread use of contraceptives, encourage and enable parents to have a smaller number of children by means of fewer pregnancies. The proportion of couples having seven or more children during the second half of the nineteenth century was 43 per cent for marriages contracted in 1925. This proportion has now fallen to some 2 per cent. In terms of broader demographic trends there will be significant implications. In 1901, 34.6 per cent of the population in the UK were under 16; in 1981 it was 22.3 per cent. Given that there is also a trend in most Western countries towards a larger section of the population being of retirement age, there will invariably be consequences in terms of dependency and generational relationships.

Birth Outside of Marriage

Given the increasing ability of women to control reproduction through contraception and abortion, it is perhaps surprising that the number of births outside of wedlock is rising (Lees 1990). Such a development would seem to bring into question the legitimacy of the idealized 'cereal box' family as the standard kinship structure. In 1961, in the UK there were 54,000 births outside marriage, while in 1971, 21 per cent of all live births were conceived out of wedlock. By 1991, the figure had risen to 236,000 or around one in three births.

The UK is not alone in this trend since in nearly all European countries the rate has doubled in the last 30 years, although it is highest in Scandinavian countries and lowest in Mediterranean Roman Catholic nations. The incidence is still growing in most countries especially among younger age groups and this may reflect the fact that there has been a dramatic decline in the age of first sexual intercourse: the median for young men and women (born between 1966 and 1975) is 17 years. Most of these births occur in stable relationships outside of marriage (80 per cent are registered by both parents). At the same time, while there is a growth in teenage pregnancy, the concept of parenthood being linked to an adult status is significantly put off with a higher proportion of people delaying parenthood until the late twenties or early thirties.

Identifying such trends is not without its difficulties. The problem of presenting data related to illegitimacy in this way is that it tends to be rather misleading in that high rates of births out of wedlock are not new. History shows that in a not untypical Dorset village, between 1870 and 1880, some 80 per cent of all the children dwelling there were illegitimate. It was not until the first half of the twentieth century that the rate of illegitimacy declined considerably.

Despite such apparent fluctuations, it has become one of Western governments' major concerns to find a way to reduce the number of teenage pregnancies and possibly attempt to increase the age that young people begin to have sex. Much emphasis is now put on helping this age group learn and understand aspects of sex especially through sex education in schools. Yet, it is feared by critics that such a strategy merely encourages young people to indulge in sex by portraying it as the norm for teenagers. The other side of the debate is the belief that young people will already be aware of sex and this is a principal way to help them participate safely in matters of choice as consenting adults, as well as encouraging it to become less of a taboo subject for discussion. In addition, there is the danger that too much emphasis may be put on the incidence of teenage pregnancies and its consequences in terms of the cost to the welfare state, alongside the problems facing teenage single mothers and the effects on the upbringing of children. While such pregnancies make news, only about 5 per cent of single mothers are teenagers (although 25 per cent of single mothers start as teenage mothers).

Voluntary Childlessness

One of the important elements of the broad 'nature versus nurture' debate of human behaviour is whether there exists anything that can be truly called the 'mothering instinct'. In short, whether nature tells a woman that it is time for her to reproduce and bring a child into the world and mother it, or whether socialization in very subtle ways puts pressures on her to contribute to the next generation upon which society relies for its survival.

Whatever the answer to this debate, it is evident that in contemporary societies having children is now more a matter of choice and even lifestyle preference than ever before. For many women, then, having children may not be their foremost life concern and may be weighed up against career considerations. This means that the conventional mandate of motherhood, where it was essential and central to a woman's identity and adult status, has been challenged in recent decades. Now it is not a question of when to have children but whether to opt to have them at all. The number of women who have decided to remain childless has been growing so that it is presently around 20 per cent of those born in 1954. The decision to refrain from having children is intrinsically tied to the freedom of women to control their reproductive system through contraception, with the pill remaining the most popular form – a quarter of all women aged between 16 and 49 take advantage of it.

Parenting

Prior to the turn of the twentieth century parenthood was not segregated or limited to certain periods in the life course. While today parents generally complete their child-raising functions with one-third of their lives to go, nineteenth-century parenthood was a lifelong career. The combination of relatively late marriage, short life-expectancy, and high fertility rarely allowed for an 'empty nest' stage. In addition, marriage was frequently broken by the death of a spouse before the end of the child-raising period.

Despite the changes over the decades, parenting and parenthood are not considered in themselves as a stage in the life course. However, they are commonly viewed as a mark of adulthood and for many people they remain crucial and meaningful aspects of life. Certainly, the birth of a first child has an enormous impact on the individual's life in a variety of ways: psychological, economic, and social. This is true for both genders, although the significance of parenthood is not the same for both. Indeed, a division of labour exists between men and women and there is still a dominant ideology that ascribes the major responsibility for parenting to the latter. Research, as we shall see below, would appear to support this view, while we may note that this engendered ideology has not always been aided in the past by the sociological enterprize. In this respect, much was exemplified by the work of Talcott Parsons who offered his theoretical contribution from the mid-twentieth century (Parsons 1959). It was crucial, maintained Parsons, that the child's intrinsic animalistic and disruptive qualities should be quelled by effective socialization. This was the way in which the child became a social being and indeed 'human'. Moreover, just as socialization was essential for the child, it was also a requisite for the social order as a totality. While, according to Parsons, socialization may take place in numerous social institutions and cultural values could be inculcated on a daily basis as a 'normal' round of social life, the family was best suited to this role. The close and emotional environment of the family was the ideal context in which the child could experience socialization and, in the case of the modern world, this meant the nuclear family and the mature female/mother role within it.

Parsons theoretical framework has, in turn, been heavily contested, not least of all by feminists who regard it as so much patriarchal ideology and the family itself as the ubiquitous and corrupting mechanism by which the patriarchal society is reproduced. The family, through socialization, subscribes childhood roles and gender structures that are far from 'natural'. Moreover, while child socialization has been a strong theme for exploration in both the disciplines of sociology and psychology, it was not until the 1970s that significant research was conducted into the preconceptions held by parents concerning their new-born children. An early study by Goldberg and Lewis (1972), for example, found that mothers of six-month-old infants expected their baby girls to be relatively quiet, clean and restrained, while their boy babies were anticipated to be more noisy and adventurous. The study even looked at parents' expectations of social roles before the child was born. Findings indicated that daughters were significantly more likely than sons to be rated as 'softer', having finer features, anticipated to be physically smaller, and to be more inattentive. Thus sex-typing and gender socialization appears to have already begun at the time of the infant's birth when little was known of an individual child's personality.

Expectations such as these are very likely to be the first stage in accomplishing a self-fulfilling prophecy. On the other hand, a persistent problem in this area of study is to establish whether parents simply treat their children in a sex-stereotyped way, or whether their actions represent a response to initial differences in behaviour between girls and boys. This is the essential nature versus nurture debate which informs so many discussions of the behaviour of both sexes.

The more learned of non-Western cultures, however, the more it became appreciated that the expected norms surrounding the behaviour of men and women varied enormously: both genders could be active or passive, aggressive or tender, sexually permissive or timid. It thus became evident that gender identity, through early processes of socialization as with other stages of life, is socially constructed. This may have detrimental consequences. For example, Gail Wyatt in *Stolen Women* (1997) has shown how the sexual identity of black women, set down from the earliest stage of life, has forged negative self-images largely as a result of dominant ideologies of masculinities in black culture. The consequences are manifested in later life with the women's sceptical attitudes towards relationships, marriage, and sexuality.

Child-Raising: Anthropological Approaches

The theme of early socialization is intrinsically linked to that of child-raising which varies considerably historically and cross-culturally, and where the evidence from Europe and elsewhere clearly shows an infinite variety of possibilities. In *Coming of Age in Samoa* (1928) Margaret Mead notes the differences between raising children in a tribal society compared to practices in the West at the beginning of the twentieth century. While Mead's work is now somewhat discredited in terms of her accuracy, at least several of her findings have been verified by comparable anthropological studies which show that aspects of child-raising are very close to how things were in Europe in previous centuries. Mead explains that the work/non-work distinction of childhood in the West is not present in Samoa. Children are gradually given tasks of increasing complexity and responsibility according to their age and in this way adulthood is not a clear stage but something that is slowly 'achieved'. Older children have responsibility for younger ones, even those aged between 2 and 3 years old. Socialization, including punishment, may be the responsibility of the next oldest sibling.

The anthropological studies by Malinowski at the beginning of the twentieth century also provided comparative evidence which further demonstrated that much of what was taken for granted in the West concerning specific age groups need not occur universally but are only established by a limited number of societies. Writing in the inter-war period, Malinowsky described the life of Trobriand children and adolescents as considerably freer and more open than that of similarly aged Western contemporaries in terms of taking responsibility for their own activities and in sexual exploration. Moreover, parental roles are considerably limited. The prime responsibility for exercising authority over the children lay not with the father but with the mother's brother. Malinowski also contrasted the relationship of father to the infant in the two cultures, noting the absence of the father from the nursery, whereas the Trobriand father offered a nurturing role, while also providing companionship for the child (Malinowski 1954).

Even today childhood in many cultures is experienced in a very different way from that of Western society. In Haiti, for instance, the children live in one of the poorest societies known. They are cherished in infancy but when they reach the age of about four years old they begin a life of hard labour, unappreciated and unrelieved work. The parents' attitude towards their offspring is often severe or at least ambivalent. Contemporary childhood in rural Haiti is one where children may be lucky enough to attend school; yet their way of life is much more like Medieval Europe than anything approaching contemporary Western culture.

Patterns of Child-Raising

Several authors have enriched our appreciation of cultural variations in child-raising in Western society. Some have seen the changes occurring with the onset of *modernity*. This is evident in the writings of De Mauss (1976), although the principal explanation for such changes in Europe he largely sees through a psychological perspective in his understanding of parenting. De Mauss' hypothesis was that transformations in parent–child relationships are independent of social and economic circumstances and constitute an autonomous source of historical change. The origin of this evolution lies in the ability of successive generations of parents to regress to the psychic age of their children and negotiate the anxiety of that age in a more effective way the second time they encounter them than they did during their own childhood. This process was similar to that of methods of psychoanalysis, which also involved regression and a second opportunity to face childhood anxieties in a more constructive way.

As De Mauss saw it, this evolution of child-raising practices followed the period of industrialization in Europe. First, there was the decline of what he called the 'Intrusive Mode' (throughout the eighteenth century) which involved a significant transition in parent–child relations. This period marked an attempt to conquer the child's mind and will. The child was raised by intrusive parents, nursed by the mother, hit but not regularly whipped 'for its own good'. Yet this harshness was accompanied by an improved level of care, and where the child was 'prayed with but not played with'.

Second, there occurred what De Mauss referred to as the 'Socialization Mode' (dominant between the nineteenth and mid-twentieth centuries). Raising the child became less a process of conquering its will than of training and guiding. Here, the father took a more than occasional interest in the child, instructing it, even relieving its mother of childcare responsibilities. The third stage was the 'Helping Mode' (which began in the mid-twentieth century). This stage involved the proposition that the child knows better than its parents what it needs at each period of development, and this fully entailed both parents in dealing with specific requirements.

In this latter stage children are neither struck nor scolded. 'Helping' involves time, energy, and negotiation by both parents. Here, De Mauus saw the influence of Freud's 'channelling impulse', Skinner's behaviourism, and Dr. Spock's writings which constituted a move from viewing childhood through adult eyes to seeing it with the eyes of the child (see below).

De Mauss believed that changing concepts of childhood were also linked to the evolution of the family. Six prevalent social attitudes were evident in Europe. First, up until the fourth century children were expendable since families were large and infant mortality high: infanticide was frequent when children (usually girls) were left to die, particularly in times of food shortage. Second, until the thirteenth century abandonment was common and amounted to the handing over of the child to be raised by others. Here, children had no social status, they were 'unseen' and childhood constituted what was perceived as an irrational period of life. Third, until the eighteenth century there was a prevailing attitude of ambivalence where the child began to enter the parent's emotional life. This was accompanied by a decline in mortality rates and generally greater economic prosperity.

Fourth, from the early eighteenth and throughout the early nineteenth century there prevailed an 'intrusive' orientation when parents attempted to conquer the child's mind and will by shaping 'little adults'. This was linked to greater life-expectancy. Beginning with the middle-classes, children begun to slowly enter social life and the period of childhood became more clearly defined. Fifth, there emerged the period from the nineteenth to the early twentieth century in which was observable an increasing emphasis on socialization that constituted the attempt to raise socially acceptable human beings and foster infant obedience. The child was seen as a miniature and potential adult, although there was a greater separation of childhood and adulthood by the emergence of the 'adolescent stage'. Finally, from the early twentieth century there evolved, as noted above, the 'helping mode' that included awareness of the child's needs and a move towards 'permissive rearing' which was at least partly shaped by psychoanalytical literature.

The problem with Mauss' psychological perspective was that it played insufficient attention to the evolution of child-raising practices in Western Europe by way of structural and cultural changes generated by the process associated with *modernity*. Before the industrial revolution families of all classes frequently sent children for some form of training at an early age – sharing in domestic and working life. The child mortality rate was high until the nineteenth century and this influenced attitudes towards child-raising where frequently there were few deep emotional bonds between parents and siblings. Industrialization had repercussions for children as many became fodder for the factories, often under grim conditions and involving many hours of work. Yet, the industrial revolution was not a simple process of the child's experience moving from the home to the factory since children were often involved in agricultural labour. The difference was that with industrialization work constituted a more tightly regulated and supervised activity.

Mauss also tended to play down the transformation in the family structure from extended to nuclear and the impact that this had on parent–child relationships. Shorter, for example, highlights changing relationships in terms of the privacy of the nuclear family, the idealized context of romantic love between spouses, the priority of nurturance given by the mother, and the more stringent boundary line between the family and the wider community (Shorter 1985). All these developments were products of modernity, as was another development – the growth of the state and its concern with child welfare.

In the nineteenth century there was little regard towards child welfare. It did not become a social issue until later in that century and the beginning of the twentieth century. Initially, the concern was only with physical welfare and this accompanied social attitudes towards women which focused on their role as wife rather than a mother. In the early twentieth century there occurred considerable changes in beliefs about motherhood and the family, and women were judged on their child-raising through medical and psychological discourses. At the same time, factory work led to state intervention in controlling child labour. Legislation eventually transformed childhood from being a time of initiation in the workforce, to a time of schooling. This helped forge a new ideology of childhood as a distinct period in its own right.

From the mid-nineteenth century there evolved a more romantic view of childhood where the working child was seen as 'unnatural'. The state acknowledged the child as unique, helpless, and vulnerable, rather than as a small adult or chattel of adults. Much was typified by the proliferation of state-run orphanages. The Factory Act of 1806 applied to orphaned apprenticeships and recognized the well-being of a class of young citizens and the state's responsibility towards them. This was accompanied by the growth of private charity organizations to help children and advance their education. In 1889, legislation was enacted in England and Wales protecting children against cruelty, while in 1895 the Society for Prevention of Cruelty Against Children received its Royal Charter.

This brief historical overview is, however, something of a simplification and there is more to consider. In his account, the historian Lawrence Stone (1977) was more concerned with the different child-raising practices employed by the various social classes that evolved particularly from the nineteenth century and where status and income proved to have determining qualities. Among the aristocracy there was something of an indifference; the child was abandoned to nurseries and the public schools. The upper middle classes displayed a greater affinity with their children but still carried the philosophy of 'spare the rod, spoil the child'. In contrast, the affluent professional classes and landed gentry from the late nineteenth century were more child-orientated: affectionate and sometimes excessively permissive – this eventually spread to the lower middle-classes. Then there were the Puritan and religiously non-conformist bourgeoisie and upper-artisans who began to put a great deal of emphasis on love and the rejection of physical punishment. The stress was more on psychological pressures of prayer, moralizing, and the threat of eternal damnation. For the lower-artisan class the attitude towards the child mixed 'traditional brutality' with sound education. Finally, the economic circumstances of the poor meant an attitude to the child that was barbaric, exploitive, indifferent, one which frequently led to widespread abandonment.

Another account of changing parent–child relationships related to social classes was that provided by Young and Willmott in which they identified the important implications of the industrial revolution for the working classes. Industrialization enhanced relationships within the extended family, brought the utilization of all family members in wage earning, and the emergence of a female 'trade union' with the strengthening between the mother and her mother and the latter's responsibility for child-raising. By the mid-twentieth century middle-class patterns begun to gradually filter down to the working classes with the husband gradually drawn back into the family unit and where more egalitarian conjugal roles slowly developed. The dominance of the nuclear family thus became established and the home became an attractive place to be in the growing leisure-based consumer society (Young and Willmott 1957).

Motherhood

Child-raising practices have long been impacted by so-called 'expert' advice as part of the development of what, as we have noted above, De Mauss designated the 'Helping Mode'. The advice presented by the specialized literature regarding child-raising practices clearly changed considerably over the years, and sometimes what they have on offer has proved blatantly contradictory. This has added to the pressure, especially for first-time mothers, of whether or not women are conforming to what experts believe are good mothering techniques. If women believe that motherhood is biological, they may do whatever they discern is best for their child and rely on what they possibly perceive as their 'material instinct'. On the other hand, as we shall see below, a good number of women are beginning not to feel this way, being quite insecure or not feeling that confident, for their own personal reasons, that they are doing the right thing. Hence, they may rely heavily on the literature and regard the expert advice as sound.

In recent decades there have been many competing ideas of motherhood supporting the evidence that it is, to some degree at least, socially constructed. Cultural, medical, political, and psychological factors all play a part in the analysis of motherhood, depending on which discourse is most favoured at any given time. For instance, in America John Watson's behaviourist psychology proved to be very influential in the first-half of the twentieth century. According to Watson, what children required was strict discipline: rigid sleeping patterns, feeding, and toilet schedules, which he maintained would build up the character of a child (Richardson 1993). He also suggested that women should become emotionally detached from their infants. For behaviourist theorists such as Watson the child would inevitably respond in a positive way and, as a consequence, the 'balanced', mature adult would develop. This stringent regulation of the behaviour and natural drives of the young infant appeared to be very much in line with the virtues of self-discipline that was practically synonymous with early twentieth-century *modernity*.

In the post-war period, especially in the 1950s and 1960s, there was a discernible move towards 'permissive' child-raising practices and much of this reflected the findings of psychoanalyst Dr Benjamin Spock who pioneered this approach. Spock suggested that mothers should indulge their children: feed them on demand and provide them with affection and attention whenever required. Above all, mothers were urged to follow their natural instincts since they were the real experts regarding their own children. This liberal stance, in turn, reflected the emergence of the so-called 'permissive society' in which a range of traditional and cherished social and political institutions were challenged in favour of 'alternatives' and experimentation.

Spock expressed concern about the use of nurseries by working mothers, stating that the environment produced within them was insufficient and superficial and failed to be as caring as the infant's family. This idea was circulated at a time when women had gained some independence in their work outside of the home. Spock had more sympathy for working mothers than John Bowlby later expressed, however he also placed emphasis on the mother as the most important figure for a young child.

Bowlby's maternal deprivation theory, which put a stress on mother–infant bonding, was also influential at one time (Bowlby 1961). The evidence for Bowlby was that the infant could only form meaningful attachments with one person and this was most perennially the mother. Disruption of the relationship with the mother in childhood by, for instance, prolonged separation will produce anxiety in the child and effects similar to grief for the loss of a loved one. Bowlby's work had a practical implication. As a result of his writings orphanages were modernized, while children's homes were reorganized into smaller units that attempted to recreate the 'family' environment rather than that of a welfare institution. Adoption and fostering laws underwent change to take the child's needs into greater account. However, critics later argued that Bowlby's work also had harmful consequences. They maintained the net result was to pathologize and marginalize any alternative form of family other than the idealized nuclear family. In short, his research and recommendations pre-supposed a two-parent family with a gendered division of labour. Other critics asked whether it was really contact with the mother that proved the decisive variable and questioned whether deprivation is simply the absence of love. The security provided by regular contact with a familiar person is similarly important, not necessarily the mother.

Despite criticisms, social agencies took on the recommendations of Bowlby's findings. Unfortunately, there were some serious implications including many documented cases of children left with their natural parents who suffered fates far worse than if they had been removed. Bowlby believed that 'children thrive better in bad homes than in good institutions'. Nonetheless, there proved to be little satisfactory evidence in support of this. Rutter points out, for example, that the reality is that many institutions provide quite satisfactory care. Although deviant behaviour displayed by children in institutional care is above average for the population, it is still less than the deviancy of children from family homes where they are experiencing disturbances and distress (Rutter 1979).

Experiences of Motherhood

For many women motherhood has become a phase in the life course, rather than a 'career', and there is increasing female status derived from occupations outside of the home. This brings challenges to patriarchal control over fertility and sexuality and marks an advance in overcoming an oppressed gender identity. The emphasis on a career outside of the family, however, is most likely to be found among middle-class rather than working-class women. In more traditional working-class communities having children and organizing the home once provided the woman with the basis of her status although, from the 1960s, there were strong indications that this was slowly changing in line with the aspirations of middle-class women, especially when the former began to rejoin the employment sphere (Young and Willmott 1962, 1973). Thus working and middle-class norms associated with mothering began to converge, reflecting changing experiences for both. As a result, by the end of the twentieth century more generalized sociological appraisals could be directed towards the 'average' mother, although important class differences remained.

Several sociological studies have looked at experiences of contemporary parenting and suggest that different attitudes can be discerned which may at least be partly attributed to class. In her work *On Being a Mother* (1983), Boulton found that mothers display four basic contrasting experiences of parenting. First, there is the 'fulfilled' mother, where the woman expresses a strong sense of meaning and purpose, and enjoys the immediate situation of childcare. Second, 'alienation', where the experiences are reversed and there is a prevailing weak sense of meaning and purpose. Here, the woman is irritated by the immediate situation of childcare. Third, some mothers describe themselves as 'satisfied' – an intermediate category between these two poles. Here, the response is one of enjoyment, but the sense of meaning and purpose is weak. Finally, there was an alternative intermediate category, 'in conflict' – where the immediate reaction is one of irritation but the sense of meaning and purpose remains strong.

Boulton discovered that roughly half the mothers in her survey enjoyed their new-found role of childcare; roughly half were irritated by it. The sources of women's frustrations and satisfaction varied. More working-class women found it difficult and stressful to resolve conflict between housework and childcare responsibilities. In contrast, a greater number of middle-class women felt that childcare monopolized their lives and made them feel a loss of individuality. In addition, Boulton considered the impact of the father's support and help on the mother's experience. In her sample only nine of the husbands gave 'extensive help', 18 'moderate help', and 23 (about half) 'minimal help'. Social class differences were important here too. Middle-class, rather than working-class husbands, were more likely to provide 'extensive help' and display more nurturing tendencies.

There is little doubt that motherhood is far more complicated a social role than ever before. Even though there is an increasing choice afforded in late- or postmodernity whether a woman becomes a mother or not, for some becoming a mother is still regarded as a significant achievement and that raising the child is the most important work they can be involved in. However, changes in the family, the departure away from the standard nuclear family, and the emergence of single and gay/lesbian mothers, means that there is no one model of what good mothering amounts to.

Some women complain of being trapped by the motherhood role or at least display mixed emotions about raising children. Paradoxically, the decision to opt for motherhood now brings even greater demands. Today, the role is often viewed as a source of personal fulfillment, identity, and a principal dimension of the psychological development of a 'normal' woman. However, normative social constructions tend to be implied, rather than clearly defining what constitutes a 'good mother' and many assumptions are made that it is the mother's responsibility to ensure that her children 'turn out correct' (Phoenix et al. 1991). Indeed, there is also increasing pressure on the mother to 'get it right'. Kate Figes, in an article in *The Guardian* newspaper (4/12/2001), reported that as a result of such social pressures as well as matters of choice, guilt has become a familiar emotion for most mothers. Such guilt relates to eating the wrong foods or living with too much stress while pregnant. Guilt comes with having to make informed choices about opting for a caesarean rather than a natural birth, concerning preferring to develop her own interests rather than engaging in vigorous interactive play with their toddler; and guilt about going back to work in the need to earn a second family income when most have little choice but to do so.

Undoubtedly, the mixed response of women to motherhood is at least partly impacted by the confusion surrounding 'expert' advice on child welfare and the status of the child. Wyness (2000) examined a number of policy reforms and professional initiatives within educational childcare and legal contexts and noted profoundly competing viewpoints of children's social position. There now exist moral ambiguities, limits to child protection, and the individualization of schooling and childhood and citizenship. He concludes that despite the impetus on protecting children, they are increasingly viewed as being more active, and as having the capacity to take on social roles and responsibilities which suggest not so much the terminal decline of childhood but its contested nature. While throughout the twentieth century there existed different forms of expert advice on parenting, the twenty-first century begins with no single or straightforward body of expert guidance on what constitutes 'good parenting' (Selwyn 2000).

Single-Mothers

As we have seen, an increasing number of women in Europe now become pregnant as unmarried teenagers, and many decide to raise their children on their own. There are various reasons advanced as to why the number of single-mothers is growing. Today, there is obviously less social pressure to embrace marriage, but possibly more so to become sexually active. It is now largely acceptable for young single-mothers to keep their babies, while the economic dimension is clearly important. Entering the job market has bolstered women's income capacity to be single-mothers and due to state benefits this is becoming at least partially financially viable.

Child benefit is payable to all mothers on behalf of children, which guarantees a mother's income, and means that they do not necessarily have to ask their husband/partner for financial assistance.

Some 23 per cent of all families with dependent children in the UK in 1994 (about one in ten of all households with children) are one-parent families – three times the proportion in 1971. Over 90 per cent are headed by a single-mother. Until the mid-1980s, most of the increase was due to divorce. But since then, the proportion of divorced mothers has remained stable, whilst that of single never-married mothers has doubled (Family Policy Study Centre 1995, 2).

Noting such changes in the 1970s, Rapoport and Rapoport (1975) saw the rise of single-parenthood as a symptom of increased tolerance of diverse family forms in contemporary society. In this respect, single-parent families may be regarded as an important emerging variant and are thus becoming accepted as a legitimate alternative to traditional family structures. However, there is little evidence that a large number of single-parents interpret their situation as ideal and actively choose it as an option rivalling dual parenthood. In contrast, Morgan (1986) suggests that the proliferation in lone-parenthood could partly be due to changing relations between men and women. Here, the important factors causing the rise include the expectations that both sexes have of marriage and the growing opportunities for women to develop a life for themselves outside of marriage and long-term relationships.

One-Parent Families and Deprivation

Much contemporary research points to the conclusion that growing up in a lone-parent family usually disadvantages children. Some studies indicate that a father and mother each make a distinctive contribution to a child's social development, so it is unrealistic to expect one parent alone to do as good a job as two working together. For instance, evidence suggests that children of lone-parent families fare worse at school and in finding jobs and are more criminally inclined than children from two-parent families. In the USA, they are also twice as likely to be imprisoned for a variety of crimes.

In the UK, in 1990, 18 per cent of families were headed by a lone mother, 2 per cent by a lone father. The problem then could be said to be the absence of the father. Sociologists such as Dennis and Erdos (1993) have even argued that in some geographical areas single-parent families are so widespread that a male generation has grown up without the discipline of a father figure. This they claimed was largely responsible, besides a number of other factors, for urban riots in Newcastle in the North East of

England during 1991. By comparison, Cashmore (1985) has questioned the assumption that children brought up by one-parent families are significantly worse off than those brought up by two by way of emotional and psychological support and in terms of overall levels of care.

Whatever the merits of the two sides of this debate, the greatest problem is a financial one. A UK government published paper (1993) indicated that there does not appear to be a link between single-parent families and criminality but that it is poverty, rather than the absence of a second parent, which is associated with young offenders. On average, children growing up in such families start out with disadvantages and end up with a lower educational achievement and lower incomes, and face a greater chance of forming lone-parent families themselves (Popenoe 1988). Despite, the observation above related to growing economic independence, for some mothers lone-parenthood greatly increases the risk of poverty, as it can limit the woman's ability to work and to further her education. Hence, lone-parents form a core of the rising problem of child poverty in Europe.

There would seem to be some evidence that the consequence of single-parenthood is also reflected in terms of the educational performance of the child. In 2001, according to a study of more than 1000 youngsters by the Institute for Social and Economic Research (ISER), children with two parents do better at school than those from single-parent families (the report studied the educational successes and failures of 1157 individuals born between 1974 and 1981). The gap between the exam achievements of children with single-parents and those from traditional family backgrounds is as wide as that between children from the poorest and wealthiest families. A child who has lived in a one-parent family at any time in his or her life has a 21 per cent chance of getting an A-level or a similar qualification. By contrast, children in two-parent families have a 47 per cent chance of achieving A-levels.

Three out of ten of the young people surveyed in the ISER report had spent time as children in a single-parent family and half of these had lived with only one parent before they reached the age of six. The report concluded that young adults who experience single-parenthood as children and those who come from families in the bottom quarter of income groups have significantly lower educational attainment on the whole. These differences ultimately translate into differences in earnings throughout the life course.

Fatherhood

It is more than significant that the topic of fatherhood seems to have been neglected by the sociological enterprize. Only relatively recently has it been established as a mainstream concern, unlike motherhood studies which are wide-ranging in their surveys. One of the reasons why this is so is because fathers are regarded as almost 'invisible' within the family unit. Even in areas which might have expected more mention of fathers, especially in terms of family studies, they are relatively unacknowledged because the family is primarily seen as a mother's domain, while fatherhood does not have the same implications in the workplace as it does for a woman who may have to temporarily retreat from it. Fatherhood, then, is perceived as more marginalized, reinforcing the idea that men's identity comes largely from the public sphere of paid work.

The traditional definition of fatherhood conforms to the social ideas and realities of the 1940s and through the early 1960s, with the exception being during the Second World War when men were drafted into the armed forces and women temporarily assumed traditional masculine occupations in civil and defence work. The time from the late 1930s up to the 1970s has sometimes been called the period of the 'absent father'. Emphasizing the significance of cohort effects was the fact that during the Second World War, many fathers rarely saw their children because of their call up for military service. In the period following the war, in a high proportion of families, most women were not in the paid labour force and stayed at home to look after their children. The father was the main breadwinner and consequently absent much of the time from the family unit. His role in the traditional home environment during this period was extremely limited.

The major image of father in the traditional appraisal was of the aloof, distant breadwinner. In the past, so much time and energy was used in this particular role that in the domestic sphere he was thought of as reserved and firm, yet benevolent. Typically, a father was respected but feared by his children, with a relationship that was emotionally remote. His interaction with his children was characterized as restricted to a brief interaction at bedtime, typically masculine work activities in the home at the weekend, Sunday outings, and the annual summer two-week vacation.

Prior to the 1960s most social scientists had mistakenly assumed that fathers were relatively unimportant in child-raising: the mid-twentieth century appeared to epitomize much and for at least some people this period is still nostalgically recalled as the 'golden age' of family life. Busfield and Paddon note the limited role of the father at the birth of a child at this time, while the extent to which fathers continued to remain peripheral within the household depended upon the way mothers coped with child-raising problems, especially in the early stages (Busfield and Paddon 1977).

From the 1980s, a father's role in the home has reflected the economics of the decade with its stress on social mobility and equality of opportunity.

There thus developed a more egalitarian approach to parenting – in theory at least, with the father taking his fair share of domestic responsibilities. There has also emerged the increasing influence of single fathers and househus-bands, and an awareness and acceptance of men in nurturing roles. Some fathers, particularly middle-class men with established careers, appear to now relish the prospect of being more actively involved in parenting – a new approach to fathering that has been frequently amplified in the media.

This fresh perspective in fathering is frequently said to reflect the emer-gence of the 'New Man' – the sensitive, caring male who seeks to escape the restrictive and dominating traditional masculine role and that this transformation is evident in more involvement in child-raising. This inno-vative orientation would seem to contradict the traditionally perceived function of fathers – one where the adult male presented a role model, especially for the young son. Here, the father's job was believed to be to prepare the child for the challenges presented by life and in facing up to responsibilities. For boys, fathers were perceived to provide a male iden-tity of competitiveness and achievement orientation. The 'New Man', by contrast, seems to be more about the self-exploration and realization that constitute the new-found attributes which are more in line with postmod-ern culture. The fact remains, however, that in terms of moving towards a more egalitarian approach to parenting, the New Man may be more myth than reality given the evidence related to nurturing the child (Table 3.1).

Boulton, as part of her research, considered the impact of the father's support and help on the mother's experience. It seemed to expose notions of the emerging 'New Man', one informed by tenderness and considera-tion, as something of an illusion. In her sample only nine of the husbands gave extensive help, 18 moderate help, and 23 (about half) minimal help. Social class differences were important in this respect. Middle-class, rather than working-class husbands, were more likely to give extensive help and display more nurturing tendencies (Boulton 1983).

It is tempting to predict that in the future men are likely to play chang-ing roles in regard to child-raising. This might be evident in growing opportunities for fathers to take paternity leave as it is understood to be

Table 3.1 Gender responsibilities for the child
(% of time in domestic sphere)

	Husband	Mother	Shared
Looking after sick children	1	63	35
Teaching discipline	10	12	77

Source: Adapted from *Social Trends*, 1996

important for them to be present for the early days of a child's life. In turn, this can be seen as an important step for the father–child relationship in starting and helping the father establish a caring role and a greater responsibility in child-raising. Paradoxically, participation might in fact be declining. Over 25 per cent of children in the UK are growing up without fathers in the home and this statistic is rising. The divorce rate and a surge in single motherhood point to more children passing through their formative years with weaker ties to their father than before. This has certainly proved to be the case in Sweden where 28 per cent of children living with only one parent never see the other parent, and the latter parent is primarily the father. By comparison, when the father has custody, the child tends to have more contact with the 'other parent': nine out of ten children living with their father had contact with their mothers. One given explanation for this is that women, who have greater contact with their children prior to divorce, are more attached to their children, and are thus more anxious to continue meaningful relationships (Hwang 1989, 133).

Fathers in the post-divorce situation face other challenges too. From the early nineteenth century men had almost complete rights over their children. Today, with the rise of women's rights and increasing divorce rates, it is the mother who is generally favoured with custody after a relationship break-up. The statistics for fathers in winning custody of their children is however increasing, depending on the circumstances. During the year 2000, in the UK, the percentage of children that went with their fathers doubled from one to two per cent. Nonetheless, this was generally in cases where mothers were not considered as reliable due to drug addiction, alcoholism, depressive illness, or health problems of comparable gravity. In a number of recent cases it has also been seen that an expectant father has been awarded control over his girlfriend's decision to abort the child.

Debate rages regarding the father's access to and responsibility towards children after divorce or separation. In 1991, the Conservative government in the UK set up the Child Support Agency (CSA) which aimed to force absent parents (mainly fathers) to contribute towards their children's upbringing. A bureau was established to administer it and collect money from absent fathers – focusing especially in the first instance on low-income fathers who were easier to locate (through social security offices). This led to considerable controversy and a highly organized campaign against the CSA (called APART, Absent Parents Asking for Reasonable Treatment). To some extent this was because the bureau did not take into account the obligations a parent might have towards a second family and that if the parent with the child was already on income support, everything collected was recouped by the Benefits Agency.

It is apparent that contemporary fatherhood is now subject to various trends. One view suggests that as a result of such variations contemporary fatherhood is in 'crisis' or at the very least is thwarted with a certain amount of ambiguity. Marsiglo, for instance, argues that after the birth of a child fathers often feel 'mixed up' or 'scared' as their feelings do not fit neatly with gender role perceptions, while there exists little by way of education as to what constitutes a 'good father' any more than a model exists for the 'good mother'. So, for the father the egocentric stage of life that may have typified youth has come to an end and he thus enters the unknown new state relatively unprepared (Marsiglo 1995).

Clearly, the transition to parenthood for both fathers and mothers is a time of change and consistency. At the birth of a child mothers are required to develop a commitment for the dependent infant. For fathers the transition is usually different as few are involved in the daily care of their young child and such participation may be viewed as optional. Society limits fathers by the influence of employment, care-giving arrangements, the economics of unequal salaries, infant activity, and residual social attitudes about men's roles. This may leave fathers feeling inadequate caregivers compared to mothers. Obviously such a dilemma is complicated in the case of stepfathers who can face emotional problems in their relationship with stepchildren – making it difficult to be the type of father figure they might hope to portray.

What may be concluded, nonetheless, is that the evidence suggests that definitions of fatherhood have evolved to one in which the importance of the fathering role is recognized as central to the child's well-being. Indeed, Lamb argues that we are currently witnessing the fourth of a series of changes in popular conceptions of the father's roles and responsibilities. That of the moral teacher, the breadwinner, and the sex-role model, is now replaced by that of the 'new nurturant father' (Lamb 1987, 7–8). The emergence of the nurturant father is not to suggest, however, that the earlier roles have disappeared entirely. Indeed, in late/postmodernity the pluralist society means that various conceptions coexist and may be shaped by lifestyle constraints and subcultural differences forged perhaps above all by ethnic cultural traditions. In regard of the latter, Delcroix (2000) has shown how Muslim Asian parents, particularly the role of the father, continue to be influenced not only by religious values but instilling a strong motivation element among their children against a background of social disadvantage and prejudice – suggesting the perseverance of the moral instructive, economic, and gender role-model of the male.

Gay and Lesbian Parenting

Cutting across notions of what constitutes the 'good parent' is the emergence of gay parenting and the debates which surround this new development. While its greater legitimacy may be linked to increasingly liberal attitudes towards sexuality, the adoption or surrogacy of children by gay and lesbian couples constitutes, for the most part, a lifestyle choice. In 1990, the number of gay and lesbian biological parents in the USA was estimated to be between 300,000 to 500,000. The number of children with a gay or lesbian parent in the same country is approximated to be between 6 to 14 million, and the number of children being raised in gay or lesbian households is estimated to be between 81–110 million. While these statistics challenge many traditional notions about the 'normal' family, they also indicate that many gay and lesbian couples perceive the same rewards in child-raising that 'straight' couples do. However, surrogacy and custody of children remains a vehemently debated issue.

In 1989, Denmark became the first country to formally recognize gay marriages as well as conferring legal advantages for inheritance, taxation, and joint property ownership. All Nordic countries have followed suit, but none of these nations allow gay couples to adopt children. In Western countries most gay couples in households including children raise the offspring of previous parents, yet many of them may be reserved about their sexuality, not wishing to draw unwelcome attention to their children. This is perhaps comprehensible since, in several widely publicized cases in recent years, courts have removed children from homosexual couples, claiming the best interests of the child.

One of the prevailing arguments is that children with gay parents do not constitute a 'natural state' of affairs. In short, children need a stable family with a father and mother providing suitable gender role models. A second contention is that 'children tend to live by what they learn': that there would be no real freedom of sexuality for the children as they grew up to regard gay relationships as the norm. Third, that the child may face problems of ridicule and bullying from his/her peers at school. Finally, with adoption it is very likely that the child's life has already been disrupted enough, and while gay people can love them as much as 'straight' people they cannot completely give them all they need.

There is a set of responses to these issues which would support the adoption by gay couples. First, that the sexual orientation is not irrelevant: the important consideration is love and commitment. Thus, society needs to dispense with the myth that somehow all gay people are automatically promiscuous. Second, gay women with partners bringing up children claim that they have grown up to be mature and stable, and usually heterosexual. Third, an argument in favour of adoption is related to sexual orientation: that if the sexuality of parents has had such an impact on children, adopted or not, how is it that so many straight people create gay offspring? Fourth, and this is perhaps the key argument in favour of gay adoption, even if there are problems, gay adoption must be better for the child than being passed from one foster home to another. In the UK, those in local authority care are 50 times more likely than other children to end up in prison and 60 times more likely to become homeless. Adoption is rigorously scrutinized in all cases for fitness of parenting. Because children in care may be psychologically damaged or particularly emotionally needy, the state has even more responsibility in selecting adopters. It may be that, in weighing the comparative virtues of prospective adopters, social service agencies will in future draw up their own hierarchy of preferences which may include preferences of married couple to a cohabitating one, a heterosexual couple as preferred to gay. What is clear from this is that the points of view advanced by both sides of the debate are couched not so much in terms of a moral criteria, as utilitarian arguments related to apparent 'harmful' consequences and the language of rights, whether the 'rights' of the adopted child not to be ridiculed or the 'rights' of gay couples in seeking surrogacy and subscribing to an alternative lifestyle choice.

Summary

Clearly, change and continuity are observable aspects of motherhood, fatherhood, and parenting in general which have obviously impacted on infanthood and the early stage of the life course. They are the immediate kinship context in which the early years of infancy and childhood are constructed and increasingly contested.

Historical and cross-cultural evidence shows that there is no single and universal pattern attached to any particular set of socially prescribed parental roles. Certainly, in late or postmodernity, such roles are seemingly negotiated and subject to numerous variations. There are more recent trends too. One is the abundance of so-called 'expert advice' on offer for parents or prospecting parents, much of which involves a therapeutic-psychological discourse that is the hallmark of contemporary society and which, paradoxically, may constrain choice. This is all part of the medicalization of the life course, one which is clear in the impact of medical ideologies from conception, to pregnancy, to infanthood. Certainly, it is evident that the formative part of the life course – early childhood – is circumscribed by an idealized view of how infants should be nurtured and socialized.

The problem, however, is that there is no agreement on what constitutes 'expert advice', since one orthodoxy is quickly replaced by another. Such advice has impacted differentially throughout the population. There exist various levels of acceptance with ethnic cultural differences remaining. These are significant alternatives to what may be perceived as white middle-class forms of child-raising. For example, Jackson and Nesbitt (1993) survey on the Hindu population in the UK show childhood experiences changing but are still informed by the distinctiveness of gender roles, food and fasting, festivals, prayer, worship, and religious ritual as essential elements of cultural transmission.

There is more to consider. Despite the volume of professional advice which exists, the younger generation is frequently perceived as one that is indulged with negative consequences: that children are spoilt through mass consumerism and have little sense of social responsibility instilled from an early age. This indulgence would seem to mark the impact of the new-found affluence for many families at the beginning of the twenty-first century. This is the theme of the book by the Harvard psychologist Dan Kindlon, *Too Much of a Good Thing* (2001), which explains how many American parents tend to indulge their children especially in their demand for material satisfaction and that this is in stark contrast to the discipline of previous generations. In his research Kindlon found that half of American parents say they are less strict than their parents were. Similarly, a poll carried out for *Time* magazine (2001) revealed that 80 per cent of Americans think their own children are more spoiled than children were a decade ago. The magazine also pointed out that parents do spend more quality time with their children than before and this may suggest a greater significant relationship between them. But this constitutes only slightly more time and probably has negligible affects.

These trends may create dilemmas for parents. In the UK, research by the Industrial Society (2001) indicated that parents now display feelings of guilt about spoiling their children and that the lack of discipline is ultimately responsible for every negative development discernible among the younger generation, from lethargy to drug abuse. Yet, in turn, children may not see being lavished with material goods as wholly beneficial, since the survey found that 77 per cent of 11–16-year-olds believe that a 'good' parent is someone who gives love and affection rather than satisfying endless material needs. As long as such contrasting evidence exists, the debate as to what constitutes a 'good parent' is likely to continue for some appreciable time. It is a debate informed by notions of choice but restricted by aspects of deprivation and circumscribed by the rhetoric of 'rights' and 'responsibility', as well as denoting increasing incidences of discontinuity and risk on the life course.

Further Reading

Lamb,M. (ed.) (1987) *The Father's Role: Cross-Cultural Perspectives*, Hillsdale, NJ: Erlbaum.
Margolis,M. (1984) *Mothers and Such*, Berkeley, CA: University of California Press.
Phoenix,A. (1991) *Motherhood, Meanings, Practices and Ideologies*, London: Sage.
Richardson,D. (1993) *Women, Mothering and Childrearing*, London: McMillan.
Weston,K. (1991) *Families We Choose: Lesbians, Gays, Kinship*, New York: Columbia University Press.

4

Childhood: Issues and Perspectives

Up until relatively recently the scope of the social sciences in respect of childhood has been somewhat limited to the inter-related topics of developmental psychology and child socialization. Both these approaches have tended to provide a rather restricted focus – one that has largely followed a cultural trajectory which viewed childhood as a natural 'stage' in the growth of the individual rather than as a social phenomenon established within the cultural and structural confines of *modernity*. Such an orientation has changed more recently in the emergence of what may be referred to as the sociology of childhood. This branch of the discipline has, in a re-latively short space of time, attracted a fair amount of interest, mostly from the social constructionist approach advanced by the postmodernist perspective. Inherent here is the conviction that childhood remains an impressive example of the 'invention' of stages of life and its accompanying social concerns, although it is recognized that what it amounts by way of a cultural construct is changing rapidly. This chapter will consider some of these changes, while also exploring aspects of discontinuity in this early phase of life through the increase in family break-up. Although much of the discussion of childhood is through the context of the family, the significance of formal education in forging experiences of the formative years, as well as future life chances, is also given consideration.

Childhood: From Modernity to Postmodernity

On both sides of the Atlantic childhood initially emerged as a distinct period of the life course throughout the early nineteenth century in the private experience of middle-class urban families. The new definition of the meaning of childhood and the role of children were related to the retreat of the family into domesticity, the segregation of the workplace from the home, the redefinition of the mother's role as the major custodian of the domestic sphere, and the emphasis on sentimental rather than the instrumental relations as the foundation of family life. In contrast, as we noted in Chapter 1, demographic, social, and cultural factors combined to produce only a minimum differentiation in the stages of life in pre-industrial societies throughout history. Childhood was not regarded as a distinct stage of life in most historical cultures. In the majority of such communities children were considered miniature adults, gradually assuming adult roles in their early years and slowly socially maturing into adulthood. Today, in many Third World countries these experiences remain much the same and children are engaged in work, often in demanding circumstances and in such a way that the Westerner would find morally repugnant.

Pre-modern Europe displayed similar attitudes towards childhood as observable in many parts of the Third World. This is cogently described by Aries, in his classical work *Centuries of Childhood* (1965). Here he provides evidence that in Medieval society the notion of childhood did not exist: children were for the most part 'invisible'. The child was absorbed into the world of adults soon after infancy and its status was not established in terms of age or physical maturity. Aries attempts to vindicate his view that children were well enmeshed in the adult sphere by pointing out that medieval art until about the twelfth century did not attempt to portray children as somehow distinct. The involvement in the adult world continued right up to the beginning of the twentieth century where, in most Western countries, children were expected to work at a very early age and for long hours and in many other respects not regarded as significantly different from adults. While an impressive example of historical sociology, Aries' work has not been beyond criticism. In particular, his claim that childhood did not begin until the seventeenth century has been rigorously opposed by Pollock who provides historical evidence to the contrary, and that the earlier integration of children into the adult world was not as complete as Aries suggests (Pollock 1983).

More recent works such as that of Chris Jenks (1996), have been able to show how in Western societies concepts of childhood are culture-specific and change and continue to change over time; from the pre-modern period, through modernity, and into postmodernity. Jenks notes that perceptions of childhood in modernity, as compared to pre-modernity, have in Western societies included philosophical underpinnings. This was exemplified by Rousseau's work *Emile* which asked and attempted to answer the question, what is a child? For Rousseau, writing in the early nineteenth century, childhood amounted to a particular orientation to the world, a distinct way of seeing, thinking, and feeling peculiar to itself. Essentially, argued Rousseau, childhood is a time of innocence – an innocence corrupted by society and the adult world. This innocent state was one that nature provided and which could not be properly comprehended because of the destructive impulse of the social order (Rousseau 1991).

In many respects Rousseau's view was unique, not to say naïve. It ran counter to prevailing Christian ideas of the sinfulness of fallen man, and the inherent evil to be found even in the newly born babe. The Christian perception was also supplemented in the nineteenth century by the idea of the child as 'a savage'. Structured by modernist anthropological 'evolutionist' writings, this notion insisted that the child was to the adult as the savage was to the civilized man. The child would grow, indeed 'evolve' into a civilized human being as long as it was taught and disciplined as part of the socializing process, just as Christians saw the sinful child in need of chastisement and instruction. What Rousseau, the early anthropologists and in its own way the Christian view had in common, however, was the conviction of the 'naturalness' of childhood.

Attitudes towards childhood were to change as modernity progressed. The new child-centredness of urban domestic families in Western Europe in the late eighteenth, nineteenth, and early twentieth centuries was characterized by the increasing focus on the parents and their children, rather than on a kinship group or lineage. For Aries (1965), this development was largely a response to two major demographic changes: the decline in infant and child mortality and the increase in the conscious practice of family life. Thus commenced the transformation of modern attitudes towards children, one later forged in the second half of the twentieth century by the growth in leisure as clearly demarcated from work, alongside the emergence in state welfare.

Even before this time, factory legislation and laws concerning the child's welfare and education proved an important factor in constructing a distinct period that we now call 'childhood' between infanthood and adolescence. From the mid-twentieth century, however, legislation went further. In the case of the UK, the introduction of the National Health Service, comprehensive child-benefit provisions, and the development of a universally applied educational system reflected a cultural concern for the child. This concern was seen to take on board fresh criteria in the 1989 Children Act which provided the child with a number of rights. It also took away the notion that children are the property of their parents and gave them the liberty to have their views taken into account, particularly in divorce custody cases.

For those living in modern societies, at least by the mid-twentieth century, childhood appeared to have become a clear and distinct stage of life. Even today childhood might be thought of as broadly the first 12 years of life before puberty and adolescence, and one identified as a distinct stage of human development and subsequently the subject of a growing body of child-raising and family advice literature. These advice books and magazine articles popularized the concept of childhood and the so-called 'needs' of children, prescribing the means to allow them to grow as children. It was clear that such accounts re-inforced generalized conceptions of a 'natural' life-cycle.

Many of these popular accounts were rooted in developmental psychology which involved a study of the development of the mental functions of the child particularly in relation to psychological problems and hence its potential social dysfunction. Much was typified by the work of Piaget who suggested that all children acquire cognitive competencies according to a universal sequence up to the state of adulthood, in particular an understanding of time, space, and causality. Within Piaget's system each stage of intellectual growth was characterized by a specific 'schema' or well-defined pattern and sequence of physical and mental behaviour in the child's orientation to the world.

For Jenks, this psychoanalytical approach to childhood epitomized the spirit of modernity. Throughout modernity the child only gradually came to know the adult world. This 'stage' of life claimed a greater duration within the total life experience. It was one that increasingly called upon cognitive and affective adult labour. Moreover, childhood absorbed growing material provision and, in Jenk's words, '... established this patterning of acquisitions as a "natural" right policed by an ideology of care, grounded unassailably in emotions' (Jenks 1996, 100).

Modernity produced a culture in which adults (especially women) were expected to 'sacrifice everything'. It was a strictly moral dimension of dependency, one produced within the family which, in turn, was a product of advanced capitalism, though loving and supportive in its self-image. Childhood, then, was part of family life that was compatible with modernity. In sociological accounts, as evidenced in Structural Functionalist theorizing, families were rationally organized as small social units, mobile, and compatible with consumerism and new forms of communication (Parsons 1959). They were also self-sustaining and self-disciplining, but public in their disposition. The ideology of care legitimized and aided the investment of economic and cultural capital in the 'promise' of childhood. It was also based upon what Jenks calls 'futurity', in short, a pre-occupation with 'caring', 'enabling', 'facilitating', as part of the nurturing process (Jenks 1996, 100).

Postmodernity brings a fresh version and vision of childhood. Partly this is because of new patterns of consumption and to some extent because there are new modes of relationships which have outgrown the mid-twentieth-century nuclear family. The family has changed and so too the character of relationships within them. Previously assumed points of attachment of the individual with the collective life, notably social class, work group, local community, as well as the family, are losing their influence in line with the demands of the post-Fordist mode of production, global economies, networks of communication, and the new techno-science which invades previously located spheres of knowledge and authority. Individuals are now more likely to be recognized through their immediate locations and activities than their group affiliations which once forged a sense of identity. Hence, there is now discontinuity rather than continuity which, in turn, impacts perceptions and experiences of childhood.

In postmodernity mass education and consumption have shortened and undermined a certain unique quality associated with childhood. It is increasingly difficult, argues Jenks, for the child to forge a sense of identity as part of the reflexive project of self. This is also observable in how adults now understand and relate to children. The fixed identities of adults, children, and families, have become transmogrified. The previous normative markers of social experience especially in the form of status are now relativized, while there has taken place an erosion of the view of childhood generated by a culture of 'progress' once synonymous with modernity. There are also many 'alternative lifestyles' informing the 'correct' way of bringing up the child – to the extent that parents are unsure what they are supposed to be 'alternative' to. Now, postmodernity has re-adopted the child, while childhood has become a site for the re-location of discourses concerning stability, integration, and social bonds. Childhood is increasingly envisioned as a form of 'nostalgia'; a longing for times past.

Jenks sees parent–child relationships in postmodernity as an unchosen, unnegotiated form of association and the site of ambiguous emotions. The trust which was previously anticipated as underpinning marriage, partnership, and friendship which have proved uncertain and transient, is now invested more generally in the child. Much is evident in the effectual prolongation of adolescence, the disputed territory that childhood constitutes during parental divorce, the uprating of children's status through advances in children's rights, and campaigns against addiction and criminality. Thus, the child has become *the* last remaining primary and trusting relationship (Jenks 1996, 107).

The subject of childhood in postmodernity has also been explored by Shorter who also puts the emphasis on the context of the family. While he warns of the 'hysterical proposition' that the family is breaking up, he does emphasise the consequences that changes have for children (Shorter 1985, 278). There are, according to Shorter two variables that have a direct or indirect impact on childhood in relation to the family. First, the sexual revolution that has undermined marriage as a permanent union, exposing children to the discontinuities that come with dissolved marriages. Second, that women are more independent economically. While this alters relationship with their husbands, it may also undermine mother–child relationship in that women's employment takes her out of the domestic sphere. Such developments have led to what Shorter refers to as 'the destruction of the nest' in postmodernity (Shorter 1985, 279).

While the variables associated with modernity and postmodernity impact childhood in contrasting ways, childhood, as Mills reminds us, is not just about historical periods or *time*, but is still inextricably linked to race, gender, class, and culture (Mills 2000, 9). Thew similarly argues that the deconstructionism of the postmodernist approach, should not be at the expense of these variables which structure inequalities and experience of childhood. Economic factors, gender constraints, and racial variations continue to impact childhood not least of all in terms of childhood identities.

The matter of childhood identities should also be seen from the child's point of view. This is Mayall's approach in his discussion of the child as a moral agent. Mayall points out that children make sense of their experiences and actions. In short, they are not passive actors, but reflective agents who are both able and willing to take account of other people's views and change their actions accordingly. Much may depend on the contexts in which the child's experiences are played out. For Mayall there are greater opportunities to act as an independent moral agent at home rather than school, since in the former there is greater scope for interpretation and negotiation of aspects of childhood (Mayall 2002, 109–10).

The End of Childhood?

The contemporary world brings contradictory images of childhood in Western societies. We might think of childhood as the first years of life, free from the burdens of the adult world, and where the separate haven of childhood still retains its predominant cultural representation. Indeed, in postmodernity there has emerged what Baos (1996) regards as a kind of nostalgic 'time warp' – a form of 'cultural primitivism' in which childhood is still idealized as some golden age. The media, in particular, reconstructs a view of the world that attempts to establish an imaginary and nostalgic celebration of childhood. Yet, this image is in stark contrast to the reality of an age of high divorce rates, where both mothers and fathers are often employed and are perhaps neglectful of their children, and where there is an increasing level of exposure to 'adult' programming on television – providing evidence that children are no longer protected from the grown-up world and encapsulated within their own culture. Today, we may therefore be seeing the development of a 'hurried child' syndrome, meaning that children have to grapple with images of sex and violence as well as fending for themselves as a result of a conjugal arrangement where both parents are working and perhaps neglectful of childcare (Winn 1983).

There is even the suggestion that childhood is in 'crisis'. Niel Postman, in *The Disappearance of Childhood* (1982), argues that there is no longer special children's food, games, and clothes, little respect for elders, where children's crimes now feature in crime statistics, and children lack a sense of shame regarding all things sexual. Critics of this view, nonetheless, counter that there is no convincing evidence of any dramatic shift in society's conception of childhood. Further, they note that the 'hurried child' thesis overlooks the fact that children in the lower classes have long assumed adult responsibilities in comparison to their indulged middle- and upper-class counterparts. The former have long been compelled to deal with many of the practical difficulties of the real world and rarely protected from life's hardships (Lynott and Logue 1993).

Another aspect of a looming 'crisis' would appear to be the increase in violent acts against children, as well as the emergence of something amounting to a moral panic regarding paedophilia, with paedophiles becoming the latest 'folk devils'. Violence may be evident in the family itself. It is perhaps curious, then, that at a time when parents are believed to increasingly spoil their children, a counter-trend is observed in the proliferating cases of reported cruelty and violence by parents against their off-spring. In the USA, roughly four per cent of all youngsters are believed to suffer abuse each year, including several thousand who die as a result. It might also be suggested that abuse entails more than physical injury. Child abuse is most common among the youngest and most vulnerable children, while the vast number of child abusers are parents, step-parents, or trusted kin (Strauss and Gelles 1986). Around 90 per cent of child abusers are men, but they do not conform to simple stereotypes. Most, however, share one trait: they have been abused themselves as children. Researchers have discovered that violent behaviour in close relationships is learned. In that sense, violence begets violence (Gwartney-Gibbs et al. 1987).

Although the statistics are rising, this does not necessarily mean an increase in incidence, perhaps only that more cases of violence are being discovered. Jenks notes that in this respect there has occurred the politicization of the 'discovery' of child abuse (Jenks 1996, 97). There would seem to be a growth of abuse over three decades: physical, emotional, and sexual. But he notes such social problems do not just 'appear'. Deconstructing this 'trend', Jenks suggests that this pre-occupation enforces the view of childhood because it assumes an abuse of dependency, which side-steps culturally sensitive issues such as child sexuality. Abuse has always been present, it has now become unthinkable. The apparent contradiction between child-centredness and child abuse is thus solved; the 'discovery' of abuse highlights the cultural concern with the welfare of the child and a prevailing ideology of the 'golden age' of childhood.

Discontinuities in Childhood: The Consequences of Divorce

Child abuse may be viewed as part of the 'crisis' of childhood. Divorce and parental separation are arguably another. The latter will be discussed here largely as an example of one of the principal discontinuities of the early life course and another inherent contradiction of a culture which is supposedly child-centred. However, divorce and separation are only one form of disruption to the family and discontinuity in an early stage of the life course. As traumatic as it is for those involved, the fact remains that in most Western societies only about one-third of family disruptions are caused by divorce. Almost all the rest originate with the death of the husband or the wife. Indeed, even though divorce has multiplied, the rate of family disruption has not. This is because the death-rate has declined more than divorce has increased.

Some commentators have interpreted divorce mostly in terms of its social consequences. Divorce generally adds to the increasing proportion of fatherless families (since in most cases children come under the custody of their mothers) and is said to be at the origin of a whole diversity of social problems, from rising crime to mushrooming welfare costs for child-support. For instance, in his book *Fatherless America* (1995) Blankenhorn argues that societies with high divorce rates are not just facing the loss of fathers but the very erosion of the idea of fatherhood with negative social consequences because many children are now growing up without an authority figure to turn to in times of need.

The question about the repercussions of divorce for the child in terms of delinquency is by no means settled. Undoubtedly there is some link, yet there is also a correlation between the death of a parent and anti-social behaviour. Because divorce and delinquency both tend to occur in low-income families, it is quite possible that other consequences of poverty are making their impact on the child rather than the specific psychological effects of divorce.

Increasingly divorce is pointed to as threatening the institution of marriage and subsequently the well-being of the child. The growing number of children living in one-parent families is not uncommonly seen as a principal source of anxiety and that divorce is one of the major reasons why. However, considerable debate rages amongst the 'experts' as to whether the estranged couple should stay married despite hostilities and unhappiness since this still provides their children with a level of stability. Some experts regard divorce as a disaster as it rips many children from their familiar surroundings, entangles them in bitter family feuds and frequently distances them from a parent they love. There is also evidence that children often blame themselves for their parents' break-up. For these reasons some experts have suggested that divorce can radically change the trajectory of their entire lives in a negative way (Goetting 1981).

La Follette (1996), a divorce specialist, believes that a child's response to divorce is always linked to its understanding of what is going on between parents and the reasons for the separation. If a child does not see any

reason why his or her parents are opting for a divorce, if there are few out-
ward signs of discord, then the child's response is to blame him/herself.
La Follette maintains that better than divorce, staying together will benefit
the child under almost any circumstance. Divorce, she suggests, rarely
brings the benefits that adults seek, and the losses can be catastrophic since
estranged spouses are often stripped of financial resources, friendships are
affected, the relationship with the family is never the same again, and all as
a result of the search for what is perceived to be a happier and more
rewarding life.

An important recent study into the consequences of divorce was conducted by the Pennsylvania State University, USA, in 2001. Based on the
research of 2,000 couples and 700 of their children who had reached the
age of 19, it found that children can suffer significant emotional damage if
one unfulfilled parent leaves the marriage early to seek happiness elsewhere. However, the study suggested that the only thing more damaging
for children was for them to remain in a family in which there was constant and violent conflict between parents who did not separate. Some
40 per cent of divorces in the Pennsylvania study involved marriages in
which there had been high levels of conflict beforehand.

Such conflict was hitherto believed to impact the health and emotional
development of children. It interfered with their schoolwork and made
them more aggressive towards their peers. In adulthood they appeared to
be more volatile in their relationships. Divorce under these circumstances
seemed to be in the long run beneficial to them. Yet, this was not true in the
Pennsylvania study for the 60 per cent of the marriages which ended in
divorce. Where it proved to be the case, however, was with couples who
often went along 'moderately happy' for many years but in which one or
both partners felt unfulfilled. In these instances divorce seemed to bring
turmoil to the children because it was not anticipated and was deemed
inexplicable. The children in the latter group showed signs of poor mental
health by the time they reached adulthood. They found it harder to make a
commitment because they did not trust relationships and tended to delay
marriage, preferring cohabitation instead. Once they did marry, they were
quicker to think about divorce if the relationship went wrong.

According to the Pennsylvania study, children are harmed more by
parents who argue rarely and then divorce unexpectedly than by those
whose disputes are violent and frequent before they split up. When
parents try to keep an impending separation a secret until the last minute,
the message to the child is that the marriage runs on lies and hypocrisy
and it is right to be deceitful in any future relationship they may have. In
any case of divorce children feel guilty. If a divorce is sudden, children will
lack confidence in their own judgement. As a result, they may grow up
finding it difficult to establish an intimate relationship. They may hold

potential partners at arm's length or will suddenly break off a relationship for the flimsiest of reasons.

Further evidence suggests that children benefit from their estranged parents going their separate ways: they might better endure a parental divorce than remain in a family torn by tension or even violence. Hayman (2001) has argued that marriages in which a couple have unpleasant rows are extremely damaging for children. Rowing parents make children unhappy, especially as they know their parents are unhappy themselves. Children are harmed enormously by conflict between their parents. In these cases, the child may feel a sense of relief when the parents eventually divorce. Hayman suggests that it is counter-productive to hide marriage difficulties from children: they need to be told that there are difficulties.

The Post-Divorce Family

In 1994, Exeter University's Department of Child Health published the results of research on 152 children in the UK aged between 9–10 and 13–14. These children consisted of 76 who lived with both parents and 76 whose parents had split up. The research also highlighted the importance of step-families. The children from the two groups were paired on factors such as age and social class. In the second group, 31 were in lone-parent house-holds, 26 had become part of a step-family, and 19 had experienced multiple disruption through at least three different homes. Of the 76 children in 'reordered' families, only a third had frequent, regular contact with the parent who had left the family home. In terms of problems of health, behaviour, and school work, those with parents whose relationship was cordial had the least problems. Those with both parents, where the relationship was problematic, had more difficulties. In addition, those in reordered families had twice as many problems. The 21 who had experienced multiple family disruption were ten times more likely than those in intact families to have a low opinion of themselves and eight times more likely to need extra help with school work and to have health complications. Of the children whose parents had separated, scarcely any had been given the chance to discuss preparations for the change and 21 per cent had received no explanation from either parent as to why they had broken up. Children from post-divorced homes seemed to fare best if they had a chance to discuss their distress, if mediation services minimalized post-separation conflict between parents, and where regular contact was maintained with the absent parent.

At the same time, there is also the issue of whether individual mothers and fathers have very different ideas on how children should be raised in the post-divorce situation. Children are now often faced with situations in which they may have to accommodate to a new step-parent who may be living with them and who bring their own standards and expectations of parenting. They may also receive care from another step-parent who lives with the non-residential parent and who may have different standards and expectations (Smart and Neale 2001). Because of such complications some Western governments, as a result of 'expert' advice, are keen on encouraging the involvement of biological fathers in the care of their children after divorce.

Childhood and Formal Education

So far, in this and the previous chapter, we have discussed childhood within the context of the family. There is more to consider however, since a good part of the experience of childhood is within the remit of formal education. Indeed, the link between education and the emergence of modern childhood is indisputable. At the same time, there is clearly a relationship between family breakdown, as well as aspects of structured inequalities and educational performance which, in turn, impact life chances in adulthood. The educational system also increasingly reflects the culture of the consumer society, so that matters of choice have recently come to the fore. Education, then, is in step with the major attributes of late- or postmodernity.

Historically speaking, childhood was only slowly to evolve in its idealized cultural form from the nineteenth century as part of the modern preoccupation with the family and the development of schooling which provided children with their own age-specific experience with school classes graduated into what might be regarded as age-sets. Today, in contemporary Western societies education is undertaken in specialized institutions from kindergarten, through to schools, to colleges and universities. Over recent decades the time which is spent in what might broadly be termed 'the educational system' has expanded considerably. This means that the social role of education and how it shapes life experiences from childhood onwards, for better or for worse, is of increasing significance: setting the stage for establishing social relationship and networks, and contributing significantly to future life-chances and the possibility of overcoming actual or potential risks.

Formal education is also central to the socializing process and provides a cultural link between the generations, supposedly imparting central values for a younger generation even in rapidly changing contemporary societies. Conversely, education generates culture in as much as it is not only concerned with the acquisition of particular skills, but is also frequently held to be a liberating experience in which individuals explore, create, use their initiative and judgement, and freely develop their faculties and talents to the full. There is, moreover, a historical link between education and employment that can be seen in the light of economic development in Western societies. As the industrial revolution created a need for an educated and skilled labour force, schooling became no longer merely the prerogative of the middle-classes and was slowly provided for the mass of ordinary people.

Education in late and postmodernity is characterized increasingly by choice or, at the very least, demarcated by the discourse of 'choice'. This would seem to be evident in legislative enactments. In the UK, the 1988 Education Act brought in a number of sweeping changes. This included, the right for schools to 'opt out' of the Local Educational Authority system if a majority of parents in a secret ballot wanted to do so and become 'grant maintained'. The main thrust of these changes was to introduce the market forces of supply, demand, competition, and parental choice into all levels of education. By more closely assessing the performance of schools and publishing the results of assessments in 'league tables' the Conservative government of the time maintained that it would generate competition between schools, as well as enabling parents to make practical choices regarding where to send their children.

The Persistence of Inequalities

Notions of choice have been related in recent years to the commitment by many governments to the equality of opportunity and the development of a meritocracy as the foundation to the Western way of life. However, there is plenty of evidence of continuing inequality in opportunity and achievement. Obviously poorer parents find it difficult to send their children for nursery pre-school training, to hire private tutors, or to purchase items like books or personal computers which give children from more affluent backgrounds an advantage. At the same time, the less affluent tend to experience greater environmental and health problems that, in turn, have repercussions on their performance at school. For instance, studies have shown that children from an unskilled or semi-skilled occupational background have a poorer diet and worse attendance at clinics to receive immunization. They also suffer to a greater extent than the average child from impaired vision and hearing and display higher rates of chronic illness which may disrupt progress at school.

There is more to consider than mere economic disadvantages. As we have seen above, recent governments in the UK have been keen on promoting a philosophy of freedom of choice in the educational system. At the same time, however, there has occurred growing central state intervention in matters linked to the syllabus and assessment. The 1992 Education Act introduced new centralized arrangements for school inspection through OFSTED (the Office for Standards in Education). This was meant to enhance the shift towards a meritocracy and a new development that is frequently labelled a 'parentocracy'. The latter amounts to a system where a child's education is increasingly dependent upon the financial capabilities and wishes of parents, rather than the ability and efforts of pupils. It is clear that such parental choice regarding their children's education may nonetheless involve social class playing a major part. Middle-class parents generally have a fuller awareness of what different schools have to offer, are more likely to subscribe to the philosophy of choice and parental rights, and are at greater liberty to reorganize households arrangements to accommodate the school life of their children than working-class families.

Parental attitude towards education has also long been seen as an important factor by sociologists in accounting for the under-achievement of working-class children (Douglas 1964; Willis 1977). More recently, Ball et al. (1994) have not substantiated the view that working-class parents were any less interested in their children's education than their middle-class counterparts. What they tended to lack, however, were the material resources and a knowledge of the educational system which made it possible for many middle-class parents to influence the secondary school their children attended and make 'choice' a reality. Many working-class parents preferred to send their children to the nearest school because of family demands and other factors which included limited transport facilities.

There is also the matter of what happens *within* schools and especially how class attributes are perceived. Influential studies applying the theories of symbolic interactions documented the perspectives of teachers and students, the processes through which school classes are constructed and negotiated, the different student roles and cultures that emerge within classes, and the impact of social stratification, whether gender, class, or ethnicity, on these interactions. What has been referred to as an 'invisible pedagogy' (Bernstein 1975), or hidden ranking system, in school culture can significantly influence academic performance and, in turn, the long-term life chances of students through a self-fulfilling prophecy. Part of this cultural differentiation is the evaluation of language. Bernstein's renowned work on linguistic differences established that people in different communities often develop distinct dialects and colloquial vocabularies (Bernstein 1961). Although groups across the class divides do this, the dialects of the more affluent gain status, while those associated with lower class and ethnic communities are judged as 'uneducated'.

Despite continuing controversy over standardized tests, many European educational systems use them as the basis for 'streaming'; the assignment of students to different types of educational programmes. The justification for this policy is to give students the kind of schooling appropriate to their individual aptitude. Hence, it is believed that the innate ability and level of motivation of some pupils means that they are capable of more challenging work than others are. Children, so it is maintained, also differ in their interest, with some drawn to particular subjects, perhaps the arts or sciences. Critics nonetheless see streaming as a way of perpetuating privilege through a labelling mechanism whatever the stated intention. The basis of this argument is that research indicates that social background has as much to do with streaming as personal aptitude does (Gamoran 1992). Streaming, therefore, effectively segregates students both academically and socially. In light of these criticisms, schools are now cautious about making streaming assignments and frequently allow greater mobility between streams.

Education and Ethnicity

Ethnic variations in achievement are evident in many Western educational systems. In the UK, as elsewhere, these variations often coincide with social status differences between ethnic groups and are frequently linked to the variables of social class and gender. For example, in respect of social class, Afro-Caribbean children are more likely to have parents in manual work and evidence suggests that many of them are under-achieving. Moreover, reports in the UK, such as that produced by the Rampton Committee (1979) and the Swann Committee (1985), have found that in general Afro-Caribbean children perform to a lower level than Asian children at school, and in both cases boys do less well than girls. Asian girls may often perform better than white boys, but black males regularly appear to be the poorest achievers. This pattern continues through to higher education. The Swann Report found a number of reasons for the general educational under-achievement of children from minority ethnic groups. These included the lack of suitable pre-school provisions, a good degree of irrelevance of the curriculum to the needs of ethnic groups, and poor communication between the school and the parents.

Ethnicity and educational performance stands as an example of the consequences of labelling. The Swann Report (1985) emphasized stereotyping and low expectations by teachers as one of the major causes of under-achievement among ethnic minorities. It spoke of the 'unintentional racism' of teachers and gave the examples of 'West Indian children will be good at sports but are not academic'; 'Asian children will be hard-working and well motivated but are likely to have unrealistically high career aspirations' and that Asian girls are 'passive'; or that 'Chinese children will be reserved, well behaved, and likely to be under pressure at home from having to help in the family business in the evening.' Such assumptions can have profound consequences. For instance, teachers often favour whites over Afro-Caribbean, by giving them much more attention and opportunities to express themselves in the classroom context. Similarly, the survey Recent Research in the Achievement of Ethnic Pupils (1996) suggested that in the intervening years black pupils often live up to their teachers' stereotype that they were more likely to behave badly and under-achieve. The resultant self-fulfilling prophecy may at least partly account for the fact that they are six times more likely to be excluded from school than other pupils.

In the 1990s, further detailed evidence showed that clear variations had emerged in the levels of educational success in the various ethnic minorities and many noted a significant improvement for some. Jones (1993) found that members of all ethnic minorities, aged from 16 to 19, are more likely to stay on in full-time education than whites. Between 1988 and 90, 37 per cent of whites compared to 43 per cent of Afro-Caribbeans, 66 per cent of African Asians, 58 per cent of Indians, 55 per cent of Pakistanis, 46 per cent of Bangladeshis, and 71 per cent of Africans were in full-time education. Jones suggests that the greater tendency for members of ethnic minorities to remain in education may be partly due to difficulties in finding jobs in a labour market where discrimination is still common. However, it may also be attributed to a greater motivation towards self-improvement through educational achievement amongst ethnic minorities and strong family encouragement to make the most of full-time education.

More than a quarter of the 130,000 adult black Africans in the UK hold qualifications higher than A-levels compared with about one in eight whites. More than one in seven Indians are educated above A-level standard. Together with the Chinese, these ethnic groups have a larger proportion than whites holding top professional jobs. Most black Africans in the UK come from highly qualified families. This means that many of the factors that benefit white middle-class children, such as financial resources, are of considerable importance. Most researchers in the area believe that the majority of Afro-Caribbeans are as concerned about their children's education as other ethnic groups. Pryce (1979, for instance, found that in Bristol the majority of Afro-Caribbean parents had considerable academic aspirations for their children, while Rex and Tomlinson (1979) failed to establish clear evidence that Asians were more interested in the education of their children than their Caribbean counterparts.

The Swann Committee stated, by way of explanation of their educational failures, that Afro-Caribbean children were influenced considerably by 'socio-economic factors', namely they were more likely to have parents from a lower working-class background. Among the other ethnic groups which have under-achieved, are Pakistani and Bangladeshi communities. Half the males and two-thirds of females of these origins have no educational qualifications. They are predominantly among the most recent immigrant groups and come largely from illiterate rural communities. When they arrived in the UK some two decades earlier, many displayed a strong 'myth of return' to their home countries. Their aim was not to obtain a university place for their children but to earn a target sum of money and then to return with cash to purchase land or with a dowry for a daughter. A good number have nonetheless abandoned this dream but carry a strong work ethic and strong value of the merits of education that sees them progressively performing well in terms of their schooling.

Part of the broader explanation of why a number of ethnic groups do not succeed as well as they might in the educational system is related to what Smith and Tomlinson term 'the school effect'. The principal consideration is that 'what school a child goes to makes far more difference than which ethnic group he or she belongs to' (Smith and Tomlinson 1989, 281). This recognizes that people from ethnic minorities are more likely to be clustered into particular geographical areas, notably the inner-cities, and that their children's educational future rests in the hands of the schools near where they live. For ethnic groups that are more likely to be poor, or immigrants concentrated in poor neighbourhoods, there may be an attempt to adjust to a new culture and this can be extremely detrimental. Since schools tend to reinforce the dominant culture in a society, students from minority communities frequently confront a confusing dilemma when trying to reconcile differences between their own culture and of the society in which they live since some may choose not to entirely cut their roots with their homeland. There are also some interesting variants such as the superior performance of young Caribbean females compared to males. The survey *Recent Research in the Achievement of Ethnic Pupils* (1996) focused specifically on Caribbean boys. In 1994, black five-year-olds in Birmingham out-performed white children in tests. Yet, by their GCSE year, the former were on average about five exam points lower than white pupils.

The Future is Female

Beginning in the 1970s, several sociological studies revealed how and why girls were usually disadvantaged at school. Stanworth (1983) looked at a mixed group of students, and found that teachers gave more attention to boys than girls even up to the standard of A-level teaching. Rosemary Deem (1980) demonstrated that education for girls in the past largely centred upon how it would prepare them for their roles with the family rather than the world of employment, while Dale Spender (1982) found curricula saturated with 'sexism' and that schools steered girls towards 'feminine' subjects. As a result of such experiences, girls learned to lack faith in their abilities. Although the education gap had narrowed in Western countries many females continue to study traditionally feminine subjects such as literature, while males pursue mathematics and engineering. In this way schools seemed to reinforce male dominance in wider society.

More recently boys appear to be doing less well and girls performing better. Statistics in 1998 showed girls outperforming boys in national curriculum tests at 7, 11, and 14 years. Girls also surpass boys at GCSE in all but one local education authority in the UK. In terms of the proportion of pupils gaining five A to C grades, the gap between boys and girls has widened nationally to 9 per cent in just ten years. In some subjects, 15 per cent more girls are achieving this academic benchmark. The gap is widest in English, where 59 per cent of girls achieve grade C or above compared to 41 per cent of boys. Yet, boys are also behind in traditionally 'boys' subjects' such as maths, science, and technology. Girls are evidently less likely to fail. In 1998, only 21,500 girls left school without any exam passes, compared to 28,500 boys. In regard to A-levels and degrees, boys seem to take greater risks. This means that they are both increasingly likely to get top grades and are more prone to failure, whereas girls are more inclined to achieve average grades.

Partly the increasing success of girls is a consequence of a shift in educational policies. The national curriculum in the UK, for instance, insists that all boys are compelled to take a language and all girls must choose a science subject; while most schools and universities now have equal opportunities policies. Furthermore, since the 1990s girls have increasingly become less family-focused, giving more importance to education and work (Sharpe 1994). No longer are they attaching primary importance to marriage and having children and now endorse the imperative of finding a job or career and emphasize being able to support themselves. Thus, much more significance is at present attributed by females to education than their counterparts two decades ago.

At the same time, there appears to be the continuing development of what is commonly called 'lad culture' (frequently discerned as responsible for under-achievement) has grown amongst boys. Almost 30 years ago Willis found that working-class boys generated an anti-school culture and 'deviant' attitudes largely centred on their masculinity. They had little respect for the middle-class school values and official qualifications which they frequently regarded as boring, effeminate, and superfluous to their immediate needs. These boys related good pupil performance with femininity and embraced deviant forms of behaviour that made them popular with their peers such as handing in work that was late and of poor quality (Willis 1977). Now the stereotypical image of the average boy appears to be one who dislikes being called 'a swot' and is more likely to be involved in non-educational pursuits at home such as watching television and playing computer games (Ghail 1995). In contrast, girls have a new-found assertiveness grounded in feminism, 'girl power', and expanding economic opportunities. The emergence of fresh identities among females, then, in contrast to enduring aspects of masculinity by way of negative consequences, are impacting in terms of educational performance.

Summary

The above discussion of childhood has ranged widely and perhaps necessarily so given the rapidly changing perceptions in late- or postmodernity of childhood and the experiences of children themselves within family life and formal education. Indeed, the evidence suggests that the early stages of life, from birth to childhood, are undergoing considerable transformations in the Western world. For instance, while stereotypical roles regarding young males and females have concerned sociologist for several generations, the improving educational standards of females indicates that attitudes are changing, while inequalities related to occupation background continue to inform life chances and opportunities. Simultaneously, significant alterations in the family structure and the breakdown of the family have transformed, for many children, experiences within childhood to one of discontinuity.

These transformations have been accompanied by different perceptions of childhood and practices of parenting with possible positive and negative aspects, alongside a great deal of cultural uncertainty as to what constitutes childhood and how children should be raised and socialized. There are, moreover, contradictory trends which make predictions regarding the future difficult to be sure about. However, it is likely that many of the developments in the decades to come will be tied to the fortunes of the family and it is this institution that will be discussed from various further perspectives in Chapter 6. At the same time there has been a restructuring of childhood which suggests that its span is shortening. This 'hurried childhood' is not just in terms of sexual or violent material that the child is exposed to, but the commodification of various aspects of childhood. To some extent this results from manufacturing nostalgic images, alongside the commodification of the early teenage years or the emergence of the 'teenie' market typified by girl magazines which deal with themes of an 'adult nature' and the preoccupation with heterosexual relationship. In the educational field, the earlier assessment of the child in many Western countries, often by way of formal examinations, would appear to bring the competitiveness associated with the adult world to the heart of the school experience. As a result of these developments childhood might be shortened at the same time that the next phase of life – that of adolescence and youth – is extended.

More broadly, in the past two decades there have been far-reaching changes in the ways in which sociologists think about children, and a growing cross-fertilization of ideas between researchers in a variety of social science disciplines is discernible. This is marked fairly recently by attempts to integrate local and global influences on the child in Western societies. For instance, Holloway and Valentine have explored how children's identities are constituted in and through particular 'spaces' (Holloway and Valentine 2000). Local cultures may include notions of masculinity and these may be played out through the home and the school, while there is the global impact of economic trends and information technologies which bring change to key areas as vocation training even from a very early age – an element that would seem to add to the processes which speed up the child's entry into the world of the adult. At the same time, studies have continued to show that even in a globalized world, the Western perception and experience of childhood is a unique cultural apparition and that an infinite variety of social constructs are to be discerned in non-Western societies, although change in these contexts are also increasingly evident (Punch 2003).

Further Reading

Chishom,L. (ed.) (1990.) *Childhood, Youth and Social Change: A Comparative Perspective*, London: Falmer.

Corsaro,W. (1997) *The Sociology of Childhood*, Thousand Oaks, CA: Pine Forge Press.

Hetherington,M. (1991) 'Coping with Family Transitions: Winners, Losers and Survivors' in Woodhead,M., Light,P. and Carr,R. (eds), *Growing Up in a Changing Society*, London: Routledge.

Lamb,M. (ed.) (1983) *The Father's Role: Cross Cultural Perspective*, London: Lawrence Erllbaum.

Mayall,B. (2002) *Towards a Sociology for Childhood*, Oxford: Oxford University Press.

Meyrowitz,M. (1984) *The Adult Child and the Childhood Adult*, London: Routledge.

Phoenix, A. (1991) *Motherhood: Meanings, Practices and Ideologies*, London: Sage.

Pilcher,J. and Wagg,S. (eds) (1996) *Thatcher's Children? Politics, Childhood and Society in the 1980s and 1990s*, London: Falmer Press.

5

Contemporary Youth

There is much in respect of the broad subject of 'youth' which engages with debates surrounding the social construct of the life course and, indeed, shifting perceptions of the different phases of life. Historical and sociological evidence also points towards the significance of youth in terms of age cohorts, alongside aspects of age stratification and differentiation. In turn, the experiences of these cohorts are cut across by such variables as gender and ethnicity. Perhaps above all, youth as a social category displays many of the changes and continuities with the life course in late- or postmodernity. Continuity is evident in that youth remains a significant and relatively 'separate' phase of life, one still surrounded by the discourse of deviance and rendered problematic by older generations. Change is observable in the growing commodification of youth culture which is itself becoming increasingly fragmented. Also apparent is change through life discontinuities and challenges facing the young, along with aspects of risk. These are all themes which will inform this chapter.

'Youth' as a Modern Invention

As a transitional period between the two stages of childhood and adulthood, 'youth' is commonly perceived of as a troubled time because it constitutes a biological period that is frequently assumed to be accompanied by emotional upheavals caused in part by abundant hormones present around puberty. It follows that the young body will develop and progress towards the 'calmer' stage of adulthood. In addition, the period of youth is also often said to be important because in the contemporary world young people must attempt to 'get to know themselves'; adjusting and recognizing their personality and identity, and constructing views about many areas of life. It is, moreover, a period for negotiating relationships with adults and friends, while it becomes acceptable for the young, at some legal age of consent (16 in the UK for both heterosexuals and gays), to form sexual relationships and thus show signs of adult maturity.

The increasing number of years that constitute the period of youth, however, now make these popularized assertions regarding biological processes and social relationships somewhat wide assumptions. The reality is that the 'discovery' of the stages of adolescence or youth occurred in the latter part of the nineteenth century and followed a similar pattern to the emergence of childhood. While puberty is a universal biological process, the alleged psychological dimension associated with adolescence was only gradually identified during that century (Hall 1920). Educators and urban reformers began to observe the emergence of young people in peer groups and identify styles of behaviour with distinct cultural attributes. Hence, there emerged a 'new' stage of life which, from the beginning of the twentieth century, became the focus of literature and the popular media, and where the boundaries between childhood and adolescence and between adolescence and adulthood became more demarcated.

Given the evidence of mutual experiences and subjective feelings of identity among the young, most sociologists specializing in the area of youth studies have worked, especially from the mid-twentieth century, within the framework which takes for granted the existence of a distinct youth 'subculture' – a term referring to cultural patterns that set apart some segment of a society's population. Thus, a youth subculture might be defined as a group of interacting individuals experiencing common shared problems and experiences and who develop particular meaning systems, forms of expression, and lifestyles. When studying the age-set of youth, as distinct from the categories of adulthood and childhood, it is apparent that this division inevitably extends to incorporating its own semi-autonomous culture which may be in some ways similar to and in other ways different from mainstream society.

Exploring the link between youth and subcultures was first evident in Structural Functionalist sociological accounts of youth groups that designated them as 'functional' in that they manage and structure, in a positive way, the increasingly prolonged transition from childhood to adulthood. Thus, Eisenstadt (1956) saw the extended period of youth as necessary in order to socialize young people into the increasingly complex values and skills required for modern society. However, the period of separation could cause identity problems and confusion. While, according to Eisenstadt, this transition is universal, in modern society it becomes especially problematic because the period of youthful socialization tends to be longer than the particular stresses that accompany it. The youth peer group, therefore, is a temporary 'container' in the search for identity. In the transition from the 'us' of the family to the 'them' of the outside world, youth groups allow young people to belong to a clearly defined network with its own internal system of values and status. According to Eisenstadt's theory, youth subcultures furnish a solution for some of the problems generated by a sense of anomie.

Hence, the group establishes support and friendship through difficult times, and more importantly, helps the individual to form a temporary identity. Therefore, personal 'difficulties' in 'growing up' towards physical and social maturity, and even group rebellion, are seen as dysfunctional but in many respects predictable. Even so, Eisenstadt speculated that most young people do, in fact, successfully negotiate the transitional phase of adolescence and settle down into the responsibilities of adulthood.

Youth in Postmodernity

Developments within late or postmodernity appear to make theorizing regarding the early youth subcultures largely redundant. On the first score there is the matter of cohort differences in a radically changing culture. As the twentieth century closed it became evident that each separate generation has its own unique identity, one defined by different characteristics which prove that the definition of the category of youth is not a fixed but a fluid age group. Recent examples of different generational cohorts are Generation X (those born between the mid-1960s and the mid-1970s) which has experienced the problems related to economic uncertainty, and the Millennial Generation (mid-1970s onwards) that found itself subject to many of the social changes at the end of one millennium and the beginning of another, in particular the conditions of a revitalized economy but with few opportunities in the job market. Because each of these generations was born and grew up under contrasting circumstances and had different social influences, they share a similar sense of identity but one radically different from earlier cohorts.

On the second count, developments in contemporary society undermine notions of 'youth' as a clearly defined stage of life. Exactly what period of life constitutes youth at the beginning of the twenty-first century is difficult to be precise about. Officially in the UK, as defined by the British Youth Council (1992), it generally includes anyone who falls within the 16 to 25 age group. The extension of youth 'upwards' denotes the proliferation of higher education opportunities which, for many young people, postpone entrance into the adult sphere of work. This official classification which extends youth in an upward direction is supplemented by developments that would also seem to take the years back into what was previously understood to be childhood. The earlier onset of puberty, and the increasing tendency of children to adopt teenage cultural styles in terms of fashion and attitude, possibly pushes the period in a downward direction.

At the same time, late- or postmodernity appears to impact the period of youth in terms of choice. One aspect of choice has been linked to youth and consumption bringing, as we shall explore below, a proliferation in terms of youth cultural lifestyles and identity constructs. Choice would also seemingly complicate the transition from youth into adulthood. Those choices related to education, training, the workplace, sexuality, and family life have opened opportunities for young people although, as we will also note, such choices are not always realized. They may be constrained by economic fluctuations, unemployment, and dimensions of opportunity and risk that restrain, or at least complicate, the experience of certain categories of youth in the transition to adulthood. Moreover, the opportunities to realize future plans and avoid risks in adulthood may depend on qualifications gained during the period of youth which, in turn, is likely to depend upon advances within the educational system at earlier stages.

Youth Subcultures

Sociological research conducted into the phenomenon of youth subcultures commenced in earnest in the post-war period. When young people began to become more affluent, they almost inevitably developed their own styles of behaviour, music, and fashion. Therefore, they were increasingly a distinctive community which allegedly caused the breach between young and old to widen into the so-called 'generation gap', and much of this distinction appears to be related to new expressions of cultural forms and symbolic expressions of distinct age cohorts (Spates 1983).

The last 50 years has seen the birth of a whole new range of marginal cultural expressions, all in one way or another initiated by young people. In the 1950s, there was more or less a homogeneous subculture identified by rock 'n' roll music and the so-called 'Teddy Boys'. This was followed by mods and rockers, skin-heads, and hippies in the next decade. More recently, there has been observable a fragmented patchwork or mosaic of youth cultures, all adopting distinctive dress, music styles, and values. This is, in turn, a reflection of wider social and cultural diversification. Thus today there is a bewildering display of youth subcultures including those referred to as modern primitives, cyber-punks, ravers, hackers, goths, rastas, grunge, skate-boarders, riot girlz, smurfs, acid heads, and New Age travellers. Certainly, by the mid-1990s, the situation was largely one of plurality or what some sociologists have called postmodernist youth styles which mix and match different genres that may even adopt and adapt previous youth cultures in a kind of nostalgic time-warp.

Contemporary Youth Subcultures

Postmodernist commentators have developed contrasting but sometimes overlapping themes in their discussion of contemporary youth cultures.

In doing so, they have made innovating contributions to our understanding of the area of subcultures which are perceived as responding to the pressures of mainstream society – a reply to a nihilistic and relativist culture. Hence there is much talk of 'alienated youth', where young people struggle to find a sense of meaning and a coherent self-identity. Alternatively, youth cultures are perceived as a product of consumption. That, in short, they have undergone a process of commodification.

There is nothing new in respect of this latter development. In fact, commodification was evident in Abram's early study, *The Teenage Consumer* (1959), where he recognized youth as an emerging consumer group with a new profile of market choices. In the relative affluence of the decade of the 1950s young working-class people, especially males, found themselves with fewer obligations towards parents than earlier generations and with more disposable income which enabled the purchase of such items as records, motorcycles, cosmetics, stylish clothes, and other recreational goods. Hence, Abrams saw youth culture as the distinct orientation of a particular leisure group whose spending choices reflected a certain hedonism and lack of adult responsibility. He also regarded the developing 'teenage culture' as in part the result of the decomposition of post-war working-class communities, a changed world in which the authority of parents over teenage children had declined. As family ties weakened, consumption and lifestyle came to construct identity rather than class, politics, or religion.

The significance of consumption in moulding and reflecting youth cultures has undoubtedly increased in recent years. In a society where economics has shifted from production to consumption, the latter brings more relevance for young people especially in the construction of identities based on style, music, and leisure – all of which constitute a visual 'otherness' and in respect of dress and forms of adornment, the use of the body for symbolic and status purposes.

It may now be argued that young people join subcultures after a period of 'surfing' the youth culture market, and then only on a temporary basis before they opt for another. Certainly, at the present time youth cultural styles are amongst the most global in the world. Partly because of a widely expressed common youth language of popular music, cable and satellite TV, and film, much of youth culture depends on borrowing from many sources in an increasingly globalized world. Young people actively play around with the dominant culture, constructing a 'bricolage' of diverse cultural strands in their own lives, mixing styles of fashion and music.

If youth cultures represent a response to the growing complexity of options, choices, and lifestyles in contemporary society, this raises a number of important questions. First, are youth groups now merely 'fashions'? Does their significance begin and end with trends in consumption and the expansion of markets amongst young people? If so, today's youth cultures are very different from those once associated with class-based deviant youth subcultures to be found in earlier Marxist and Social Action accounts that stressed a response to sentiment at the 'roots' and in giving expressions to the frustrations experienced by young people. In rephrasing such questions, it can be asked whether consumption has become the key means by which youth identities are defined and distinguished in terms of both adults and other young people.

A related question is whether youths are now 'slaves' to consumerism. It can be argued that youth markets are manipulated by the corporate world, where 'street' styles are appropriated and commercialized by big business. Some commentators, then, have portrayed youth cultures as completely manipulated and generated by music and clothing corporations that have sought to exploit a specific 'youth market'. The saturation of youth as a market by global capitalism thus makes them highly vulnerable to those selling what Furlong and Cartmel (1997) call 'identity scripts'.

To be sure, from the 1980s there was a shift in focus from manufacturing to marketing. The goods became unimportant or secondary. What increasingly matters today are the brands and people's emotional attachment to them and it may appear that young people are particularly brand conscious and some would contend noticeably vulnerable to the dictates of the large corporates. Companies such as Nike, Apple, Disney, Calvin Klein, Gap, Microsoft, Starbucks, McDonalds, Virgin, and Intel represent not so much their 'products' as their brand name and image – many attractive to a younger generation.

This consumer aspects of youth culture now seems to be increasingly moved down to the younger teenager age range. Identification of the so-called 'tweenies' market is a current case in point. Niche publications such as *CosmoGirl*, *ElleGirl*, and *Teen Vogue*, aimed at 12- to 16-year-old girls, appear to take for granted their hyper-awareness of brands, while the 'teen market in the UK alone is estimated to be worth some £8.4 billion annually. The problem with this top-down, corporate–consumer emphasis, however, is that it tends to make young people 'cultural dupes' without any real sense of agency and creative power. At the very least, it fails to differentiate between an 'authentic' youth culture as opposed to mainstream culture on the one hand, and the youth culture industry which creates fashions and market products on the other.

Youth Cultures as Political Resistance

While the period of youth has frequently been comprehended as an emotionally difficult period, the rebellious attitudes displayed by the young may be seen and understood as a way of coping with a time of personal confusion and turmoil. In this regard, the more interpretist sociological approaches have always provided a less reductionist account and viewed the radically inclined youth cultures as largely constructed and negotiated by young people in a meaningful way. Such cultures are, therefore, active ways in which youth deals with the problems generated by both the wider culture (with all its pushes towards obtaining jobs, consumer goods, 'getting on' in school, becoming mature males and females), and the immediate 'adult' culture of the parents.

Youth cultures, in the words of Cohen, 'express and resolve, albeit magically, the contradictions which remain hidden or unresolved in the parent culture' (Cohen 1986, 82–3). In other words, youth is a stressful time, and young people have to develop and negotiate their own responses. In doing so, youth styles may come to be seen as a form of resistance, in which the young consciously and purposefully work out their own cultures as a way of handling a string of diverse problems. Whether, for example, the style of dress is the drain-pipe trousers of the teddy boys, the 'bother' boots of the skin-heads, or the outlandish attire of the punks, all are saying something about the felt need to establish a distinct identity.

It is evident that at least some youth subcultures possess their own unique cultural orientations and some are inclined to be counter-cultural in the sense that they can be opposition, political, and explicitly challenging the conventional values of mainstream society (and the values of adults in particular) and the status quo. Since the hippie movement in the USA which campaigned for peace during the Vietnam war in the 1960s, there has been the punks of the 1970s who often overtly supported the anarchist movement and brought direct opposition to traditional moralities and structures of law and order, and the more recent 'slacker' culture of so-called Generation X and the sheer hedonism and individualism of the Rave culture of the Millennial Generation.

In all these examples we find a defence of the idea that the primary meaning of youth culture is protest, even if merely symbolic in nature, against one set of social processes or another. Despite their different cultural styles these groups would seem to register protest against the alienation and dehumanization of late-capitalist society. Having acknowledged that some youth subcultures are culturally resistant, the relationship between subculture and politics has changed dramatically. Rave, hip-hop, and hackers seemingly carry little of the aggressive and overt political assertiveness of the earlier hippies and punks.

Even in the case of the more radical groups, consumerism quickly appears to take up, popularize, and effectively dilute stylistic and creative subcultural aspects. For instance, it may be that punk music and style of dress was originally the product of unemployed working-class youth but, within a very short space of time the movement was commercially exploited in the youth marketplace by corporate interests. Thus, when a subcultural symbol like punk music is commercialized, instead of providing a long-term focus on which the movement can coalesce and identify, the symbols are rendered harmless by the popular music industry. It is reprocessed and repackaged to a wider audience which does not associate in any meaningful way with its original protest and rebellion.

An early key text in the area of counter-culture youth groups is *Resistance Through Rituals* by Hall and Jefferson (1975). Here the authors stated a case for seeing youth cultural resistance as a 'symbolic' or 'magical' solution to the problems and contradictions facing youth in late-capitalist societies. They call it magical because it is their belief that the counter-culture does not address the real material basis of subordination and has failed to subsequently develop properly organized political action, that is, it is not political in any ideologically 'Left' leaning, 'progressive' or radical sense. Indeed, what Hall and Jefferson claim youth culture is essentially doing is distracting youth from genuine political action. Instead, what remains is resistance through rituals operating via the sphere of leisure. So it is 'political' but in a very misguided way.

One explanation for this decline in radicalism and what appears, certainly to the baby boomers who formed a more earnest counter-culture rump in the 1960s, as apathy and passivity, is that in today's economic climate there is now a greater uncertainty, too much pressure to succeed, and too few real opportunities for having a real influence on one's life and on political processes. To put it simply, protest and the call for change is perceived by the young as not even worth attempting. The politics of turning one's back and a mentality of regression, according to Hall and Jefferson, is exemplified in the infantilism of the 'rave' culture with its excess of alcohol, 'designer drugs', and cartoon t-shirts. Here, there is an attempt to forget the problems of being a grown-up and a desire to live entirely in the present. It amounts to pulling back on hope and trying to put off the future rather than taking up the challenge of attempting to shape it.

Redhead (1993) also comes close to this view in his appraisal of contemporary youth cultures. There is, he explains, a kind of 'cultural contradiction' that young people now face where a gap opens up between the ethic of hard work and thrift on the one hand and the economic reality of youth unemployment, under-employment, and poverty on the other. Faced with this, Redhead suggests that young people, middle-class and working-class alike, resort to a politics of pleasure, a hedonism in hard times (Redhead 1993, 57). Readhead argues that if the feature of resistance can be seen in contemporary youth cultures, then it is void of anything as dated as 'class consciousness' and lacks specific reference to a head on assault on industrial-capitalist society. Nevertheless, some aspects of resistance do appear to be very real. Much is epitomized by the so-called 'primitives' who oppose the culture of contemporary life and the de-humanizing consequences of mass consumption. This is attempted by the symbolic bodily use of physical resistance associated with tattoos, piercing, and hair sculpting. Another form of resistance might be the invention of new and ever-more unbearable sounds and styles (at least to some) which resist appropriation (thrash metal, punk, rap, hard-core appears too aggressive and alien for adults to endure). Here there is an endeavour to deliberately divorce from capitalist market forces and seemingly it constitutes a reaction to their incorporation by youth cultures since the 1970s. If this assertion is true, it is possible to suggest that the range of youth subcultures that are observable today may be subsumed under three broad typologies identified by their reaction to mainstream culture; the culture accommodating, the culture-resisting, and the retreatist subculture.

Gender and Ethnic Youth Cultures – Variations on a Theme

Female Subcultures

One of the most significant limitations of many of the earlier studies of youth subcultures was the absence of any meaningful analyses of females within them. In the vast majority of studies girls scarcely received a mention and were largely referred to only within the context of their dependent relationship with young males and even then primarily as sex objects. In fact, in sociological works they were usually merely portrayed through the eyes of the 'lads' (Heidensohn 1985). It may well be that girls simply occupy subordinate positions in youth subcultures, reflecting their lower position in wider society (McRobbie and Garber 1976). At the same time, distinctively female youth subcultures took a less public, less street-based, and therefore less observable form as a result of the greater social restrictions placed upon girls. In addition, feminists have also pointed out that the invisibility of girls in youth subcultural analysis is attributable to the long-time monopoly of this field by male researchers.

Despite these observations it is clear that the female peer group has a distinct and significant existence within the larger teenage youth group itself. Evidence suggests that girls share much leisure activity in common. They are more likely than boys to know details of the top popular music recordings, to read teenage magazines, and to be familiar with the latest dance routines – which they perform, usually in a kind of 'protective togetherness' at discos and other venues. This togetherness has been high-lighted by a number of feminist sociologists who have provided insights into a rich female subculture that has underlined the close relationships of girls within the peer group (McRobbie 1978a; Ward 1976). Here they offer each other intense and long-lasting friendship, contributing emotional and practical support, trust, and loyalty over a protracted period of time.

There are a growing number of sociological accounts demonstrating the importance of friendships between girls in the creation of coherent subcultures. In this respect, Leonard's study of young girls found that when 'going steady' and courting there is still a clearly allocated 'girls times' and 'boys times' (Leonard 1980). After leaving school, the girls went to sixth form college, Technical or Art college, youth employment schemes, or paid employment. The pressures on the girls to lose touch with their close friends may be particularly strong at this point since the daily contact is broken. Leonard found that this was when a steady boyfriend is most likely to take over from relationships with girlfriends. However, Griffin (1985a) discovered the persistence of much previous friendship, particularly those of best friends who lived in close proximity to each other. She found that friendships between girls did not break down, but were largely maintained alongside boyfriends – the girls using various strategies to retain them.

Griffin suggests that young girls' relationships are divided into clear stages, according to their age and how well they know other girls. From 'going round with a boy', usually in a mixed sex group at the age of about 13 or 14, the girls 'progressed' to the more coherently delineated 'going out with a boy' from about 14 or 15, and from there to more regular boyfriends and 'courting' which might lead to engagement. The girls were very clear about the boundaries that existed between one stage and the next. Whilst largely taking for granted that they would end up getting married, the girls were nevertheless able to use the stages to keep control in relationships with boys and to simultaneously maintain their friendships with their girlfriends. 'Going around with boys' posed no threat to the girls' friendship and at this stage there was even boyfriend swapping. 'Going out with' often involved undertaking social activities in foursomes and a kind of chaperoning. Relationships were longer lasting and this allowed the retaining of the close interdependences between the girls (female friendships and relationships are also discussed in Chapter 6).

Ethnic Subcultures

Although the greater majority of youths from the ethnic minorities are manual-class as measured by parental occupation, it is not appropriate to treat them exclusively under the rubric of working-class youth because of the importance of racial and ethnic factors largely related to problems of identity. While all young people have the difficulty of forging a workable identity, for black and Asian youth it is particularly acute. Many are frequently presented with two potentially conflicting adult models. The first is that of a citizen in a Western society, sharing equal rights and duties with whites; second is the matter of identity of black, Asian, or some other ethnic group, visibly distinct, and with a unique cultural heritage. Achieving a workable balance between the two is difficult. The problem is made worse by the experience of prejudice and rejection, since self-identity partly depends on how others appraise the individual and collective to which s/he belongs. Hence, the cultural life of ethnic, mostly immigrant groups, and particularly of the young, cannot be properly understood without bearing in mind the distress and frustration that discrimination can provoke.

Love of music, a preference for religion, and a liking for street-based social activities are well known aspects of Afro-Caribbean culture in the UK. Unemployment or irregular employment, are also part of the familiar background of life, and young blacks are accustomed to dealing with them in their unique way through the development of distinct youth cultures. However, there is the danger of constructing stereotypical images. Common, largely negative characterizations of Afro-Caribbean culture tends to present two polarized stereotypes which are perceived as responding in their own way to social disadvantage and discrimination. First, the 'hustler' copes with the difficulties of the job market by 'hustling' a living out of dealing in drugs, gambling, pimping, or stealing. He is characterized as living in some style, sporting smart cars and well-cut clothes, and displaying a 'laid back' attitude to life. This popularized image has, however, a certain amount of legitimacy as suggested in some of the sociological literature. The work of Wallace (1990), for instance, suggests that unable to fulfil their patriarchal responsibilities as providers and heads of households, black males may retreat to a compensatory hyper-masculinity, centred on sexuality and violence, living through 'Black Macho' fantasies. This is often at the expense of black women, their sexuality, and negative self-perceptions. Such aggressive masculinity has, according to Wallace, emerged as a cultural norm that is passed down to younger generations.

This delinquent culture contrasts sharply with the religious fervour of another Afro-Caribbean youth subcultural figure, the Rastafarian. The 'Rasta' movement illustrates the defensive, retreatist trend which is almost an inevitable part of the cultural tradition of a group actually or potentially subjugated. Rastafarians trace their spiritual roots back to Africa as exemplified by their plaited hair and some aspects of dress imitate African origins (Cashmore 1979). Between these two polarized youth cultures, most Caribbean youths are influenced by a wide variety of mainstream values and other youth subcultures. Moreover, it undoubtedly remains the case that most young Caribbeans, much like their parents, are fairly well assimilated into mainstream culture.

Assimilation, whatever its merits, clearly has its difficulties for the young of various ethnic groups who might find themselves being caught between the pressures of two different cultures. Asian youths, for example, may be pressurized by dominant Western culture, including youth culture, on the one hand, and the values of their parents and grandparents on the other. Culture in the West may be identified by its egalitarian ethos and permissiveness. Asia culture, typified by the religious values of Islam or Hinduism and patriarchal family structures, run counter to Western expectations. Young people may find themselves having to choose between these contradictory cultural values making 'growing up' a particularly difficult process and the forging of distinct youth cultures among ethnic groups relatively unlikely.

Despite the difficulties that some ethnic groups have in forging distinctive youth subcultures, the frequent social construct of such subcultures as a social problem is a subject highlighted by recent research of what appears to be the growing phenomenon of ethnic 'gangs'. Alexander (2000), for instance, has shown how the Asia gang has been 'discovered' as a 'new' and urgent social problem. The image portrayed in the media has proved to be one which sees their emergence against the backdrop of urban deprivation and an underclass, combined with fears of growing youth militancy and masculinities-in-crisis. The result has been to position Asian and especially Muslim young men, as the latest 'folk devils'. The 're-imagination' of Asian male youth has focused on violence, drug abuse, and crime set against a backdrop of cultural conflict, generational confusion and religious fundamentalism. Alexander, however, does not interpret the Asian gang as deviant or constituting 'resistance'. Rather, it is much more mundane and ordinary, a source of peer group identification but where the broader family is still very much of a concern and where a response to a multi-ethnic society, via non-deviant activities, is at the centre of youth identification. This is a source of belonging which carries a great sense of loyalty and community but where religion is not a particularly important element. The gang thus gives expression to Asian youth cultural ambivalences and contradictions of identity and marks a way of dealing with broader social exclusion.

That stereotypical views of ethnic youth subcultures are so widespread, may partly be attributed to the mass media. Henry Giroux (1997) in his account of the ways that black youths are perceived puts particular emphasis on the role of the visual media which saturates contemporary cultural life. Such media brings negative portrayals through a complex deconstruction of black youth image when associated with film characters, tarnished real-life idols such as O.J. Simpson, alongside sexualized presentations of black youth as permissive. In terms of 'race' and ethnicity this means that from childhood they are constrained by a negative perceived role of alienated outcasts and thus prejudice is reproduced over the generations in a distinct, public, generalized, and very damaging way. Giroux reports that such characters may frequently lead to a self-fulfilling prophecy in that some young blacks may act out these negative role models, so that they constitute part of a subculture of resistance.

Youth and Deviance

In the context of youth cultures, 'resistance' suggests aspects of social deviance. However, deviance and non-conformity are part of a much larger concern of sociological enquiry. Here, we consider the area more broadly with reference to the creation and repercussions of 'moral panics' as periodic social constructs of deviance. While the subject of 'moral panics' has been addressed with reference to contested childhoods (Chapter 4) and implicit in the creation of the 'folk devils' of ethnic youth subcultures discussed above, the earliest studies related to the first youth groups. Here, the term 'moral panic' was given to mean an amplified fear that cherished social values were under threat by 'outsiders'. Amplification is accentuated by media sensationalism. In this regard, youth are generally viewed as a problem in contemporary society: they are either seen as trouble, or in trouble. The young, then, are beset by predominantly negative images and stereotypes: media talk of rising juvenile crime and various other problems which serve to increase the chance of them 'acting the part' and reinforcing this disapproving appraisal through self-fulfilling prophecies.

Stanley Cohen (1971) was perhaps the first to consider moral panics regarding youth cultures through the conflict between mods and rockers in the early 1960s and where the media amplified gang violence and vandalism. More recently, there arose the moral panic surrounding the acid house movement of the late 1980s. The movement was largely centred on a distinctive form of music associated with a particularly raucous lifestyle and frequently with the 'designer drug' ecstasy. According to Redhead (1993), one of the reasons why the movement was so heavily persecuted was because it threatened the peace and quite of respectable suburbia and where dance meetings were regularly described as 'rural riots'. Police action led to over 2000 arrests in 1987–88 in the UK. The music fused two forms; 'Chicago house' dance styles and the 'Balearic beat' of the Ibizan jet set. The media presented the movement in such a way as to exaggerate its danger. It was portrayed in chilling dimensions as 'killer music' believed to be closely associated with ecstasy. The victims, according to the tabloid newspapers, were 'youths', 'teenagers', and 'schoolchildren'. Media reports presented their news in such a way that young girls were seen as losing their innocence to drugs. In fact, in the development of the narrative of a moral panic, girls were regarded as the targets of a double threat, of drugs and sexual abuse.

Despite the danger of labelling, modern research highlights the fact that a comparatively high number of young people suffer from a range of social and psychological maladies which stress the 'risk' of being young, some of which are linked to negatively perceived conditions of mental health. For instance, depression is a common illness amongst adolescence with an estimated prevalence of four to six per cent in the UK. This is possibly because many 'teens feel that they do not fit into the peer groups that surround them, or as a result of feeling obliged to comply with the strict internal regulation of such groups. At least from a medicalized perspective, this may also explain why one in 1000 of the population experience the onset of schizophrenia between the ages of 16 and 25.

There is also the area of self-harm. The number of boys who commit suicide in the UK each year is greater than those killed in road accidents. The number of young males taking their own lives is three times that of females (in 1996 3640 men: 1232 females). Male suicides have risen from ten per 10,000 in 1976–81 to 20 per 10,000 in 1996. Among younger women it has decreased, while their level of 'deliberate self-harm', drug overdose, and attempted suicide is up to four times more common than men (although this is increasingly commonplace among males). Regarding soft drugs, *The Face* magazine survey in 2002 found that over 50 per cent of young people in the UK have used cannabis, around 15 per cent with the drug ecstasy, but in the case of 'hard' narcotics such as heroin only 1 per cent has experimented.

At the same time, young people are frequently linked to high levels of crime and delinquency. For instance, the UK Home Office research in 1997 showed that one in two young men and one in three young women aged 14 to 25 admitted to having committed at least one criminal offence. The 1996 Audit Commission estimated that those under 18 years old commit seven million offences each year. Ten to 14-year-olds represent 14 per cent of all known offenders. Self-report studies show that the crime ratio between males and females of 14 to 17 years is about equal even if official statistics indicate males are higher.

Within a medicalized framework, some scientists may find biological reasons for youth delinquency, reducing such difficulties to the abundance of volatile hormones as young people reach puberty. However, sociological research, as we shall see below, has found other factors that may be more important. In the time of economic uncertainty of the past few years the young have experienced a harsh financial climate which greatly adds to or even precipitate these troubles. State benefits for young people have been cut, while the recent introduction of tuition fees and abolition of grants has had the effect of reducing the number of applications to universities, and youth unemployment is high even for university graduates. Thus, at present young people may have to rely financially on their parents for longer and in general are living at home until a later age, which causes the period of adulthood, and all that entails in terms of adult responsibilities, to be suspended.

Youth and Sexuality

Youth sexuality is a contested area related to the subject of deviance. This is significant since sexuality is vital to the individual in terms of identity. Whether it is their sexual drive or their sexual preference, it will impact a person's life in some shape or form. Sexuality for young people in the early twenty-first century seems to increasingly present a risk with a rise in teenage pregnancies, debates over the age of consent for heterosexuals and gays, fears of sexually transmitted disease – primarily AIDs, and the increase of people commencing sexual relationships at an earlier age. It is probably true to say that sexual activity among adolescents is a matter of anxiety for adults who feel it is their responsibility to regulate and protect teenagers from many of these tribulations. In turn, the increase in sexual activity at a younger age could at least partly be due to the need to rebel, knowing that adults would disapprove. Thus many teenagers may experience the compulsion to follow paths that adults would disapprove of; sexual permissiveness, drinking, smoking, drugs, and so on. Whether a true or false appraisal, the sexuality of the young has become a social issue which has extended the repertoirs of perceived deviant behaviour and may be a source of yet another moral panic, this time resulting from the contested area of the 'young' body.

With the teenage pregnancy rate high in most modernized countries (in the UK 10 per cent of women are pregnant by the age of 20), teenage sexual relations are becoming a concern to parents and governments alike. Young couples apparently rarely consider the age of consent as a deterrent, although it may act as a rough guideline. What is seemingly the case is that the young are starting to have sexual relationships at an earlier stage. One of the main reasons is that puberty is emerging earlier and hence young people reach sexual maturity at an earlier age. Now one in eight girls and one in 14 boys start puberty by the age of eight. The figure compares to roughly one in 100 a century ago.

Today, in the UK one in four girls and one in five boys have had sex by the time they are 16 years old. In 1997, there were 65,500 conceptions to women under 20, including 8300 under the age of 16, while 62 girls per thousand aged between 15 and 19 conceived. About half of all under-16-year-old conceptions, and a third of all teenage conceptions end in abortion, with socially deprived girls three times more likely not to have an abortion. This may feasibly be due to a lack of education regarding alternatives to giving birth or a cultural emphasis displayed by girls from a poor background in opting for children rather than following a professional career. Although there are negative aspects, it might be argued that the general trend towards sex at an early age is inevitable in a society which is so focused around adulthood. With the increasing availability of contraception and access to advice from doctors and family planning clinics, adolescents are becoming easily capable of receiving sexual advice possibly encouraging the ease at which teenagers can lead an active sex life.

Attitudes towards sex are to a large degree engendered. While young males are often regarded as the sexual predator and the female the passive actor, a higher number of girls have sex at an earlier age than boys. Arguably, this could be because girls in particular associate relationships and having a boyfriend as part of being 'grown-up', and therefore it is a direct way for them to feel mature. One could however conjecture that this may be due to the sexist role models that girls are subjected to throughout childhood, in particular, it is expected that it will be the women who nurture the children and the men who earn the income to look after them. Griffin (1985b) also sees finding a boyfriend and being sexually active as proof of young women's 'normal' heterosexuality and more 'grown-up femininity'. Establishing a steady relationship may simultaneously be a way of protecting a girl's reputation from the label 'slag' whereas promiscuous boys are often praised by their friends and viewed as merely reckless (Lees 1986).

The 'Burden' of Youth

From School to Work: Changes and Discontinuities

Since the early 1990s in the UK, successive governments have continued the process of marketization in higher education: introducing student loans and fees ideally to make students responsible and enthusiastic consumers, while simultaneously saving public money. In sum, the education policies in recent years have supposedly further tied the aims of the educational system to the needs of a developing and competitive economy. Here, the alleged virtues of the dynamics of the free market are seen to precipitate economic growth, while simultaneously establishing a meritocracy and enhancing equality of opportunity.

Supposedly in order to advance these aims there has been the expansion of further and higher education for young people. In 1973/74 approximately one-third of all 16-year-olds and less than four in ten females participated in some form of full-time education in England. By 1993/94 70 per cent of males and 76 per cent of females that were 16 years old undertook full-time education. Moreover, full-time participation among 17- and 18-year-olds more than doubled during this period. These changes have not been confined to those from privileged class backgrounds. Young people from all social classes now tend to remain in full-time education until a later age and, whereas higher education was once the privilege of the better-off, it is now rapidly becoming a mass experience.

Expansion in higher education took off in the late 1980s to the extent that the term 'mass' higher education has enjoyed common currency. Peter Scott (1996) gives various reasons for this expansion. Perhaps most obviously, there is the need for acquiring personal transferable skills in the ever-changing post-Fordist economy. In addition, Scott argues, participation in higher education is now a key component in the manufacturing of social and personal identities. In particular, attending university is presently not so much about being middle class, but related to occupational and cultural credentialism. In short, as Western societies have become more technologically based, culturally diverse, and socially mobile, diplomas and degrees supposedly say a great deal about 'who you are'. Moreover, qualifications such as advanced degrees serve as a shorthand way to differentiate between those who have or do not have the 'correct' manners and attitudes sought by many employers. In short, credentialism operates in much the same way as family background by way of a gatekeeping strategy that restricts prestigious occupations to a small and privileged segment of the population. Finally, higher education has become part of what Scott calls the 'entertainment-learning-leisure-heritage complex'. This means that education has now emerged as a powerful cultural commodity which is produced and consumed as a segment of a developing educational marketplace.

The expansion of higher education has had considerable bearing on the life course and what it means to be 'a young person'. It has impacted upon relationships with family and friends, the sphere of employment, leisure, and lifestyles, and the ability to become established as an independent young adult. Lengthening the period of education means that the young can find it difficult to forge adult identities, maintain coherent biographies and develop strategies to overcome obstacles. Much is linked to the fact young people today have to negotiate a set of risks which were largely unknown to their parents: this is true, irrespective of social background or gender.

From the 1990s, even those with relatively few qualifications at the age of 16 years frequently opted to stay in full-time education, although in many depressed areas this is partly because there are so few credible alternatives in the labour market (Furlong and Cartmel 1997). Yet, those who venture into higher education often find themselves entering employment with crippling student debts that could take years to pay off. In addition, the risks and opportunities which the young now face are very different from those which were encountered by their parents. In the 1960s and 1970s experiences in the school and the labour market were clearly connected to social class. Those from working-class families tended to leave school at the minimum leaving age with few qualifications and found the transition to becoming manual workers relatively easy. Since the 1990s the well-established relationship between the family, school, and work seem to have weakened and young people embark on their journeys into adulthood along a wide variety of routes, many of which appear to have unpredictable outcomes. These changes in the experiences of the young are clearly discernible in the world of work. The youth labour market has changed so drastically that it would be almost unrecognizable to those of previous generations.

In line with Beck's notion of 'individualization' (Beck 1992), educational experiences are becoming individualized and packaged as a consumer product. Performance 'league tables' encourage parents to 'shop around' for the best school for their children, and a growing range of educational credentials and courses may lead young people to regard educational services as 'products'. As a consequence changes in the delivery of education and the increased use of certification means that they and their parents are obliged to take personal responsibility for educational achievement. Consequently, failure is equated with poor choices or a lack of effort or talent rather that being influenced by social class.

Yet, despite the far-reaching nature of changing educational experiences, there is little evidence that the relationship between social class and educational attainment has weakened. Statistics from a nationally representative youth cohort study has shown that among those who reached the age of 16, during the 1991/92 school year, staying-on rates varied from 64 per cent for young people with parents in professional, managerial, and technical occupations, to 51 per cent among those with parents working in semi- and un-skilled and personal service occupations.

Neither is higher education void of the consequences of social inequalities. The history of higher education in such countries as the UK is one that has long been overshadowed by class inequalities. It appears that the recent transition from elite to a mass system has done little to erode class differentials in access. Despite increasing numbers of working-class students, particularly those from ethnic minority backgrounds, applying to university their experiences of the choice process are qualitatively different to that of their more privileged middle-class counterparts. Access to the best universities and the better quality teaching and research departments are still the preserve of the middle-classes, rendering considerable restriction in freedom of choice in education (Reay et al. 2001).

There is a broader consideration however, one related to the realization of choice and opportunity. A report entitled *The Burden of Youth* (2000) suggested that young people are struggling against ever-increasing pressures to make the most of their lives. It argued that today's youth, the so-called Millennial Generation born between the mid-1970s and the mid-1990s, have far more opportunities than previous generations and in general are increasingly affluent, confident, and ambitious. Yet, the expectation to succeed is also far greater, with teenagers under considerable pressure to do well at school, college, and the job market.

The popular emphasis on young music and television celebrities, who achieve fame and fortune in their late 'teens and early twenties, also encourages young people to have high aspirations. The world appears to be at their fingertips, with more choices, more chance to travel, and the trend towards delaying marriage and parenthood. However, *The Burden of Youth* report maintained that young people are searching for absolutes in terms of identity, lifestyle, and morality, yet struggle to find them. Moreover, a significant minority of disadvantaged young people are excluded from the opportunities open to their counterparts and face an uphill struggle to live life to the full. The report pointed out that one in 16 leave school without any qualifications and any prospect of a decent job. This means that, in terms of youth as a social category, there is a growing gap between the 'haves' and 'have nots' – further fragmenting an increasing varied 'stage' of life.

Youth and Changes in the Labour Market

Today, few young people make smooth and easy transitions from school to work. There are various reasons for such disruptions. For one thing, unemployment has become much more common, even among graduates, and it is normal for those who leave full-time education before the age of 18 to spend time on government training schemes. The recession of the late 1970s and early 1980s was a turning point in youth employment opportunities, marked by a radical change in the need for youth labour. Prior to the late 1970s, there was a strong demand for relatively unqualified school-leavers in many areas of industry. Since the mid-1980s patterns of labour requirements have changed significantly and opportunities for young workers are increasingly linked to the demand for flexible specialization and the growing use of part-time and temporary employment contracts. These have weakened the collective employment experiences of the young.

Since the 1980s the opportunities of 16- to 21-year-olds have become characterized by variety and flexibility. Until the 1970s, when the majority of 15- and 16-year-olds made 'traditional transitions' straight into jobs, the kinds of employment they entered were relatively predictable and often associated with their places of residence, gender, and education (Ashton and Field 1976). These transitions have now been restructured and this age category has subsequently experienced a number of routes into employment, or at least alternatives to the workplace, after leaving school.

Besides the route of full-time education which has been the option with some young people unable to acquire employment, young school leavers (perhaps some ten per cent), may find themselves in part-time employment for months or even years, before securing full-time work (Roberts et al. 1989). Others may enter a youth training scheme where geographical locality and rates of unemployment are important. Indeed, employment schemes have become central to an understanding of transitions from school to work, and young people today tend to follow much more complex routes into the labour market. Such changes mean that the collectivized transitions which were once common among young people from working-class families, in particular, have become increasingly rare as they begin to make transitions to a highly differentiated skill market, as opposed to a relatively undifferentiated labour market.

The significance of all these options is that if occupation is viewed as the main indicator of achieving adulthood, then that transition has become infinitely variable and flexible. In 1993, 67 per cent of 16-year-olds in England stayed on in the educational system, 12 per cent opted for training schemes, and only 7 per cent went straight into employment. As a result of the diversity of routes between school and work, young people are thus confronted with an increasing range of options which force them to engage with the likely consequences of their actions on a subjective level. The young often face these routes with a growing sense of unease and insecurity. Although transitional routes have remained highly stratified with respect to social class, these changes have again impacted personal orientations as the range of experiences encountered at this phase in the life course become much more individual in nature.

An important contribution to the understanding of the transition of young people to adult life is the work of Banks et al. (1992), albeit limited to a survey of a small sample of 16- to 20-year-olds. The survey suggests that there are few significant differences within this age group regarding attitudes and experiences. The average 16-year-old has far less social and emotional development than those in their early twenties: few experiences of longer-term close relationships outside of the family, and display little sense of the moral responsibilities often associated with adulthood. Managing their own money, their time, and their lives generally are not problems that many have faced. A good number of 20-year-olds, by contrast have moved closer to adult identity. Yet, within this age group there was found to be a wide variation in the rate of transition from full-time schooling to employment. Banks et al. note the various routes to transition, at least some of which have long-term repercussions in terms of life opportunities. On the other hand, there are choices which are, in the short term, less consequential. These choices include political party allegiances, leisure activities, patterns of spending, and personal relationships. Such choices constitute part of a whole range of life options which are unstable and frequently reversed when adult identity is achieved. However, in terms of aspects of social identity it is clear that some attitudes are already forged by the age of 16 and therefore only reinforced afterwards. These attitudes include orientations towards authority, gender, commitment to employment, and views towards fatalism (Banks et al. 1992, 179–85). This picture suggests continuities of values and opinions, but at the same time differences in experiences of major transformations result largely through various routes to the workplace.

Other sociological studies have researched the significance of risk and choice and found that social variables may influence how they are negotiated. Longitudinal research by Thomson et al. indicated that across a number of different backgrounds there are 'critical moments' in young persons' biographies which have implications in processes of social inclusion and exclusion. Yet, there is a relationship between social and geographical location and the events that they report as having particular biographical significance. The character of these 'critical moments' as part of reflexive project of self is socially constructed, as are young people's response to them. The case studies showed an interaction of choice, chance, and opportunity. The notion of 'critical moments' forges a middle path between the way young people talk about their lives and what actually happens to them. Whilst most young people make references to individual choice, the required resources and opportunities are not necessarily available, and this is recognized by young people as they anticipate the future (Thomson et al. 2002).

A study by Du Bois-Reymond (1998) also indicates that young people vary in the way that they think about time – in particular in relation to their present condition of being young and the way they envisage their future adulthood. In the case of less economically privileged young women, attitudes were found to be very present-day orientated and perceptions of their future lives were taken by an unquestioning acceptance of how they saw their parents' situation. They did not think in terms of choices and opportunities or of seeing the future as being something of their own making. Rather, the future was perceived as a fairly scheduled, standardized life course. Du Bois-Reymond concludes that for many of the young people the navigation of the transition to adulthood is influenced by their perception and experience of time and involves planning and making choices but that this incorporates the very real restrictions that may be present. This clearly throws doubt upon simplistic notion of the reflexive self in late modernity – an observation also made in a comparative study by Branem and Nilsen (2002) of young people in the UK and Norway. Among their conclusions was that among less privileged young females notions of a negotiated future involving opportunities and risks was almost entirely absent. Such young girls tended to envisage their future in terms of their parents' circumstances while, far from considering future prospects, the emphasis was very much present-orientated.

Summary

'Youth' is not the only stage of life (if it may be regarded as such) where individuals experience major physical and psychological changes and are obliged to make readjustments to social roles and expectations. Motherhood, mid-life, and the transition to old age are all accompanied by such readjustments, although it could be said that the adults involved in these changes will adapt to social norms more easily and retain a strong sense of self, having had more life experience. Under such conditions then, it is perhaps not too surprising that youth subcultures develop as a response to unique challenges. Moreover, where everyday life experience is one of subordination and low status, it is evident that subcultures emerge to deal with inter-generation tension.

The situation in late- or postmodernity is now more complex. If youth has historically been interpreted as a 'crisis', then the nature of that crisis may have changed. It is one informed by choice, opportunities, disconti-nuities, and problems of identity – all of which may be impacted by periodic moral panics and negative appraisals which cut across the positive image of looking and 'being' young. It is also clear that just as the stage of youth was initially associated with Western-style *modernity*, the experience of youth in late- or postmodernity in Western societies is in many ways radically different. Nearly eighty years ago Margaret Mead (1928) was able to contrast developments in the West with pre-industrial societies. In Samoan society that stage of life known as 'adolescence' simply did not exist. Those older children who had not reached adult maturity lived in a kind of 'temporal no-man's land' which had an ambi-guity of status that involved a significant rite of passage into adulthood. It may be many young people the West now feel that they are in a kind of 'no-man's land', as a result of discontinuity and disruption, without even the psychological support of a rite of passage.

Further Reading

Cotterell,J. (1996) *Social Networks and Social Influences in Adolescence*, London: Routledge.
Irwin,S. (1995) Rights *of Passage: Social Change and Transition from Youth to Adulthood*, London: UCL Press.
Redhead,S. (1993) *Subcultures to Clubcultures: An Introduction to Popular Cultural Studies*, Oxford: Blackwell.
Singh, Ghuman P. (1993) *Coping with Two Cultures: British Asians and Indo-Canadian Adolescents*, Clevedon: Multilingual Matters.

6

Relationships, Sexualities, and Family Life

Given the significance of social change and the transforming nature of a number of important key social institutions in late- or postmodernity, it is increasingly difficult to divide the broad period of adulthood into sub-stages such as 'young' or 'older adulthood'. Perhaps above all, the range of discontinuities now evident early on in adult life renders it arduous to be precisely sure where adolescence and youth ends and adulthood begins, while later adulthood also extends through mid-life and old age. Hence, the theme of adulthood is perhaps best approached via a survey of several settings in which adult life is experienced. This will allow an exploration of the major variables that shape adulthood; opportunities, risks, and discontinuities.

In regard to family life, it is clear that the family is one key social institution which is today undergoing significant transformation, indeed something of a structural and cultural revolution is taking place. We have already considered changing aspects of family life in respect of infancy, childhood, and parenting. In this chapter we will look at the family largely in as much as it influences experiences of adulthood and this will permit a consideration of changes in family relationships and structure, alongside historical developments through an overview of the critical literature, much of which has been of a postmodernist or feminist persuasion.

The theme of relationships is also approached from a broad perspective and there is a sense in which this chapter is primarily about relationships, not least of all because they form integral and vital aspects of self and identity. In this context, the growth of individualism both as a social value and social structural arrangement is important. Because of social and geographical mobility, people are not always able to keep up a close connection with parents or wider kin as in the past. Communities and family networks continue to break down, while life-long friendships are difficult to sustain. At the same time, late- or postmodernity is a society of choice not just related to what consumer durables we wish to buy or holidays that we take, but choices of lifestyles, of morality, and relationships which may have profound consequences for the life course.

The transforming nature of relationships is not restricted to family life. Sexual relationships and mate-selection patterns are also changing. There are various trends to consider. For one thing, we now live in a permissive society clearly less concerned than in the past about a person's sexual orientation, who has relationships with whom, or the consequences of an illegitimate child. Yet, the risk due to the spread of the HIV virus has made people more cautious, forcing them to think again about the repercussions of a permissive lifestyle. As a result, views of morality and relationships are often confused and uncertain.

Friendship

In a world characterized by loss of community, of increasing social mobility, and of choice, friendships are important for individuals to develop a sense of belonging and identity. In short, they are a significant means by which a concept of self is forged. In an ever-changing world it is increasingly difficult to sustain friendship and relationships for life, while social isolation becomes a problem for a growing number of people.

Human relationships clearly come in various forms. We may speak of those within the family which involve emotional relationships between co-residing kinship members, between husband and wife, and spouses and children. 'Friendship' by contrast, can be defined as a non-sexual relationship built upon common interest and intimacy, freely entered into. Giddens believes that the pursuit of personal happiness and stability through such one-to-one relationships is of increasing importance in late modernity with the decline of a cohesive moral and social world, and where family structures are continuingly eroded. Social relationships are now freely entered into for their own sake largely for what can be derived by each person from a sustained association with another; one which is continued only in so far as it is thought by both parties to deliver enough satisfaction for each individual to stay within them (Giddens 1992, 58).

Giddens' notion of the 'pure relationship' is, however, open to criticism. His tendency is to approach the subject of relationships, especially heterosexual relationships, in a simplistic way which also says little of non-heterosexual relationships. It is an approach that views relationships as large, culturally unmediated constructs (apart from being largely individualistic and instrumental in orientation) and void of many of the engendered and negative repercussions which may negate notions of a meaningful enhancement of self-identity. A broader sweep has informed of the complexity of contemporary relationships. Lees, for instance, writes that much theorizing about identity and relationships has overlooked the contradictions inherent in female identity. Forming an identity as a young girl involves establishing a firm sense of self – in opposition to the popularized depiction of girls as sex objects and in opposition to the characterization of women as no more than sexual beings. The dilemma for young girls in particular is that they tread a very narrow line: they must avoid being called a slag, but equally they do not want to be thought unapproachable or sexually cold (Lees 1993, 16).

Popular discourse supports the view that non-heterosexual friendships should be equal, intimate, and based upon affectionate mutual bonds. This is implicit in Gidden's theorizing. However, this assumption overlooks the fact that personal life is continuingly engendered. A range of sociological literature shows that males and females feel different obligations towards friends and associates, while opportunities and identities impact on the manner and dynamics of friendship. The research suggests that men's cultural upbringing and experiences of the workplace encourages the formation of social relationships with others but limits the number of close friends and the depth of relationships, as well as restricting what they disclose about their personal life and how much emotion they are prepared to show. In comparison, women appear to 'really know each other', and are ready to genuinely provide a greater self-revelation and empathy (Hey 1997).

Clearly, friendship constructs are forged in childhood as part of the socialization process. Boys are likely to be active in large groups where they are competitive and often aggressive; girls will mix in small groups which tend to be close and intimate, communicative, and co-operative. In adult life, friendships are further structured, particularly in terms of the display of emotions and in such a way as to reflect cultural expectations of gender roles and, according to feminists, the patriarchal structure of society. There are important differences of class and ethnicity which also have to be taken into account. However, research suggests that gender is largely the determining factor.

Seider (1989) argues that males constantly fear that they are not 'man enough' and are relentlessly under pressure to affirm their male identities. This has an impact upon their relationships in wider society. Seider argues that men are the dominant inheritors of the foremost value of *modernity* – rationalism. The Enlightenment vision of modernity was shaped around a secularized ascetic Protestantism which brought a disdain for the body and the emotional life. Mastery of the self and the body has perennially been constructed as an ideal to which all individuals should aspire but which men, rather than women, are likely to achieve. Within the rationalist tradition, men may choose to live without emotions at all, treating them as 'distractions' that take them away from the path of reason. For men it is always 'others' who have emotional needs, but they also often have to learn to deal, frequently inadequately, with emotions and feelings of their own. According to Seider, as far as relationships between male and female are concerned, it is women who are, more often than not, relied upon to do the emotional work in order to keep the relationship going. Men are dependent on partners to interpret what is developing in a relationship and to sustain it, while they often feel that it is self-indulgent for them to attempt to fulfil their emotional needs. This can create problems within relationships, for example, it may leave women feeling guilty about satisfying their own needs. While men very often subscribe to notions of romantic love it is, more often than not, associated with sexual conquest.

Aggressive emotions are not limited to male adulthood. Boys growing towards adulthood may feel compelled to prove that they are not 'weak' since weakness is a form of humiliation. According to Seider, boys must defend themselves or they might have to seek alliances with older brothers or stronger peers to come to their aid. In turn, this helps generate a male hierarchy. Aggression is especially important in the traditional working-class context (Seider 1998, 203). Here, the emphasis may be not on control but being 'out of control' – sometimes purposely amplified by alcohol consumption or indulging in dangerous sports to create 'hardness' or display the lack of emotions.

The 'Emotional' Female

In Western societies emotions are frequently associated with weakness of will and loss of control, the irrational, the physical, the female, and the 'chaotic' nature of women's bodies and their perceived capitulation to desires. By no means is this a new cultural view. The Greek philosopher Plato, some two and a half thousand years ago, spoke of the dominant emotional drives of women that made them 'lower' than men and predisposed towards evil and the baser desires. By contrast, men naturally had 'higher' rational capacities which were conducive towards creating a more civilized and spiritual character. In recent centuries, this cultural perception has often been legitimized by scientific medicine that draws parallels between uncontrolled emotions and the female reproductive system. For example, in the Victorian period hysteria was frequently associated with the malfunctioning of the uterus (see Chapter 8).

According to feminists' accounts, in a patriarchal society it is acceptable for women to display emotions; for this only confirms their weakness and shows that they need men to be independent, self-sufficient, and relied upon. The 'home' has been predominantly portrayed as the sphere of the emotions and the polar opposite to the public sphere of work and is associated, in binary opposition, to the 'emotional woman' and 'unemotional man'. It is not that men are perceived as having no emotions at all. Yet, those which are acceptable in man, such as anger, aggressiveness or triumph, are frequently regarded as 'unattractive' in women. Thus, there is a strong link between perceived femininity and emotionality. Women are regarded as being 'naturally' good at dealing with other people's emotions because they are themselves inherently emotional and that this is most discernible in the supposed natural mother–infant bond. At work, men have to prove themselves to be independent and self-sufficient and in competition with other males. Any sign of weakness could be threatening, for rival men could so easily use it to their advantage to 'put someone down'. Thus they have to be constantly 'on guard' ready to defend themselves from other males who might threaten their status and hence their masculinity (Nauright and Chandler 1997).

This self-assertiveness and display of the unemotional self would seem, however, to conflict with notions of the 'New Man' and the caring nurturing male expressing a different side of his nature, particularly in the domestic sphere. Yet, there is a parallel contradiction. As women increasingly enter the workplace the cultural norms that traditionally informed their behaviour and orientation, one of nurturance and submissiveness, may be reversed, creating its own 'crisis' of identity in the competitive world of work.

Changing gender norms may well be impacting heterosexual relationships. Certainly, Sue Lees speaks of a 'crisis' in the relationship between adult men and women. In particular, that men's attitudes to women have not kept up with the dramatic changes altering women's lives. Explanations include rapid social transformations in the economy, the breakdown of traditional morality, and the growing confidence of women to contest their subordination in the family. Lees sees the 'crisis' as part of the transforming nature of male identities especially in the restructuring of working-class families and the proportion of women entering the job market from which is derived a new-found economic power (Lees 1993, 1–2).

Mate-Selection

Throughout the world, families have historically formed around the institution of marriage – a legally sanctioned and ideally enduring relationship involving economic co-operation, as well as normative sexual activity and child-bearing. Historically embedded in Western culture is the belief that marriage alone is the appropriate context for procreation. Traditionally, cultures have attached the label of illegitimacy to children born out of wedlock and although of far less concern to Western societies today, the evidence suggests that in every known human community a child born outside of marriage is likely to be stigmatized.

In industrialized societies, laws prescribe monogamy, a form of marriage joining two partners. Much results from Christian religious proscriptions, economic factors, and idealized views of romantic love. The high level of divorce and remarriage, however, suggests that 'serial monogamy' may be a more accurate description of Western marital practices today, signifying the ease by which divorce can be attained and perhaps the consequences of an increasing life-span.

Marriage Patterns

Other changes and trends have also been observable related to the typical 'Western marriage'. During the twentieth century there occurred a remarkable increase in the marriage rate. Between 1911 and 1954 in the UK, the portion of women aged between 20 and 40 who were married grew by nearly one-third in the age group 20 to 39. In 1931, the figure was 572, in 1951 it became 731, and in 1961 it had reached 808 per thousand. Today, 95 per cent of women and 91 per cent of men have been married by the age of 40. In 1996, the number of marriages in the UK was, however, at a 70-year low. There were 201,000 first marriages in 1994, half that of 1970. People are now also marrying at an older age: the average age in the European Union in 1993 was 28.5 for men and 26.1 for women. Such statistics render the lower age of marriage in the early and mid-twentieth century as something of a historical curiosity. The current later age chosen for marriage brings wedlock back to the patterns observable in the seventeenth and eighteenth centuries.

Generally speaking, people will marry someone of similar age, education, social class background, and lifestyle. Goode argues that since the marriageable population of the Western countries is segregated into pools of people with similar class origins, even a free dating pattern with some encouragement to fall in love does not threaten the stratification system; generally people fall in love with 'the right kind of people' (Goode 1982, 80–90). In fact, there never is a completely free-market in courtship or mate-selection. Rather, as in some economic exchanges, there are many smaller markets in which only certain people are eligible to participate. It is within each such a 'market' that the greatest freedom is to be found. In the USA, according to a Gallop poll (1998), at the end of the twentieth century marriages were: 99 per cent racially endogamous, 90 per cent religiously homogeneous, and 50–80 per cent social class homogeneous.

The Changing Nature of Courtship

Western society today still places considerable premium on marriage as a source of meaning, purpose, and fulfilment, and where love is believed to be a vital ingredient in mate-selection. However, the concept of romantic love and indeed the general notion of love are especially difficult to quantify, to confirm its presence, or to deny. It is obviously not an entity which can be measured empirically. Certainly, love has a personal subjective expression for the individual but what is certain is that in the West there remains a cultural code of romantic love which is reaffirmed by the media and popular discourse.

Throughout earlier ages, romantic love had been historically recorded as enhanced by the use of love potions and usurped by the illicit fantasies of the rich. In a great deal of Western literature, over some three centuries, it was insisted that love was compatible with marriage and an important factor in choice of partner. Christian Canon law, created and written centuries ago, stated that love should be a precursor to wedded union. Similarly, in Europe in the seventeenth and eighteenth centuries documentary evidence confirmed that it was believed that love was a natural expression and something that would develop *after* marriage and hence even meant to develop in arranged marriages. This suggests that the notion of being romantically attached through pre-marriage courtship is an invention of early modernity.

Goode (1982) believes that the main connections between the element of romantic love and developments associated with modernity in the West are as follows. First, the family unit is relatively independent of the larger kinship group, so husband and wife are free to love each other without serious competition from kin. In many other societies the husband–wife tie is accorded less emotional prominence. Second, the parent–child tie is strong in Western societies, and falling in love permits the young person to free her/himself from this attachment in order to enter the independent status of spouse. Third, compared to pre-industrial societies, Western cultural patterns give considerable freedom to adolescents, thus increasing the likeliness that they will fall in love. And, of course, love may be viewed as a mechanism for filling the gap left by the decline of arranged marriages. Young people, who in another marriage system would be pushed into marriage by their elders, are motivated to marry because of love.

Romantic love may be a cultural value more readily enculturated for females. Indeed, one constraint placed upon female youth would appear today to be the popular pressures to meet the 'right man' and fall in love. This is frequently presented as the norm through the media and, by way of example, idealized in Angela McRobbie's analysis of *Jackie*, a magazine for young girls which shows that

> the stories consist of isolated individuals, distrusting even their best friends ... and in search of fulfilment only through a partner ... Jackie stories ... elevate to dizzy heights the supremacy of the heterosexual romantic partnership (McRobbie1978a, 17 and 20).

Much of such literature states that girlfriends take second place or are dropped altogether as girls start going out regularly with boys. The model which emerges is a polarized one: girlfriends or boyfriends. The two are seen as incompatible, and inevitably the boyfriends win in the end – just like the magazine stories. The picture which comes across is that women are passive victims of ideological pressures, totally seduced by the cultures of feminity and romance.

The link between romantic love and mate-selection has, however, been supplemented by more recent developments. Dating in the 1970s and 80s changed in three ways. First, there were greater opportunities for informal opposite sex interaction such as the workplace. Second, dating behaviour became less formal than in previous generations and no longer a set progression of stages from first meeting until the time of marriage. Third, it was more and more acceptable for women to initiate dating activities and be responsible for the economics of the date and, arguably, a greater equality within the relationship.

Over the last decade there have been indications of a return to a more conservative system of courtship, while the feminist movement has increasingly carried weight with its emphasis on the sexual alternatives open to women. The spread of AIDs, as we have noted above, has also made people acutely aware of the potential dangers of promiscuous behaviour and multiple partners. The future, however, looks quite different altogether and may be determined by factors once believed to be limited to the realm of science fiction. Technology may develop to allow certain knowledge of a person's genes, thus becoming part of mate choice – perhaps through dating agencies. While the indirect information concerning looks, age, and academic achievements would still be important, with more genetic information accessible decisions can be based on an exact certain knowledge. Relationships, then, are increasingly exposed to information technology, lifestyle preferences, and perhaps the growing commercialization of romantic love which culturally contradicts with sexual permissiveness and choices open to sexual lifestyles.

In other respects aspects of mate-selection may not have changed. Elizabeth Jagger in her deconstruction of heterosexual dating advertizements suggests that in the postmodern consumer culture men are furnished with a wide range of resources in which to create 'desirable' identities but that for women reflexive self-fashioning is more problematic. Men stressed financial and occupational resources, alongside more traditional masculine images. In contrast, female self-image in 'selling themselves' is quite restrictive and more closely associated with sex role stereotypes based on physical attractiveness and body shape (Jagger 2001).

The new technologies clearly play their part in contemporary dating. Wysocki (1998), for example, has considered how people participate in sexually explicit bulletin boards on websites or 'sex on-line'. She concludes that they subscribe for various reasons. The most common is to fulfil particular fantasies that were not being fulfilled in their relationships off-line and to share their fantasies with the like-minded. Thus the relevant websites have become 'fantasy lands' for people to talk about sexual activities which they could not live out in real life. However, once contact is made, face-to-face meetings might ensue and the fantasies become a reality.

Given many of the changes noted above, Mary Evans may well be correct in identifying what she sees as a 'crisis' in heterosexual relationships. Evans argues that the cultural practices underlying love have shifted. Contemporary culture has personalized and sexualized love, and unhitched it from marriage – the coupling of which began in early modernity. At the same time society has de-eroticized sex and in doing so undermined emotive bonds. The result is that people now have impossible expectations which may ultimately be emotionally damaging. It is now romanticized and commercialized love void of care and commitment. Evans concludes that in terms of relationships, Western society has produced a confused culture which, through love and sexual relationships, has brought emotional insecurities that do not bode well for future generations (Evans 2003).

Alternatives to Marriage

Cohabitation and the Single Alternative

Even if marriage has enjoyed a continuing popularity in Western societies, various alternatives have also emerged. One is cohabitation, though it would seem to neither significantly undermine or replace marriage. Cohabitation may be defined as the sharing of a household by an unmarried couple. This arrangement has become more popular in recent years. The proportion of all non-married women aged 18 to 40 cohabiting has doubled since 1981 to 25 per cent of all couplings, although it is most frequent among young women in their twenties and divorced people. Cohabitation rarely lasts more than two years, and usually ends in marriage. In Europe, almost half of those between 25 and 44 years of age have cohabited at some point. This is all evidence that social attitudes towards this arrangement have changed considerably. A generation or two ago, it would most likely to have been described as 'living in sin' which indicated its disapproval of sex outside of marriage generally. Attitudinal surveys now find a generational difference – with older people (those born before 1950) disapproving, but younger ones overwhelmingly in favour of it. Around 61–64 per cent of the former group would advise marriage without living together first; only 17 per cent of the younger group would now advocate this (*Social Trends* 1997, 45–6).

With cohabitation currently carrying far less stigma than even some 30 years ago, it may be regarded by many as a 'trial marriage', whilst others reject the institution of marriage altogether. A fair few may be influenced by the high levels of divorce and believe that should they wish to end their relationship sometime in the future, then it would be less traumatic than if there were a formal union. The reality is that 70 per cent of first partnerships are cohabitations lasting on average two years, while 60 per cent of all cohabitations moved into marriage. In 1980, 2 per cent of women had children while cohabiting. In 1997, the figure had risen to 22 per cent (UK Office of National Statistics (2002) and the Institute of Social and Economic Research, University of Essex (2002)).

As an alternative to marriage or cohabitation, a greater number of people are living alone in Western Europe now than ever before. By 1995–96, a quarter of all households in the UK housed just one person living alone (about half of these were pensioners). Elderly widows have always represented a large share of single people. But a new group of divorced men under the age of 65 has become the second biggest group to live alone: there were two and a half-times the number of men living a single life in 1996 than in 1971 and it is anticipated that this group will continue to rise. It seems to be men in particular who choose not to marry. Included among the main reasons are that sex is available without marriage – a man can acquire a 'wife' without marriage through cohabitation; that they wish to avoid the risk of divorce and its costs; that men want to wait before having children; that marriage requires change and compromise; and that men want to own their own house before finding a wife (*National Marriage Project*, Rutgers University 2002).

'Alternative' Sexualities

To discuss what might be termed 'alternative' sexualities, such as a gay orientation, under the rubric of 'alternative to marriage' is perhaps unsatisfactory. This is largely because to do so would suggest that the relationships involved are unstable and fleeting, whereas, in reality, many gay people are seeking to have their permanent relationship endorsed by the legal arrangement of marriage. Hence, a discussion of 'alternative' sexualities is perhaps best viewed as in contrast to the popularized view of the heterosexual marriage.

Although same sex relations have existed across cultures and throughout history with varying degrees of acceptability and frequency, in the West is has for centuries been opposed. For nearly 2000 years this condemnation was derived from the Christian church which regarded homosexuality as a cardinal sin. From the mid-nineteenth century same sex relations added to this negative view through a medical framework that interpreted it as pathology. Throughout this period homosexuality was strongly condemned by law in most European countries and all the states of the USA. It was not until the more permissive society of the 1960s that the legal position began to change. The scientifically imposed designation 'homosexual' was shifted to the preferred self-designated term 'gay' at a time when gay men and lesbians started to 'come out' and subsequently became accepted in mainstream society. However, a survey in 1996 found that 64 per cent of lesbians and gay men concealed their sexuality from some or all of their colleagues at work. This is perhaps understandable since the survey also found that 21 per cent of gays stated that they had experienced discrimination in employment and some 33 per cent of heterosexual employers insisted that they would be less likely to employ a lesbian or gay person (*Mori Poll* 1996).

If gay equality has been achieved in law, there are other indications that parity with heterosexuals has not yet been achieved including the issue of gay adoption (overviewed in Chapter 3), the field of biomedicine, and criminology. Waites contends that in late-modernity so-called 'expert' discourse circumventing the subject is less likely to confirm that a 'fixed' gay, and for that matter bi-sexual identity has been established by the age of 16 in a way that it is assumed for heterosexuals. Hence, legal equality does not imply recognition of homosexuality and heterosexuality. Moreover, it also suggests an increasing medicalization of gay sexuality (Waites 2003).

Despite the evidence of continued discrimination, sexual variants are gaining legitimacy in Western culture and may, in fact, be a product of it. Indeed, Storr goes so far as to see bisexuality as essentially 'Postmodern'. Storr explains that the existence of a self-conscious bisexual identity by way of community association, organization, and politics came with the advent of postmodernity of the 1970s. Indeterminacy, instability, fragmentation, and flux are all part of the postmodern condition. If modernity had structured heterosexuality, postmodernity brings its own form of sexuality that is increasingly varied and challenges the ideal heterosexual relationship forged as part of the ideological construct of modernity (Storr 1999).

Epstein has, by contrast, placed a greater emphasis on the medicalization of 'alternative' sexualities. The social toleration of sexual variations such as lesbians, gays, bisexuals, and transgendered people, seems to have been increasing. Such differences have also been legitimated by health services. Nonetheless, as Epstein notes, in the USA the development of health policy for 'special populations' has led to the medicalization of the identities of such people who are consequently excluded from biomedical citizenship. While the rights of these groups can be traced to gay and feminist movements since the 1970s, they are now subject to medical scrutiny. The consequence of medicalization is to encourage the public to see sexual and gender identities as fixed biological or cultural types, and as an illness category. Far from becoming 'sexual citizens', the medicalization of the sexual alternatives may turn out to be yet another form of social control and exclusion (Epstein 2003).

Marital Breakdown

Divorce

Divorce has various consequences and in Chapter 3 we considered the implications of the end of marriage for children. Another obvious repercussion is for the estranged spouses themselves. Most divorcees report divorce as an extremely painful experience, but that the most traumatic period is when spouses separated for the last time. After divorce, it is men who generally feel more detrimental effects. Both parents may experience emotional distress, and psychological and heath problems as integral to the process of adapting to new roles and perhaps new relationships as part of a settling down period which may average some two years. After divorce, moreover, females seem to adapt more readily than men. Married men, compared to married women, live longer than single men, have better mental health and report being happier. Yet, this is reversed after divorce with men finding it more difficult to cope on their own and display deteriorating levels of physical and mental health (Hetherington 1991).

Divorce however, is only one expression of marital breakdown. Couples may separate but remain married indefinitely: the number who does so is impossible to estimate. The incidence of spouses who stay together in the same household, even though their marriage is 'dead', for practical and financial reasons or for the 'sake of the children', is likewise impossible to estimate. Divorce rates, nevertheless, can be monitored and they are undoubtedly increasing in most Western societies.

There is a tendency for rising divorce rates to be seen as an essentially Western phenomenon. In reality, many pre-industrial societies have been known to have substantially higher divorce rates than any measurable in the West (Goode 1961, 404). Neither is there anything particularly new in increasing rates in Western societies. There had been a long-term upward trend in the number of civil divorces in the nineteenth century. However, prior to 1914, the annual number of divorces never exceeded 10,000 in England and Wales, and 1000 in Scotland. There were substantial increases in the wake of both World Wars, but the numbers fell back during the 1950s. From the early 1960s the trend has been upward, with the 1970 figure more than doubling that of 1960.

Over the last few decades there has occurred a rapid increase in the divorce rate in the UK, as in other Western societies. The peak period for divorce in the UK was the 1970s, although the rapid rise has stabilized since the mid-1980s (at around 160,000 per year). Between 1971 and 1994, the divorce rate more than doubled, so that by 1994 the UK had the highest divorce rate in the European Union (but not as high as USA). It is now expected that 40 per cent of recent UK marriages will end in divorce. The most common reason for women to be granted divorce is the 'unreasonable behaviour' of the man; for men, it is the adultery of the wife (*Social Trends* 1997, 48). Roughly a quarter of children can now expect to find their original parents divorced by the time they are 16, though the trend of ending marriage may have slowed down at the beginning of the twenty-first century, it does nonetheless seem a stable Western pattern.

More general explanations for divorce include the following. First, divorce is legally easier to accomplish and is cheaper than before. Changes in cultural attitudes towards marriage have created a climate of public opinion in which it has been possible to pass laws making it increasingly easier to opt out of marriage. The long-term background to the erosion of marriage as a permanent and binding commitment is the decline in formal religious belief. Marriage is less often seen as a sacred, spiritual union, but more as a personal and practical commitment which can be abandoned, as a matter of choice, if it failed. This attitude to marriage has resulted in a series of changes in the law, making the grounds for divorce less strict and the administrative procedure for obtaining it less complicated and less time-consuming. In financial terms, especially with Legal Aid, divorce is now a cheaper process.

In the UK, the Divorce Law Act of 1969, which took affect in 1971, gave a sharp upward shift to the total number of divorces. The Act established that it was sufficient to claim an 'irretrievable breakdown of marriage' to obtain a divorce. It is a phrase general enough to be interpreted to include virtually all conceivable reasons for divorce. Although there was an upward rise in the divorce rate after the legislation, it did not 'cause' the increase since there were underlying social factors responsible.

Second, there are demographic changes that have increased divorce rates.It has been common to exaggerate the stability of marriage in the past, when the early death of a spouse ended as many marriages after a few years as divorce does now. When people did not live as long as they do at present, marriages were obviously of shorter duration. These days, without divorce, most people's marriages could last some 50 years or more – given current life-expectancy and marriage rates.

A third factor is the value placed on individualism. Beech sees the rise of a contemporary society where people expect choice, control over their lives, and where beliefs in equality are important factors in explaining rising divorce rates. As a culture we have become more individualistic, seemingly more concerned with personal happiness and success than with the well-being of families and children. Fourth, there may be the factor of diminishing romantic love. Western culture has long emphasized romantic love as a basis for marriage, rendering relationships vulnerable to collapse as sexual passion subsides. There is now widespread support for the notion that one may end a marriage in favour of a fresh relationship simply to renew excitement and romance.

Fifth, women are now less dependent on men and display changing expectations.Increasing female participation in the labour force has reduced a wife's financial dependence on her husband. In addition, women have largely come to expect more from life than being merely the homemaker. They are more likely to demand freedom from the dominance of the husband, making it easier to walk away from unhappy marriages. Up to the time of the change in divorce legislation in 1969 twice as many men filed for divorce than women. This figure was reversed after the change in law. Finally, there is the stress factor. With both spouses working outside the home, jobs consume time and energy. Raising children can be difficult in this context. Thus, divorce is most common during the early years of marriage when working couples have young children (Beechy 1983).

Family Life

So far we have discussed the significance of the family in the life course largely in relation to childhood and infancy, as well as its link to marriage as a social convention. Here, we consider the topics of the historical development of the family, contemporary family diversity, and some of the possible dysfunctions that it may have for the life course. First, however, something needs to be said about the development of the culturally idealized structure of the family as a key social institution which, in late- or postmodernity, has become a contested site of political and moral discourse.

In sociological terms, the family is frequently described as a basic social arrangement which unites individuals into co-operative groups overseeing the bearing and raising of children. These social units are, in turn, built upon kinship, a relationship bond based on blood, marriage, or adoption that integrates individuals into primary relationships. Although most societies contain family structures, just who is included under the umbrella of kinship has varied throughout history and differs in the contemporary world from one culture to another. Nonetheless, on a universal basis individuals are initially born into a family composed of parents and siblings – an arrangement that is generally referred to as the *family of orientation* because this group is central to the socialization process. In adulthood, people forge a *family of procreation* in order to produce or adopt children of their own. What is termed the *conjugal* or *nuclear family* is founded on the unit constructed around a married man and woman with children and is grounded, at least ideally in Western societies, in life-long marriage and parenthood.

Structural Developments

As early as the mid-twentieth century the Kinsey reports (1948, 1953) showed a considerable difference in family organization and values according to class, ethnic, and occupational variations, as well as divergences in sexual behaviour. There has also been evidence produced of a fair amount of dislocation and change throughout the life course of the family in the mid-twentieth century (Weeks 1985, 84).

An ideal-type model might suggest that family life begins with courtship, followed by the settling into the realities of married life. Next comes the task of raising children, leading to the later years of marriage after the children have left home to form families of their own. But such a model does little justice to the dynamics of change and variation evident at the beginning of the twenty-first century. Thus, for example, cohabitation may lead to a family with children yet then, after divorce, a lone-parent family frequently forms or, on re-marriage, a step family or re-constituted family could possibly result. As more and more people forge non-traditional family ties, many are currently thinking of kinship in terms of 'families of choice', with or without legal or blood ties, and comprised of individuals who feel they belong together and wish to define themselves as a family (Weston 1991). What does or does not constitute a family, therefore, is a moral and political matter that lies at the heart of the contemporary 'family values' debate.

In the 1980s, Robert Chester (1985) argued that while changes in the family had been far from minor in the previous few decades, there were signs of a reversal of some of the trends in what he called the 'new conventional family'. Furthermore, Chester suggested that the contemporary life course makes it inevitable that at any one time, some people will not be members of a nuclear family household. Yet, he argues there is little evidence that people are choosing to live on a long-term basis in alternatives to the nuclear family. This was a view which was not always substantiated by the evidence. A decade later in the USA less than one in four households in the USA approximated the traditional image of a married or cohabiting couple with children. Stacey (1996), for instance, suggests that in the United States only 7 per cent of households conformed to the modern patterns of bread-winning father, home-making mother, and one to four children under the age of 18.

Into the new millennium, however, things may have changed again. In the USA, census data (US Census Bureau 2000) estimated that the percentage of children living with both their biological parents jumped from 51 to 52 per cent. These findings tentatively hint that family relations in the United States could be entering a new era of stability after two decades of transformation. This report may indicate that change in family structure is levelling off. In 1990 for instance, 22 per cent of the nation's children lived with single-mothers, while six years later it had risen only an extra one per cent.

In the USA, researchers attribute the possible re-emergence or at least consolidation of the nuclear family to many factors including the fact that the divorce rate has fallen from its peak in 1980 when there were over five divorces for every 1000 people; by 1999 the rate had dropped to four in 1000. Also, out of wedlock births have been levelling off. In 1970, roughly one in ten births involved unmarried mothers. Although that rate surged to one out of three in 1994, it has since virtually stayed at the same level. The apparent return of the nuclear family should however be cautioned as it could be exaggerated by other factors. The economy, for example, may have played a significant role. Between 1991 and 1996, the average financial situation of many families improved considerably. These improvements reduced the number of divorces since spouses will invariably feel more economically secure.

Despite mixed evidence about the endurance of the nuclear family, it is clear that considerable diversity does exist. Earlier studies suggested that social class was a major determining factor. Rubin, for example, identified not only a difference in financial security and range of opportunities, but that class could also affect the size, structure, and values embraced. In turn, these variables forged attitudes towards family and married life, reflecting differential levels of education and work satisfaction and accompanied, for the middle classes at least, a greater emphasis on verbal skills, flexibility, and initiative. In addition, middle-class couples shared a wider range of activities, while traditionally working-class domestic life was more sharply divided along gender lines. In such homes, Rubin explains, convention masculine ideas of self-control stifled emotional expressiveness on the part of working-class men, prompting women to turn to each other as confidants and develop strong bonds between them. The privatization of middle-class family life, by comparison, was highly compatible with extended friendship networks and was displayed in the relative lack of involvement in the social life of the immediate neighbourhood: it is more organized and less spontaneous (Rubin 1976). Over the last 30 years however, the predictions of Young and Willmott have undoubtedly been fulfilled in the shifting of working-class families to conform closer to the middle-class stereotype, although outcrops of traditional working-class family structures and norms may be observable among semi- and unskilled workers (Young and Willmott 1973).

As with social class, we must be aware of the dangers in generalizing about ethnic minorities and their family structures. Just as there is enormous diversity behind the so-called 'white nuclear family', so there is great variety among the families of the major ethnic groups. At the same time, ethnic family forms in the UK, for instance, have been subject to change over the past 40 years. In the early days of mass migration (1950–70) there was a severe disruption of family life, as patterns found in the former homes began to disintegrate. Nonetheless, subsequent new forms of stable family types have emerged. Having recognized this, there are some differences that are quite striking compared to the standardized Anglo-Saxon family.

The Asian population across the world generally has a very strong extended family system. There are, however, cultural differences between Bangladeshis, Pakistanis, Punjabis, Tamils, and other ethnic groups and nationalities regarding family structures, values, and norms which are as great as their similarities. Irrespective of structure or tradition, Westwood and Bhachu (1988) identify a number of transformations including the tendency for some Asian families to have become more nuclear in structure, to display a greater diversity of family life, and a more open attitude to women working outside the home.

Afro-Caribbean families account for less than one per cent of all families in the UK, but do provide a stark contrast to other ethnic groups (Skellington and Morris 1996, 20). Today, around 37 per cent are headed by a female (compared with 9 per cent of white families). In such families, marriage is often weaker, female-headed households are more common, and the husband/father role is likely to be less pronounced than Asian families. There is also a parallel in the USA where Afro-American families are of a similar structure. This is often seen as linked to the cultural legacy of Caribbean society. Originally, whilst marriage is much valued in the Caribbean, other patterns of sexual union were always possible. There are still common law family households with unmarried cohabitation, as well as women-headed households.

Problems in Family Life

The Myth of Conjugal Roles

Rising divorce statistics suggest an underlying problem in family life in terms of marital relationships. Other difficulties would also appear to be evident and to some extent undermine the rosy picture of the idealized nuclear family. One would seem to be in the area of conjugal roles where notions of egalitarian gender roles still appear to be something of a myth. In 1993 and 1994, the Mintel market research group produced two survey reports called *Women 2000* and *Men 2000*. They found the following. First, that 80 per cent of women claimed that they take, or share equally large financial decisions with their male partners. However, fewer than 40 per cent have their own bank accounts. Second, 42 per cent of married men claimed to share at least one domestic task equally with their wives, but only 26 per cent of women thought this was the case. Third, 85 per cent of working women said that they almost always do all the laundry and ironing. A similar proportion maintained they are entirely responsible for cooking the main meal. Some 25 per cent of husbands were 'happy cookers' who preferred entertaining and experimenting rather than cooking daily meals. Fourth, it was discovered that 50 per cent of husbands admitted to being 'sloths' over housework. They were predominantly to be found in the 35 to 54 age group. Finally, the liberated 'newish man' was most likely to be middle-class and young. Men under 34 without children were best at sharing jobs in the home, yet were still not particularly interested in taking the share of childcare.

Dysfunctional Aspects

One argument is that the contemporary nuclear family is dysfunctional and this has resulted in its breakdown. Hence, it is not emotionally supportive of its members but claustrophobic, emotionally over-charged, and generates stress and conflict – problems exacerbated by the isolation of the family unit. The family may be seen as limiting freedom, preventing self-actualization, and narrowly defining intimacy. This theme was explored in R.D.Laing's renowned work, *The Politics of the Family,* which in so many ways epitomized the critiques of the family that came out of the 1960s and 70s. Laing believed that many of the problems of family life are linked to the tension of a child's early dependence on its parents and its eventual strivings towards independence. Parents were depicted by Laing as being highly ambivalent about letting go of the child and in encouraging its independence and the development of an individual identity.

This ambiguity around independence raises problems for the child, while his/her concept of the self is undermined by the destructive intimacy of the nuclear family (Laing 1976).

Violence epitomizes the darker side of family life. During the 1970s a 'new' family problem seemed to have been 'discovered': men's domestic violence against women. This trend appeared to accompany increasing rates of violence against children (see Chapter 3). A study by Mooney (1994) in North London found that about half of all women surveyed had experienced threats of violence or actual violence – though many of these women failed to tell anyone of their experiences. A campaign against domestic violence in 1994, called Zero Tolerance, estimated that in London alone almost 100,000 women a year seek treatment for violent injuries inflicted by their partners. In the past, the law regarded domestic violence as a private, family matter. Now, even without separation or divorce, a woman can obtain court protection from an abusive spouse. Although the majority of battered women in this particular report left home to escape their husband's violence, most are forced to return, because of the stigma attached to leaving, lack of childcare facilities, and economic dependence on the husband.

Studies such as that of Dobash and Dobash (1980) indicated that as men learn to explore hegemonic white, heterosexual masculinities they come to recognize the necessity for domination. Often men need to be in control not only of themselves but others in order to affirm their male identities. This creates a fear of emotions which are readily identified with the 'feminine' and are often treated as a sign of weakness. They expect to be respected by their partners and children not so much for what they do but the positions they hold. While the link between masculinities and male aggression may lay behind domestic violence, the phenomenon is a socially constructed one since, as in the case of child abuse, it has been 'discovered' to the extent that discourse around the subject tends to designate it as a new and emerging 'problem' and thus playing down the incidences in the past which, in reality, may have remained largely unreported.

Summary

One of the principal insights that sociology provides into non-emotional relationships is that they are a social product created by societal needs and cultural trajectories. It is much the same, moreover, with relationships of a more intimate nature. This is not to pretend that biological and psychological processes do not play a part, not least of all in the matter of sexual impulses. Nonetheless, societies structure, encourage, and constrain these impelling human needs according to time and place. Today, some

cherished institutions such as marriage and the family unit which historically channelled and constrained sexuality – uniting it to reproductive
functions, are clearly being undermined and alternatives present themselves. Whether single parenthood, cohabitation, or any other variation to
the family are for the long-term benefit of society remains to be seen.

Founded on recent trends, some predictions for the future may be
conjectured. First, divorce rates are likely to remain high. There may be
some erosion of support for easy dissolution of marriage, although in 2000
the Labour government in the UK abandoned its idea of compulsory
marriage guidance because it was unworkable. Several generations of
high divorce rates have seriously weakened the idea that marriage is a
lifetime commitment. Looking back over history, however, marital relationships are about as durable today as they were a century ago, when
many marriages were cut short by death. Yet, it is unlikely that marriage
will regain the durability that it sustained before the 1960s, so that divorce
now marks one of the main discontinuities in adult life. Second, there is
increasing acceptance of sex outside of heterosexual, monogamous, life-
long marriage, and the growing legitimacy of marriage as a terminable
arrangement. While extra-marital sex may still be frowned upon, 20 to
50 per cent of women in the UK will have at least one relationship outside
of marriage, while 50 to 65 per cent of men will stray before the age of 40
(*Mori Poll* 1998).

A third prospect is that family life in the twenty-first century will be
highly variable. This represents new conceptions of family relations as a
matter of choice. There have now emerged new, flexible, highly individualistic, and sexually variant relationship patterns (Cancian 1987). An optimistic view of the future is one which predicts that relationships will
emerge where men and women are equal and interdependent; where their
child-raising is altogether part of a more egalitarian and democratic
arrangement, and where sexuality and love become more 'plastic', diffuse,
and open. This is a relationship of choice, closely allied to individualism
and one which may forge a kinship arrangement that some sociologists
term the 'postmodern family' (Stacey 1996, 8). Whatever its precise
designation, it is one which is unpredictable and part of a broader context
of relationships where alternatives to marriage present themselves.

All in all, at the beginning of the twenty-first century, families seem to
be undergoing very significant changes while, some traditional patterns
are still observable. Clearly, transformations in the family have stimulated
a great deal of debate in sociology, the realm of politics, and social policy.
For some with informed opinions these changes amount to a disaster, to
others they mark social progress, bringing individualism and the end of
patriarchy and restrictive gender roles, as well as enhancing a culture
where choice is of paramount importance. Whatever the merits behind

changes in the family and attitudes towards sexuality, their increasing diversity and exposure to choice has considerable impact on the life course in terms of risks and discontinuities, alongside increasing opportunity and challenges.

Further Reading

Chodorow,N. (1994) *Feminities, Masculinities and Sexualities*, London: Free Association Books.
Goldthorpe,J. (1987) *Family Life in Western Societies*, Cambridge: Cambridge University Press.
Lees, S. (1993) *Sugar and Spice: Sexuality and Adolescent Girls*, London: Penguin.
Wilton,T. (1995) *Lesbian Studies: Setting An Agenda*, London: Routledge.

7

Work, Leisure, and Consumption

Employment

Work is an important status marker of adult life. The capacity to earn an income, the undertaking of responsible roles, independence from kin, and integration into the adult world come through the opportunities offered by employment. In turn, occupational reward will determine life-chances and opportunities throughout the life course and, where applicable, to younger dependents as well. This is true of late- or postmodernity, as in previous times. Whether one can realize meaningful choices, fulfil lifestyle ambitions, avoid the unwanted consequences of risk or can forge the identity of one's preference, will largely depend on rewards in the employment marketplace.

A wealth of sociological literature has grown up around the theme of the relationship between work and identity. One emphasis has been on the link between identity and status. It is the status of a person's work which frequently determines how they perceive themselves and the means by which others can tell so much about them; life opportunities, income, and lifestyles. Although the time spent at work has greatly diminished over the last hundred years or so, for many people it still occupies over half their waking hours. It is not surprizing then, that work overspills into other areas of life and that 'we are what we do'. Moreover, our sense of self-esteem and personal well-being is wrapped up with the work that we undertake.

In late- or postmodernity the stress on adult identity is not restricted to the workplace. The shift from production to consumption, and the rise of the consumer society and its accompanying culture, means that consumption and lifestyle rival work and work experiences as the major variables behind identity and identity construction. 'We are what we do' is supplemented by 'we are what we consume'. In turn, consumption, to one degree or another, impacts upon leisure pursuits as an important variable shaping 'non-work' experiences. It is the overlapping themes of work, leisure, and consumption, as pertinent to adult life, which informs the discussions of this chapter, particularly in tracing their relevance in the change from modernity to late- or postmodernity.

Experiences of Employment: Work and Identity

In 1992, the UK *Labour Force Survey* found that the proportion of people active in the workplace in Europe to be around 165 million or 60 per cent of the population. Such statistics suggest that well over half the population in the European community spend a good part of their waking lives at work. Employment is obviously an economic activity not least of all in determining, via income reward, life chances, life experience, and the limits of lifestyle constructs. Yet, there are many other considerations too for life opportunities and this chapter discusses not only the changing nature of work and experience of the workplace, but some of the positive and negative ways in which employment shapes the life course through the implications for identity and social integration – forging great significance also for age cohorts and relationships with other generations.

Career patterns change over the life course. For example, in the past, within a more coherent life-cycle model associated with *modernity*, men between the age of 55 and retirement may have been described as being at a stable 'career maintenance stage'. It still remains the case that those already in high-status jobs with successful careers are likely to be at their peak employment period and will maintain a high level of involvement with their work. Others disappointed in their career ambitions may be less concerned. It is probably the latter, realizing the reduced potential for further advancement in their current occupations, who are likely to turn to other sources such as family, leisure, or community for fulfilment in their lives. In the workplace such lack of advancement may lead to what Robert Merton called 'ritualism', whereby individuals merely go 'through the motions' – lacking work interest and ambitions (Merton 1969).

Particularly in more prestigious white-collar occupations, a career is a frame of reference frequently used by individuals to interpret where they are in the life course and what they expect to happen to them at any future point of time. Here, there is a discernible link between career regularities, the negotiation of risks and choice, and the construction of personal identities. Of all occupational categories it is professional people who most of all may attempt to make sense of who they are in terms of their location along a career route and possibly draw comparisons with others in the workplace. Whatever the specific occupational path embarked upon, the regularized career pattern associated with it helps the career-minded to evaluate life performance to that point and allows an anticipation of likely future possibilities in a reflexive way. However, a rapidly changing economy and job structure means that this sense of future certainties has for most professions been undermined since discontinuity and career change are the experiences for many people today.

Constant house moves, a characteristic of the early career stages in many occupations, will obviously limit the employment possibilities open to men's wives since it is the husband's work that is frequently held to be the priority. Women, including working wives, face their own challenges however. We have seen in the previous chapter how being 'feminine' is associated with a range of discernible emotions. Entering the workplace changes some of these cultural ideals of the nurturing and caring female. Like their male colleagues, female career-orientated women are increasingly expected to be rational, non-emotive, and competitive. The working wife and mother, therefore, may find herself having to display different sides of the 'self' in working and domestic life. This provides an important counterpoint to the alleged 'crisis' of male identity; the inherent contradiction of the 'New Man' in the domestic sphere and the competitive careerist male in the workplace.

Work and Mobility

Despite high levels of risk and unpredictability in economic life, late- or postmodernity is often perceived as a social order driven by choice and equality of opportunity. Hence, it is associated with high levels of social mobility, alongside the growth of a meritocracy and the 'open' society. There is mixed evidence as to the degree in which these alleged positive attributes of late- or postmodernity are realized in any meaningful sense.

Ken Roberts (1993) has explored career trajectories and social mobility in terms of social class background and sees class as an enduring significant variable. He concludes that since the 1980s the proportion of children from working-class homes going on to higher education has increased – allowing mobility into skilled and high-level jobs. Regarding younger people of all social classes, those with high-quality professional training are in a better position for work retention and progressive careers. The opportunities for working-class youth have come not from enterprise initiatives from business or government but the extension of high-level employment and educational or occupational training.

On the other hand, Roberts found that there were increased risks of unemployment and survival on property incomes for those who failed to enter careers and reasonably secure jobs. The possibility of middle-class long-range downward mobility was only remote since the contraction of manual employment means more mobility for working-class youth. For middle-class youth, the expansion of professional and management jobs confirms that their positions were less venerable than before. Their typical problem was to choose between the widening range of occupations at this level and the possible routes open to their attainment.

While Roberts draws a relatively optimistic picture of social mobility through occupation, Cote and Allahar (1996) highlight the dilemmas facing marginalized and alienated youth. In North America, Western Europe, and Japan, many youths can expect to have a lower standard of living than their parents. They are conditioned to stay younger longer and have, as a result, become socially and economically marginalized, finding it difficult to establish adult identities. A good number of young people amass credentials regardless of employment prospects and continue to live at home, often dependent on their parents, into their thirties. With fewer jobs available, the young are ironically targeted by businesses, but increasingly as consumers rather than producers. As new technologies continually reduce the workforce and transform the social fabric, an entire generation of young now find it difficult to keep up with developments. Given the marginalized role of many young people, Cote and Allahar suggest that the pertinent question that emerges from these developments is, 'what does it mean to come of age?'

The Growth of the Service Sector and the Dual Labour Market

The arrival of the post-industrial society has certain profound repercussions in the sphere of employment not least of all on different forms of employment, varying experience within the occupational sphere, and a greater insecurity which add to the risks of the contemporary life course. Industrialization in the nineteenth century meant the dominance of labour in the form of manual factory workers. By the first decade of the twentieth century, however, more than 45 per cent of the UK workforce was involved in the service sector (with 40 per cent in industry and only 15 per cent in agriculture). At the beginning of the 1970s, while some industries like agriculture declined to around 4 per cent, that of the service sector had increased to approximately 54 per cent of the working population.

The expansion of service occupations is one reason for the growth of the middle-classes. Many of these jobs can be described as 'white-collar' and essentially different from factory work. However, a great deal of service work including sales positions, clerical, and secretary employment, offers income and status closer to that of most manual workers than that of the professional. Put another way, an increasing number of occupations in these post-industrial times provide only a modest economic reward that constrains life course opportunities, levels of consumption, and lifestyle preferences. Simultaneously, the infinite fragmentation of the workforce in terms of income has undermined coherent class structures which were, for instance, exemplified by the 'classical' accounts of working-class communities (Young and Willmott 1962).

The decline of class, income, and reward in the marketplace has, nonetheless, been supplanted by new divisions in terms of work experience, opportunities, and income. The change from factory work to service employment constitutes a shifting balance between two classifications of work. First, there is the smaller primary labour market which appeals to those in the traditional white-collar professions and high management positions. These are jobs that people may regard as constituting life-long 'careers' and are synonymous with high incomes, job security, and are generally intrinsically personally satisfying. Such occupations require a broad education rather than specialized training and usually guarantee the possibility of career advancement.

In comparison, there is the secondary labour market that is comprised of jobs providing the minimal benefit to employees. This segment of the labour force is employed in the low-skilled, blue-collar type work found in routine assembly line operations, and in low-level service sector jobs including clerical positions. It is a sector which tends to offer little by way of income, demands a longer working week, and affords less job security and hence life course discontinuities and less opportunity for personal advancement. Moreover, it is in this sector that workers are most likely to experience alienation and job dissatisfaction. Such negative experiences at work most commonly beset women and ethnic minorities who are overly represented in this quarter of the labour force (Kohn and Schooler 1982).

Most of the developing areas of employment in the post-industrial economy fall within the secondary labour market, and they involve the same kind of unchallenging tasks, low wages, and frequently poor working conditions once identified with factory employment. To this is added a greater job insecurity in a rapidly changing economy which has few parallels in the past. It has also led to more part-time and flexible work practices. Simultaneously, over the last decade, part-time work has become more common – especially for women. By comparison, it was not too many years ago that employees could more or less take for granted security at work – a 'job for life' – often in the same firm for the duration of their lives until they retired. Economic developments have changed all this. Companies now relentlessly compete and the dynamics of the global economy means that the larger firms have to 'down-size' and de-centralize in order to gain the necessary flexibility to survive. These trends invariably lead not only to cutting the number of people on the payroll, from managers to shop floor workers, but also replacing long-term employees with temporary workers. By hiring 'temps', companies can 'cut corners' by not having to provide insurance, paid vacations, or pensions.

Female Employment

Since the industrial revolution the position of men and women in employment, and the benefits that they have derived from it, have differed considerably. During the war years of the twentieth century women carried out many jobs that were previously the exclusive province of men. On returning from war, men again took over most of those occupations, but the earlier established pattern had been broken. In the UK, between 1961 and 1975, the working population grew from 23.8 to 25.6 million. Practically, the whole of this expansion is accounted for by the increase in the number of working women by 30 per cent, from 7.7 to 9.8 million. In 1931, 10 per cent of married women were economically active. By 1951 this had risen to 30 per cent, and in 1987 it stood at 60 per cent.

It would appear that these trends towards female employment are increasingly breaking down the conventional view of the woman being the home-maker and man the breadwinner. This is underscored by legislation in the UK, as in other Western societies, which has both reflected changes and encouraged future change. The Equal Pay Act, the Matrimonial Proceedings and Property Act, and the Child Benefits Act – all legislations since the late 1960s – have attempted to enforce gender equality in the workplace. Yet, despite what appears to be genuinely greater opportunity for paid employment, women are still to be found in typically 'female' occupations – supportive and caring roles: administrative support work (for example, secretaries, typists) and service work perhaps exemplified by waitressing, food-service work, nursing, and childcare. These jobs lie at the low-level of the pay-scale, offer restricted opportunities for advancement, and are subject to greater supervision.

Inequalities in employment opportunities for females can be measured in various other respects. First, whilst many people in the European Union are employed in the service sector, the figure is 76 per cent for women and 52 per cent for men, and the latter are more likely to be found in higher status and better-paid employment. Second, there is insecurity of employment which may bring disruptions and discontinuities throughout the life course. In measuring the working experiences of women, feminists, particularly those of a socialist variety, have argued that they constitute a 'reserve army of labour'. Put succinctly, women are a spare pool of potential recruits that can be brought in or released into the economy through the periodic cycles of booms and recession. One of the main functions of this reserve army is to reduce the wages of all members of the labour force since a group of unemployed people creates competition in the workforce and allows employees to reduce wages (Beechy 1983).

Third, as mentioned above, women are more likely to work part-time. In Spring 1996, only 8 per cent of male employees worked part-time, compared to some 45 per cent of women (*Social Trends* 1997, 71). Although more women in the UK work outside the home than in other EU countries, this growth in part-time employment practically wholly accounts for the increased employment of women with dependent children since the 1970s. (Table 7.1)

Fourth, slightly more women (11.9 per cent) than men (9.8 per cent) are employed on temporary contracts and there are significant pay differentials between the sexes, with women more likely to receive low pay and minimum wages (*Eurostat* 1995, 109, 121, 137). The report *Men and Women in the EU* (1995) found that women's representation in the labour force in the European Union rose from 39.3 per cent in 1987, to 41 per cent by 1992. The most significant rise has been among married women: the over-all rate for the UK is 53 per cent and more than 40 per cent of married women with children aged under three years are now in employment. The proportion of women in the paid labour force, nevertheless, is still well below that of men: Around 74 per cent of the male population between 25 and 60 is in paid employment, and the proportion of men in paid employment has not altered a great deal over the past century. Fifth, another difference is the proportion of women who work from home compared to men. In 1995, 9 per cent of employed men and 24 per cent of employed women in the UK worked some time at home (*Social Trends* 1997). Here, there are also ethnic variations. For instance, whilst East African and Indian women often work, taking them out of the domestic sphere, Bangladeshi and Pakistani women's lives – more restricted by Islamic rules which do not

Table 7.1 Part-time work and gender, 1993
(in millions)

	1986	*2001*
Males		
Full-time	11.3	11.8
Part-time	0.3	1.0
Females		
Full-time	5.3	6.4
Part-time	3.9	4.8

Source: adapted from *Social Trends*, 32, 2002

permit women to be in close proximity to non-family men – lead to a much stronger home-based commitment, including a preference for homework.

Probably the key problem facing women's equal opportunities centres on the difficulties of balancing work and private life. A woman's family situation shapes her work experience in ways that it rarely does for men. Child-bearing and child-raising especially in countries with little childcare provision can substantially weaken women's career structures and hence life opportunities. Age also affects labour force participation. Typically, both men and women join the workforce in their 'teens and early 20s. During their child-bearing years, however, women's participation lags behind that of men. After about the age of 45, the working profiles of the two sexes again become similar, with a marked withdrawal from the labour force as people approach 65 years old. After that point in life, only a small proportion of each sex continue to perform steady income-producing work.

Opportunities for greater opportunities at work might be forthcoming in the economic and social policies of the European Union. However, despite equal opportunity being one of the pillars of Europe's new employment policy, it has been applied differentially. While Rubery et al. speak of the 'feminization of the workforce', they acknowledge that in the member states of the European Union in the 1990s there were significant national differences in the four major dimensions of gender equality: care and wage work, occupational segregation, pay, and working time (Rubery et al. 1999). Hence, despite an allegiance to the economic strategies of the EU, the rights of women in the workplace varied considerably between countries of Western Europe.

It is not all bad news however. Rosemary Crompton has found that throughout Europe women are at last moving in increasing numbers into managerial and professional occupations. These changes are both cause and consequence of wider developments in the family, the relations between the sexes, and social attitudes more generally. However, past differences in national policies, and 'gender culture' attitudes mean that both trends in women's employment, as well as social attitudes, show considerable variation across Europe. Certain cultural distinctions nonetheless seem to be fairly universal even among professional people, especially those in a caring capacity such as doctors when compared to the business world of female bankers. Variations in the demands and ethos surrounding these jobs impact differentially, with those women involved in the former seemingly having a greater responsibility for domestic tasks. Domestic conjugal roles are also a consequence of life course planning offered by the two occupations. Women who go into medicine make a career decision at a fairly early stage – allowing a combination of employment with family life – especially by choosing particular medical specialties that do not make excessive time demands. Under the pressures of the financial world, however, female bankers are 'forced' to involve their partners in childcare (Crompton 1999, 209–11).

While at least some professions could be said to allow women more freedom in negotiating their careers in the life course, it has brought restrictions in other respects. Martens, in her comparative study of Holland and the UK, discovered that in some professions notions of work commitment favoured masculine concepts of a career and what it stood for by way of work continuities and, by contrast, women's discontinuities, due to childcare responsibilities, enhance the idea that women are less committed workers and are more suitable for part-time employment (Martens 2000, 215–16).

Unemployment

Every industrialized society has some degree of unemployment which, in turn, now marks one of major sources of life discontinuity. Much of it is temporary. Few young people entering the labour force find a job straight away and some (usually female) workers temporarily leave the labour force to raise children. Yet the economy itself also generates unemployment. Jobs disappear because occupations become obsolete, as businesses close in the face of foreign competition, and as recessions force lay-offs and bankruptcy. Mass unemployment, which has been evident from the 1970s, has now become a fact of economic life. In the UK, in 1992, unemployment peaked at 10.8 per cent (3 million people), yet one of the more serious features since that time has been the growing proportion of those unemployed for more than a year as is the case with over 40 per cent of the unemployed in the European Community.

Youth and Female Unemployment

During the onset of mass unemployment in Western societies, Adrian Sinfield (1981) suggested that there are five major groups who are more

Table 7.2   Unemployment by ethnic group (of 16–24-year-olds)

Ethnic group	%
Black	36
Pakistani/Bangladeshi	31
India	27
White	14
Others	28

Source: *Social Trends*, 28, 1998

likely to become unemployed in Western industrial societies: those who experience redundancies due to economic change, older workers who face enforced retirement, unemployed women, those who have experienced irregular employment over a long period of time, and unskilled youth attempting to make the transition from school to work.

Perhaps of those sections of society most likely to be disadvantaged are the young who are impacted by negative aspects of the economy in other ways as well. Many young workers must put up with low pay, and in the UK the minimum wage is lower for people aged under 18 years than it is for older people, and does not even exist for those under 16. In the early 1980s, with the beginning of recession in the UK, 28.9 per cent of males under 20 were unemployed compared to 10.3 per cent of those aged between 25–54. The official figures for youth unemployment understate the extent of the problem. In the face of growing youth unemployment one solution has been to raise the school-leaving age, thus eradicating substantial numbers of young people from the labour market and extending entrance into the adult world. Recently, the methods used by UK governments to remove large numbers of youngsters from the labour market have included the Youth Opportunities Programme and the Youth Training Scheme. These schemes, depending on how they are interpreted, may well hide the true number of young people unemployed.

Various factors need to be taken into account in explaining why the young are disproportionally disadvantaged. Youth unemployment is more often than not higher than adults partly because younger people are entering the labour market for the first time and are consequently more at risk from unemployment. Second, many jobs entered on first starting work are unskilled and semi-skilled in the manufacturing and service sectors – those traditionally associated with high rates of labour turnover. In addition, in times of relatively full employment some youngsters may change jobs either to find variety in work or until they settle down, again placing themselves at risk of unemployment.

The Repercussions of Unemployment

Unemployment in Western industrial societies is a fact of life. Nobody, whether manual worker, professional, or management, is entirely safe from the possibility of being cast out of work and subject to its subsequent negative implications. When it does occur, unemployment can wreck havoc in the lives of individuals and their families. Many studies have suggested that those unemployed will suffer an experience akin to that on hearing of a serious illness; an initial shock, followed for a short while by denial and optimism. There may even be a sense of being on holiday for a period and a feeling of freedom. Nonetheless, this is soon followed by distress and anxiety. If the unemployment continues for a long time, it may lead to resignation and the need to adjust in practically every area of life.

Unemployment has been linked to ill-health, psychological problems, premature death, attempted and actual suicide, marital breakdown, child-battering, racial conflicts, and even presented as a reason for football hooliganism. In terms of ill-health, Laurance (1986) found that unemployed school leavers in Leeds experienced higher levels of poor mental health and a higher mortality rate compared to the unemployed irrespective of social class, while in Edinburgh the suicide rate is known to be 11 times higher than for employed men.

Perhaps the most obvious effects of unemployment are financial. The Office of Population, Census and Surveys (1990) found that over two-thirds of families with parents under 35 were in debt after three months of unemployment. In the UK, relative to wages, unemployment benefits have been declining, causing a great deal of poverty. There are many other social consequences as well and these are less easy to measure than financial ones. They include a loss of sense of identity since work provides a social role and is a source of relationships outside of the family. Unemployment tends to reduce social contacts and activity. According to Fagin and Little (1984), in their study of unemployed men, most of those surveyed discovered it immensely difficult to create a framework which would impose a regular, purposeful activity and they found it hard to occupy themselves. A subculture of despair can emerge, sometimes linked to the development of an under-class of those who feel that they have no stake in society and fail to enjoy all the things that other people expect, while unemployment tends to hit hard those who already have fewer resources to cope.

A closely related aspect of work which is lost with unemployment is its ability to structure 'psychological time' – an important aspect of the life course. Work divides the day and week into time periods. Fagin and Little discovered that the unemployed had difficulty organizing their time without this framework. The men they studied spent more time in bed but their sleep was restless and they experienced greater tiredness than they did when they were working. Fagin and Little also recognized that work provides opportunities to develop skills and creativity and offers a sense of purpose. This tends to be lost with unemployment and was reflected in some men making statements like 'I'm surplus to requirements'. Moreover, according to this particular research, income from work provides freedom and control outside of work. In particular, it creates the possibility of engaging in leisure activities much of which cost money. Unemployment negates these opportunities.

Finally, studies have found that only certain types of activity increase with unemployment (Hill 1977). The unemployed spend more time watching television, doing housework, reading, or engaged in hobbies. Social life decreases, as does participation in sport and spectator sports. Overall it appears that leisure is not an adequate substitute for work because most of what it entails is solitary and passive and fails to compensate for the loss of contacts at work.

Dealing with Unemployment – Matters of Youth and Gender

Unemployment impacts on different social groups in diverse ways depending on their previous experiences and expectations. The young are a good example. Roberts et al. (1989) accept that young people do not enjoy unemployment, but are in many respects better equipped to deal with it than older workers. For school-leavers there is no work identity to be undermined and fewer financial obligations. Many of their peers may often be in the same situation, while some can rely on the generous support of their families.

As we have seen (Chapter 5), a good deal of sociological analyses of youth has considered the school-to-work transition and the significance of youth cultures. Increasingly, unemployment would seem to complicate this transition and the move from youth to responsible roles, and the self-sufficiency associated with maturity and adulthood. As early as the 1970s, Willis showed how difficult it was for young people, void of the status, roles, and financial resources, to aspire to adulthood and to carve a stake for themselves in wider society. The young are denied the opportunity to become independent from parents and often experience long periods of poverty. They are refused the occasion to take on family responsibilities, while planning for marriage is postponed. Nonetheless, the majority of young people manage to keep a level of self-respect and not suffer extensively from the range of social and psychological maladies often associated with unemployment (Willis 1977).

The view of Willis is that contemporary youth unemployment has, however, a profound effect on family life and gender relations, as well as on young people's position in education, training, and the job market. Willis uncovered evidence that unemployed young men do not, as might be supposed, cling to the traditional cultural sources of masculine pride and adhere to rigid gender roles simply because they are obtuse, apathetic, or unaware of their new situation. Their responses reflected the potential benefits of creating mythical 'macho' exploits such as marathon drinking sessions. Factors like these may account for the increase in substance abuse and crime, and provide a convincing argument as to why the period of youth may be difficult. Willis believes that financial hardship prevents young men from enjoying a normal social life. Without work, leisure activities have less meaning and increasing amounts of time are spent in the home. Perhaps the most important consideration, however, is that young people are left in limbo unable to look forward to or make the transition to adult status. They become bored, frustrated, and demoralized. This often leads to stress and conflict within the family.

The recession of the 1980s spurred research into areas that were understudied, particularly the implications of unemployment for women. Partly, as Sinfield suggests, this is because female employment rather than male unemployment was less often seen as a problem (Sinfield 1981). Women are expected to be primarily committed to being housewives and mothers rather than workers. Work is often regarded as a central source of identity for men, but not for women. Women might be expected to suffer less from unemployment because domestic life offers them a sense of identity and purpose. In the 1980s, new research started to challenge such assumptions.

Using data from questionnaires and interviews, Henwood and Miles (1987) compared the situation of unemployed men and women. For women who seek work as a means of escape from the home, unemployment can be especially harsh. Women, like men, respond by trying to meet a broad range of people, attempt to keep occupied most of the day, lack a sense of contributing to society, feel that they are not respected by others, and suffer from not having something regular to do during the day. Indicative of changing attitudes by younger women, Warr et al. (1985) also found that unemployed 17-year-old females reported more distress, depression, and anxiety, and were considerably more concerned than their male counterparts about the stigma of being unemployed.

Work Satisfaction

It might be argued that boring, mundane work is part of the payment that people living in advanced industrialized societies have to endure for their high material standard of living, and that these standards can only be achieved by the systematic utilization of machine technology that, in turn, has its negative repercussions. Hence, there will be certain costs, including the degradation of a great deal of work and a considerable sense of personal dissatisfaction in order that sufficient surplus be produced to allow opportunities for leisure and high levels of mass consumption.

'Alienation' is the term usually associated with low degrees of work dissatisfaction, especially the lack of creative and social capacities, and a failure to freely develop a physical and mental energy. Marx's prediction that work under capitalism would become more alienating is at least partly justified in the area of today's mass production. The increase in processes of de-skilling is evident in the Ritzer's exploration of 'McDonaldization' (Ritzer 1983). Ritzer linked the initial meaning of the concept of McDonaldization to the repercussions of a shrinking global market. Large-scale commerce and manufacturing, dominated by the developed countries of the West, now penetrate almost every region of the world in a globalized economy. Typified by McDonald's, the US fast-food chain, what is produced is a fairly standard package, while market dominance dispels the myth that a free global economy brings endless variation and upholds consumer choice through competition. It is the same all over the world – the same image and the same product. One of the principles of the standardizing impulses of McDonalization is 'control'. This suggests that the behaviour of employees is reduced to a series of machine-like actions. The implication here is not just in terms of de-skilling, but the de-humanization of workers. In other words, alienation. The advantage of such strict control for the business is that variation is reduced to a minimum, costs are kept down and efficiency increased. The price in terms of the loss of work satisfaction is, nevertheless, incalculable.

Writing at the beginning of the twentieth century, Max Weber also offered his own account of alienation and interpreted it more in terms of the growth of bureaucratic organizations that were experienced as impersonal for white-collar workers and mirrored the experience of manual workers in the factories. Weber portrayed a picture of a growing bureaucratic society where human beings were trapped within rationally-based organizations with their strict roles, rules, procedures, and hierarchies. This meant that the middle-classes could also be subject to alienation. Such a theme was subsequently developed by C.Wright Mills (1951) who, in *White Collar: The American Middle-Classes*, maintained that the expansion of the service sector of the economy in advanced capitalist societies had led to a 'shift from skills with things, to skills with persons'. Just as manual workers become like commodities by selling their 'skills with things', a similar process develops with non-manual workers who sell their 'skills with persons' on the open market. Mills referred to this sector of the economy as the 'personality market'.

According to Mills a market price is adjoined to personality characteristics, and as a consequence people sell small fragments of their personality. Individuals are employed not merely because of their academic qualifications and experience, but for their ability to interact with other people. However, since aspects of personality are bought and sold like any other commodity, individuals are alienated from their true selves. Their expression of personality in the workplace is insincere and false. Mills thus draws a picture of men and women prostituting their personalities at work in search of personal gain.

Fairly recently there has been considerable debate as to the ramifications of the emerging technology upon employment levels and work satisfaction.

It may well be that the new technologies will call upon constant employment retraining throughout the life course. However, not all commentators believe that it will. Some question whether the new technologies bring the much-heralded flexibility and require new and innovating skills. In this regard, Pollert argued that if flexibility is occurring then it may come to rely more on traditional skills, at other times it may even de-skill workers (Pollert 1988). Many jobs have not been re-skilled but have simply been expanded to include a greater range of tasks that require little skill. At the same time, according to Atkinson (1985), flexibility may mean more job security for some but not others. Managers, designers and technical sale staff, technicians, and craftsmen are likely to be multi-skilled employees who are capable of working in different areas within a firm. In contrast, clerical, supervisory, and component assembly workers are less secure in their work. They are easier to recruit, are more likely to be offered short-term contracts, and can readily be laid-off in times of recession since their skills are in plentiful supply.

Those who have to work in boring and tedious jobs are faced with the daily need of coping and there are various ways by which people do so. The interactionist concept of 'managing the self' and 'others' provides some insights into how people survive the monotony of work: daydreaming, sabotage, and the frequent changing of jobs are all ways in which people cope. Absenteeism is another. For example, in car assembly work rates of absenteeism and labour turnover are commonly very high. Similarly, rates are high among psychiatric and geriatric nurses when compared to more prestigious and satisfying nursing specialisms such as paediatric nursing.

Perhaps the most popular form of escape from work for many people is to lose themselves in leisure time activities. It is in leisure, as a result of work void of meaning and expression, that people can indulge in what they wish and involve themselves in more pleasant pastimes. C.Wright Mills' *White Collar: The American Middle-Classes* explored this theme and provided the image of people selling little pieces of themselves for money during week days and attempting to re-claim themselves in the evenings and at weekends. He described this differential attitude that most people have to work and leisure as 'the great split'. Today, leisure appears to have greater social significance than ever before. The subject will inform our discussion in the rest of this chapter.

Leisure

In recent years a growing body of literature has been concerned with the link between leisure and identity. Shanir (1992), developing Stryker's earlier work (1987) on the connection between identity, roles, and relationships, has proposed that 'leisure identities' can become highly salient to the self-concept for three reasons. First, these identities express and affirm individual talents and capacities. Second, they provide some degree of social recognition. Third, they affirm the individual's central values and interests. Other writings in the area suggest that people are motivated to develop and maintain a consistent and positive self-concept or identity and consequently, they engage in a form of leisure behaviour that allows them to affirm or validate their own 'desired identity image'. Indeed, it has been shown that participation in certain types of leisure activities allows this through physical appearance, personality, skills and abilities, while others wish to prove something to themselves by 'sign value' (Haggard and Williams 1991).

Life-Cycle and Leisure

Speculation as to which social variables enhance or prohibit the realization of the advantages of leisure has long informed the relevant sociological literature. There was a tendency in the early sociological work, perhaps exemplified by the research of Parker (1973), to relate leisure patterns to experiences and satisfaction in the workplace, with manual and non-manual occupations constituting the major divergences. Alternatively, a life-cycle approach seemed to be an attractive framework by which to understand leisure patterns. Such a perspective was offered by Rapoport and Rapoport (1975) who argued that the life-cycle, along with family life, was largely responsible for shaping leisure, although other factors such as class and gender might be important. At different stages of the life-cycle individuals exhibit varying attitudes to work, family, and leisure. The Rapoports identified four main stages in the life-cycle with each having implications for leisure pursuits: *Adolescence* where the major preoccupation was a quest for personal identity; *Young Adulthood* where the principal interest is with creating a social identity that reflects the concerns with occupation, relationships, and friendship; the *Establishment Phase*, between roughly the ages of 25 and 55, during which time people try to establish satisfying lifestyles where home-centred leisure activities are more central; and the *Later Years*, the final phase, commences roughly at the age of 55 or with retirement, and includes a sense of social and personal integration. Patterns of leisure nonetheless vary, according to the Rapoports, and depend on such variables as health and income which may restrict some people in their activities.

Ken Roberts (1978) took a wider view of leisure than Stanley Parker or the Rapoports. While not denying that work and the life-cycle were important, he also stresses the variety of leisure patterns which were available and that leisure was increasingly open to choice. Individuals are engaging in leisure when they feel they are choosing a meaningful activity in their free time. Roberts therefore attempts to allow for the significance that people gave to leisure. Thus, activities such as gardening and home decorating should not be seen as leisure activities unless an individual defines them as such. Moreover, there are many different social factors which display an enormous variety of leisure interests. Leisure activity is, for example, influenced by variables such as class, gender, age, ethnicity, education, and marital status.

Gender and Leisure

Until the 1980s women were largely conspicuously absent from sociological studies of leisure activities. Early feminist contributions critiqued the work of Parker, especially his distinctions between work and leisure (Green et al. 1990). There were various observations made concerning women's experiences. First, women's work is often not involved in earning a living, thus women in full-time housework are automatically excluded from Parker's framework. Work (domestic) activities of the housewife tend to overlap with and undermine the quality of a woman's leisure. Second, the distinction Parker makes in his categories of work and work obligations was found to be fairly meaningless for housewives. The domestic part of work obligations is a large part of the housewife's total work at home. Third, the central feature of the life of women is that of domestic activity which allows few escapes into leisure since there is little real free time.

While both men and women have very high rates of participation in watching television, visiting or entertaining friends or relatives, and listening to radio or music, there are important differences in regard to the leisure activities of males and females. Not only do men and women tend to take part in different types of leisure, but women also have less access to leisure opportunities than men do. The General Household Survey (1993) indicated that the sport and physical activities that women took more part in than men were indoor swimming, keep fit/yoga, and netball. Some 59 per cent of men, but only 38 per cent of women participate in one activity other than walking. At the same time there is less variation in home-based leisure patterns between men and women. There is a marked difference between participation in DIY (Do It Yourself), predominantly preferred by men, and dress-making, needlework or knitting, overwhelmingly undertaken by women. This seems to reflect conventional conjugal roles.

The General Household Survey also indicated that there is now little difference in the amount of time available to either sex or the circumstances in which women and men can engage in leisure. There is, however, more to the equation. Green et al. (1990) claimed that it is much harder for women to forget about work and put aside specific time periods for leisure. For them, leisure time has a greater possibility of being interrupted because they are constantly at the demands of the family. Women also have less money to spend on activities, and many wives remain financially dependent on their husbands and this obviously limits the forms of leisure they could engage in. Furthermore, the attitudes of men restrict the options open to women. Many women are expected to choose their leisure time pursuits largely from a limited range of home and family-orientated activities that are socially defined as 'proper' family pursuits. The social control of a male-dominated society thus extends to leisure. Nonetheless, women are slightly more active than men in voluntary organizations and are more likely to attend evening classes, all of which plausibly free women from dependence on men in the sphere of leisure.

Green et al. believe that gender is not the only variable influencing leisure. Among others considered important is ethnicity and this may cut across gender variables. Although women of Asian and Afro-Caribbean minorities share common cultural attributes, traditions suggest that their leisure patterns are frequently very different. In some Asian families cultural and religious factors may mean less autonomy and equality. According to Green et al., Asian men are often reluctant to encourage women to be mobile and may restrict what they can and cannot do. In contrast, Afro-Caribbean women are rather less limited in their leisure. Green et al. maintain that they have more power in their families than Asian women and encourage this independence. Leisure is less home-based than for Asian women but is still restricted.

To conclude, while women would appear to be disadvantaged in the sphere of leisure, by no means is gender the only variable bringing limitations to leisure pursuits. Various constraints on leisure have been differentiated by Crawford et al. (1991) as structural, interpersonal, and intrapersonal. The former relates to fairly obvious restraints such as time, money, health, and the opportunities on offer. Interpersonal constraints in leisure activities arise from relationships with others including family responsibilities, absence of a leisure partner or a mismatched leisure partner. The intrapersonal includes such variables as low self-esteem and personal ambition. All may converge to either encourage or restrict leisure activities.

The Consumer Society

In the opening chapters we briefly considered the emergence of the consumer society and its relevance to late- or postmodernity. At this juncture we might explore the significance of consumerism for the sphere of leisure. Until very recently the traditional approach to the economy by sociologists centred around the production of goods, with a focus on either particular industries or workers and work experience. More recently, they have increasingly come to recognize the importance of not just what the economy produces and how it produces, but what and how we consume. Western societies, both economically and culturally, are increasingly 'consumer societies', and consumption and shopping have become one of the most popular leisure activities in the UK (*Social Trends* 1997). Part and parcel of all this is the growth of the shopping mall with megastores such as Virgin Records, hypermarkets like Tesco, chain stores including Argos, retail parks, and DIY centres. There is also the vast expansion of all kinds of commodities; sports clothes geared to sports of every kind, electronic technology including computers, and ever more sophisticated technology aimed at home amusement. New forms of entertainment and leisure complexes are emerging everywhere. There are now new modes of eating out, from fast foods to upmarket dining, in addition to centres geared towards pure escapism as typified by theme parks and Disneyland holidays.

Today, the tendency is to use credit cards to pay for many of these commodities and services. This has huge economic repercussions. In the UK, at least a third of all consumption is based on credit and there are some 25 million credit cards currently in circulation. Despite the increasing popularity of shopping malls, other innovating forms of shopping are becoming widespread. After purchasing a digital television set-top box decoder, or an up-to-date computer, one can buy into an array of 'armchair services' – from shopping and banking to travel and public services now on offer. Hundreds of channels with interactive shopping services come 'on line' through the television and the Internet, and all are available through credit card purchases.

The Commodification of Leisure

For Clark and Critcher (1985), leisure, in much the same way as work, is forged by capitalism. It is now big business and an important source of profit. The commercial provision of leisure is dominated by large companies which have a wide variety of leisure activities to offer. These companies enjoy the power to persuade consumers of their leisure needs. The leisure industry creates new products and services and then tries to convince consumers that they should purchase them through widespread advertizing. In some areas of leisure provision such as entertainment, a few large companies dominate the market and therefore, according to Clark and Critcher, actually restrict consumer choice.

More recent critiques of the consumer society may not be so radical, but nonetheless raise pertinent questions as to whether it has really brought positive change. It is evident that the extension and development of the consumer culture in the late twentieth century onwards has depended upon the creation of new markets, not least of all through the production of images and advice on lifestyles. However, the emergence of so much consumption has given rise to a great deal of speculation as to whether it has added to the quality of life for most people.

It might be conjectured that commodification enhances choice in a more genuine way. In short, that choice is extended. Consumption has become the means for a higher standard of living, as well as a chance not to stifle culture but to enhance it. Goods and brands spread through the world, liberating the consumer through choice. With the packaging of CDs in megastores, for instance, global music has developed and, consequently, the sheer range of music presently available has dramatically increased. The same is true of food, with supermarkets now making available ingredients and recipes unknown two decades ago. Thus contemporary culture can now be seen to be enriched – giving the great majority of people a greater choice and more control over their lives than ever before.

One growing dimension of the consumer culture, which arguably has proved a mixed blessing, is personalized technology. It is partly linked to lifestyle preferences, although it has influenced contemporary life in other respects too. The scope of technology in opening up new markets has also added to the 'modelling' and remaking of the body beyond what medical science now has to offer. In this sense technology can bring a certain 'personalization' for the individual and this is typified in the realm of entertainment. Hitherto, entertainment has been social: the music hall or cinema, or family TV, whereas there is now the 'personal computer' or the Sony 'Walkman' and even the mobile phone. All are significant through the media of personalized consumption.

There is a counter view to that which argues that the consumer society generally enriches human existence. It is one that states that consumerism is having a detrimental effect; destroying traditional culture, human relationships, and civic responsibilities (Bryman 1995). Some critics maintain that the new culture is one of instant gratification and, with the market dominating, leads to a general 'levelling down' of life – destroying social differences and communities. In short, it is the 'Coca-Colarization' of the world, where children mass consume McDonald's fast-foods and learn to become the unquestioning consumers of tomorrow. Much can be seen to lead to the weakening of shared and moral values and the rise of a crass materialism. Arai and Pedlar believe that this is part of the 'crisis' of postmodernity and, in particular, that leisure has lost its community edge. In fact, from the latter years of the twentieth century, the social relevance of leisure has diminished as consumption and individualism came to dominate leisure and recreation (Arai and Pedlar 2003). The change from work to leisure, where individuals invest their life activity and meaning, would therefore seem to be linked to levels of alienation and accompany the shift in the economy from production to consumption.

Certainly, some commentators have stressed aspects of alienation in the consumption of leisure. This is fairly implicit in Featherstone's account of the various forms of escapism into fantasy and dreamworlds (Featherstone 1982, 28–9), while for Baudrillard (1983) commodification undoubtedly represents a distinct narrowing and convergence of cultural experience, rather than its widening, and in the postmodern society 'there is nowhere to go but to the shops'. So much of mass leisure activities are orientated towards astonishing, exciting, and titillating in a spontaneous way – creating a kind of fantasy world into which people can escape. Within consumer culture one tendency is the fragmentation and differentiation of markets. In its most extreme formulation this is seen as entailing the end of the social connections and the emergence of consumption as an endless series of signs and images which do not cohere and cannot be used to formulate a structured and simple lifestyle and set of tastes which, in turn, undermines coherent and stable concepts of self.

Another, more negative view is not to see variety in consumption, one enhanced by globalizing processes, but the dominance of a particularly Western and rather standardized lifestyle. Thus, far from globalization impacting the West through consumption, Latouche (1996) sees it as an integral part of the growing hegemony of Western culture. In short, the spread of Western influence is not just in economic terms but a sameness of styles of dress, eating habits, architecture, music, urban lifestyles, mass media, philosophical ideas, a range of cultural values, and attitudes about liberty, gender and sexuality, science and rationality, which have all impacted global cultures.

Summary

This chapter has been concerned with a number of broad overlapping themes. It has attempted to show how work shapes our lives and gives expression to structured inequalities in discernible and less obvious ways. Work can also provide the foundation of subcultures, social relationships, and perhaps above all help forge notions of self and identity especially as so much time is spent at work. As much can be said about leisure. The experience of leisure and consumption has changed as rapidly as the world of work and is likely to continue to do so for the foreseeable future. Leisure, especially through consumption, increasingly dominates our lives as well as offering new opportunities of choice. It is now possible to suggest that leisure is replacing work to a greater extent as a central life interest in the postmodern society as people appear to have the time and money to at least seek a greater fulfilment throughout the life course.

Not all social groups, however, are able to escape into more and more leisure and it is clear that work continues to shape leisure activities. Some professional jobs have become more demanding, while many people find themselves having to work longer to afford what the consumer society has to offer including its alluring leisure pursuits. Contrary to what is popularly believed, the number of hours worked per week has been rising in recent years: in the case of the UK from 44.5 hours per week for a male in 1985 to 45.8 in 1996 (*Social Trends* 1997, 79). Moreover, as leisure becomes increasingly dominated by market forces some people enjoy better provision and opportunities, yet some people may find themselves at a profound disadvantage.

Further Reading

Bently,T. and Gurumurthy,Y. (1999) *Destination Unknown: Engaging with the Problems of Marginalised Youth*, London: Demo.

Cohen,P. (1997) *Rethinking the Youth Question*, Education, Labour and Cultural Studies, Basingstoke: McMillan.

Cote,E. and Allahar,A. (1996) *Generation on Hold: Coming of Age in the Late Twentieth Century*, New York: New York University Press.

Crompton,R. (1999) *Restructuring Gender* (ed.) Oxford: Oxford University Press.

8
The Challenge of Mid-Life

Commonsense discourse surrounding 'mid-life' has frequently focused on notion of 'crisis', 'ageing', and 'decline'. As with generalized perceptions of youth, those of mid-life are informed by assumptions regarding physical, mental, and emotional change in which traumatic aspects are often held to be observable. While such attitudes to mid-life may begin with negative appraisals which perceive it is a 'turning point', popular views, at least up to relatively recently, have been largely shaped by the medical profession, alongside the cultural emphasis on the virtues of being young. The result is that mid-life often becomes problematized, where health risks are seen to be increased and the challenges of inevitable decline on 'all fronts' have to be negotiated. These risks, if the medical frame of reference is accepted, confront above all women and the 'handicap' of their 'declining' reproductive system and the dreaded onslaught of menopause.

Undoubtedly, Western culture has impacted and shaped accepted wisdom related to mid-life – one where it is frequently assumed that early adulthood is a relatively stable and calm period following the trials and tribulations of adolescence, and that mid-life heralds the uncomfortable decline of old age which invariably follows. For this reason and others, most of the images used to describe middle age are essentially negative ones. In late/postmodernity, however, some of the common assumptions and perceptions regarding mid-life are beginning to change. Partly this is because of more optimistic views forged by aspects of choice in terms of lifestyle, so that in the consumer society it may now be possible to talk of a plurality of mid-lifestyles. On the other hand, changing perceptions of mid-life result from the problem of pinning down precisely where it begins and ends. This chapter considers some of the debates surrounding mid-life – discourse which confirms the social construction of this 'stage' of life, changing perceptions regarding its taken-for-granted disadvantages, and what still appears to be the influence of medicalizing processes and the inability of some people to fulfil many of the alleged promises which mid-life is now believed to bring.

Cross-Cultural Perspectives

Throughout Western history and up until relatively recently, mid-life was not regarded as an especially difficult time. Today, it is frequently referred to as a climacteric or 'crucial period'. In simple terms, it is perceived of as a juncture between physical and mental growth and decline in the life course. Biological changes take place during mid-life, but they are by no means absolute or entirely predictable. Moreover, mid-life would seem to be shaped by negative connotations which overlap with patriarchal cultural assumptions that the desirable social function of the woman in mid-life is one that is home-based, where she looks after the family and performs a set of socially proscribed roles as her reproductive functions come to an end. Simultaneously, through medicalization, accompanied by the interests of the pharmaceutical industries, mid-life is regularly approached as a list of medical complaints some of which at least are understood to be 'curable'.

Anthropological and cross-cultural research has found that the popular Western view of mid-life is in fact quite unique. Even amongst technologically advanced societies the meaning and symptoms of mid-life vary considerably. Lambley provides the fascinating example of Japan. This modern industrialized nation is in many respects comparable to the societies of the West, with similar economic values and not dissimilar standards of living. Yet historically, mid-life, especially amongst women, has not displayed the same meaning in Japan where it continues to be regarded as marking the commencement of maturity rather than just the onset of old age. Until they have reached the age of 50, Japanese men and women are not generally considered as fully mature. Although the cessation of menstruation in Japanese women is seen as part of the change of life, it fails to be attributed the same implications that it assumes amongst Western women. Even the symptoms are different. Hot flushes – the single most frequently reported complaint amongst Western females – are uncommon amongst Japanese women during the menopause, where as others, notably constipation and diarrhoea, are familiar conditions (Lambley 1995, 9–11).

Attitudes to mid-life are by no means uniform, even amongst Western societies. One cross-national study in Europe, for example, discovered that over half the women questioned had found the menopause psychologically upsetting, but while two-thirds of French and UK females experience it as distressing, this was not the case with German women, amongst whom fewer than half had found it particularly difficult (Komesaroff et al. 1997). Even within these societies patterns related to mid-life varied considerably. Women whose menstruation commenced late, those who never married, those who had never fallen pregnant, and those who had a child after the age of 40 seemed to be less affected by the menopause than other women. Wealth and education also appear to help women at this stage of life as they do during earlier times. Thus, more affluent and better-educated women tend to report fewer physical and psychological problems associated with the menopause (Lambley 1995, 10).

While accounts of mid-life would appear to be radically different, even in Western societies, notions of a 'crisis' are notably missing from the pages of the history books. Evidence that the so-called 'change in life' was a challenge at best and 'curse' at work are not evident. Certainly, there is little to suggest that women experienced menopause in the past along with all the 'unwanted' biological and emotional baggage which is assumed to go with it. While it may be true that women have been 'absent from history', it is clear that throughout most of its course the life expectancy for females (and of course for males) was little more than what is designated as mid-life today and where reaching 40 years was regarded as an achievement and not infrequently undesirable. As far as many women were concerned, a cycle of pregnancy and childbirth was quickly followed by old age and death.

The Medicalization of Mid-Life

The mid-life climacteric in women has long been regarded differently from that of men. This is perhaps inevitable given that women have also traditionally been thought to display a contrasting psychological as well as physiological nature to men based on broader commonsense notions regarding their reproductive system. One legacy of this is an almost Western cultural preoccupation with the womb which has often been blamed for a good deal of what men do not understand about the behaviour of women. Above all, it has been held responsible for a broad scope of female emotional problems. Indicative of this negative view of the reproductive system is that the term 'hysteria' derives from the Greek word for 'womb'. In ancient times, the womb was regarded by the Greek physician Hippocrates as sustaining practically a supernatural authority over a woman for much of her life until it was no longer productive.

Such discourse surrounding the womb has endured throughout the centuries and was to eventually surface with the 'advance' of medicine and with wide-ranging implications. In Western societies, an interest in mid-life and all its perceived woes has not just arisen because people are observably living longer but because of the gradual rise in the status and power of medicine and the medical profession which coincided with the advent of *modernity*. Under the auspices of the medical profession menopause became something of a mixed blessing. On the one hand, it was perceived as a time when a woman was exempt from her natural reproductive functions and related emotions. On the other hand, it was evidence that her period of fertility was over and this had implications for her social purpose and status, for good or for bad.

In the early medical writings, mid-life came to be designated as a 'problem' and the great majority of so-called health difficulties were seen as connected to a women's reproductive system. In the eighteenth century, there were periodic references to the familiar symptoms which are today associated with the menopause. John Leake, an English physician, suggested in one of the earliest published medical textbooks (1777) that women during mid-life sometimes experienced headaches, dizziness, chronic pains, and a range of 'female' hysterical disorders. Leake was also one of the first to refer to the association between the appearance of chronic disease and the loss of menstruation in women, and this helped to bring about the common assumption that physical as well as emotional problems occurred at about the same time. It was not, however, until the nineteenth century that doctors typically came to believe there was something more than mere 'hysteria' happening during the mid-life of a woman.

The 'Pathology' of Menopause

Gannon writes

> ... a woman's menopausal status has become a crucial component of her identity. In many disciplines, a woman's career, roles, and accomplishments, and lifestyles are being reconstructed within a hormonal paradigm (Gannon 1996, 68).

With reference to this medicalized context, Gannon explains how, in the past, mid-life might have been concerned with age-related physical deterioration, such as diminished energy and cardio-vascular changes which have become redefined as part of the 'menopausal syndrome'. This involves the transformation of menopause from a predictable, expected, and normal life event, to a progressive disease with manifestations in every sphere of life consistent with sexual and, indeed, medical politics – defining and pathologizing women according to their reproductive status as biologically disadvantaged.

Most doctors in Western Europe and the USA once held the conventional view that little of medical interest occurred during the menopause.

Nonetheless, in France in the early nineteenth century, medical reports appeared describing a 'menopausal syndrome' that required medical treatment. By the mid-century, UK and American doctors followed suit and the medicalization of the mid-life period began in earnest. This association of organic pathology and emotional problems with the menopause slowly gained popularity in medical circles as the nineteenth century progressed. Two broad medical approaches to mid-life emerged, the gynaecological and psychiatric. This obviously reflected the medical fields which had most to do with mid-life women and the problems of which they apparently complained.

Gynaecologists, seeking to understand the workings of the womb from an early stage, focused on the role played by the ovaries and hormones in the female reproductive cycle and purported that 'problems' encountered by women in mid-life were largely due to changes in these. Typifying this is the fact that at least one school of gynaecological thought regarded the menopause as a mid-life 'disease'. However, it was not until the 1960s that effective hormone-enhancing medications became available, but once they were, they aided the grip of gynaecological interpretations of the menopause.

Psychiatry, on the other hand, arose almost entirely out of the monopoly acquired by the medical profession to deal with those deemed to be psychologically disturbed and this played a major part in the theories, which were to be developed about mid-life with much focus on assumptions regarding mid-life problems and their alleged prevalence in menopausal women. As they turned their attention to the subject, a possible link to the more extreme forms of mental instability became increasingly acceptable. Continuing in acceptance throughout the twentieth century was the view that the menopause amounted to an important medical and psychological issue. It was deduced that during the menopause women experience the almost compulsory symptoms of hot flushes, depression, headaches and dizziness – all of which could be put down to hormonal changes (typically associated with the drop in oestrogen and the effects of testosterone).

The second half of the twentieth century saw the growth of the 'psychoanalytical revolution' and its belief that practically all human ailments could be reduced to psychological factors. Evidence of this, in some regards discernible in the influence of psychoanalysis on public opinion and discourse in respect of the female menopause, has been even more important than the contributions of gynaecology. Part of the growth of this medical specialism was due to the fact that psychoanalytic thought influenced far more people and penetrated more areas of society than those of the other professions. Hence, the psychoanalytic approach impacted upon a whole range of non-medical groups, especially those in the cultural sphere such as writers, artists, and filmmakers.

The Social Construction of Mid-Life 'Crisis'

Perhaps more than any other 'phase' of life, mid-life is associated with a detectable 'crisis'. While the medical profession has helped construct such a 'crisis', popular perceptions have also been forged by the view that mid-life is some 'half way stage' and this invariably includes a process of intensive transition of the self including the interpretation of time perspectives in as much as it frequently brings a reevaluation of life values and goals. In the past this may have led to reflexive re-orientation, involving planning for the 'second half' of life, and a realization that death was an inevitable future event which has to be come to terms with in the present. The dominant underlying perception, at least up to recently, may have been time was 'running out' or that 'the best years were behind'. However, this orientation now appears to be disingenuous given the fact that life expectancy is increasingly rising. Hence, beliefs in a 'crisis' are less easy to sustain and the years associated with mid-life, the forties and fifties, may now be approached with perhaps far more optimism than before.

While positive appraisals regarding mid-life are perhaps evident, commonsense views related to what it entails still carry negative stereotypes. Perhaps impacted by medical discourse, there exists a generalized cultural belief that mid-life is synonymous with a psychological 'crisis'. Symptoms and behaviour often attributed to mid-life crises seem to range from boredom, exhaustion or frantic energy, self-questioning, irritability, to unexpected anger. It might, so it is assumed, be related to various excesses including alcohol, food, or other compulsions, considerably decreased or increased sexual desire, and greatly decreased or increased ambition. Many of these so-called psychological and adult behavioural 'problems' are, of course, subject to the invariable medical 'cure'.

Women's 'Experience'

The ageing body has implications for an individual's social identity and social status, and the physical changes which take place at mid-life can provide a signifier of age. The cultural stress placed upon the need to look young and beautiful impacts in a derogative way for women and help shape mid-life as a 'crisis' point via its alleged universal biological consequences. Neither is the overarching shadow of medicalizing processes entirely absent and is observable in popular conceptions of the 'biological clock ticking away'. It is with such perceptions that thoughts of being just 'older' give way to being 'old' – a negative appraisal enforced by the cultural belief that the biological clock turns women from fertile into infertile females. The repercussions for women's self-appraisal may be severe given the confluence of proscribed perceptions of the decline in beauty, sexuality, fertility, and all that counts as femininity. Accompanying these appraisals are other social constructs related to gender, most notably ascribed domestic roles in later life which, in turn, have led to assumptions that it is women who have to make the greatest changes during mid-life.

Much by way of cultural evaluations were uncovered in earlier sociological works on the subject. Nowak, for instance, found that a person's attitudes towards their body vary according to their age and that such attitudes are linked to levels of concern about physical attractiveness. The pre-occupation with attractiveness was discovered to continue well into the mid-life period. During this stage women appear to far more likely to express a 'below-average body' image than men of the same age. Nowak examined the relationship between a person's definition of 'attractiveness' and 'youthfulness'. She found that the mid-life period, and particularly the years between 45 and 55, is a time in which women exhibit a greater concern with facial attractiveness than at any other point in their lives. Perhaps surprizingly, women over 65 were the least fretful when it came to looking old compared to young and middle-adults. Nowak concluded that women under 45 are more preoccupied with their attractiveness but seldom see this affecting their youthfulness, and while women over 65 worry in just the opposite direction, middle-age women worry about both (Norwak 1977).

Although there may be perceived changes, some responsibilities prescribed to women are not relinquished in latter life, thus limiting the so-called choices and greater freedom that contemporary lifestyles are supposed to afford. Older mothers frequently continue to shoulder the burden of domestic labour and house work. They still have to deal with demands from grown-up children and are more likely to be responsible for dependent older relatives. The fact that gendered multiple roles carry on into mid-life may be evidenced in different ways. A fascinating study which bears witness to the negative consequences of such roles is Hislop and Arber's work on women's sleep patterns. Drawing upon empirical data from focus groups and 'sleep diaries', sleep is shown to be a socially patterned phenomenon which reflects the gendered nature of women's roles and responsibilities. For many women in mid-life, the reality of sleep is one of disruption and where their sleep needs are compromised by unpaid physical and emotional labour associated with family duties and obligations (Hislop and Arber 2003).

It is also evident that women experience mid-life in different ways, responding to the so-called 'challenges' of mid-life as a result of a range of factors. Indicative of this is Daly's interview of 150 women in the USA regarding the way they encountered mid-life (Daly 1997). The respondents fell into three categories. A small minority claimed to be 'gliding through mid-life'. Nearly two dozen felt 'besieged by problems'. The great majority (105 women), however, were 'battling through problems', suggesting that the alleged difficulties were far from insurmountable. While Daly's study indicated that there was nothing deterministic about women's experience of mid-life, it also provided evidence of how this stage of life was circumvented by medical processes and discourse and that women had not infrequently internalized the language of 'crisis'. Interview finding showed that women's perceptions often concentrated on the 'problems' of menopause, ageing processes, domestic responsibilities, and accompanying references to such treatments as tranquillizers and hormone therapy.

Men's 'Experience'

In recent years more has been made of men's experiences of mid-life. Again, there is evidence of this stage of life being associated with 'crisis'. Now there is a developing discourse around the male menopause based upon research into men's hormone levels and the 'andropause' – the consequences of which are supposed to be manifest in irritability and depression among other negative signs. Men, like women, then, are increasingly seen as deficient either biologically or emotionally, while the notion of the male menopause is gaining currency, although a distinction needs to be made between the male mid-life 'crisis' and the male menopause, more correctly referred to as the andropause. The two may occasionally overlap, but the causes are perceived as different. The medical argument is that andropause has a hormonal origin. Testosterone levels fall, while too much testosterone present is in a form which cannot be used by the body. Vitality ebbs, fatigue and weariness are commonplace, and together with depression, loss of libido and irritability are the apparent hallmarks of the andropause mood. Much still remains unproven however. Unlike the equivalent menopausal condition in women, the existence of the male counterpart has by no mean yet received full endorsement and remains an area of contention even within the medical profession itself.

While the 'discovery' of the male menopause to some extent marks the extension of medical interests into the male mid-life domain, there is also the cultural baggage of mid-life where men supposedly 'go off the rails'. Clearly there is much which is engendered here. While women's menopausal state may be perceived as a danger to herself and those around her, popularized views of men's 'crisis' is often couched in frivolous terms, articulating a kind of mid-life 'ladish' disposition or return to adolescence. Moreover, mid-life for men is increasingly defined in sexual or reproductive terms. Thus male menopause also has its alleged 'cures'. Apparent waning of biological drives may be addressed by the 'wonder drug' Viagra. Despite this parallel with the female 'crisis' men, if not ascribed some kind of new attractiveness in their maturity which provides a stark counterpoint to perceptions of women, may often be excused extramarital affairs in the need to stave off the effects of ageing and 'prove something to themselves'. If recent newspaper reports are to be believed, the increasing incidence of such affairs and a growing divorce rate among mid-life men can be blamed on the extensive use of Viagra. The same drug may also have had the effect of medicalizing 'dysfunctional' sexuality among older men. In this respect Barbara Marshall argues that ideas about 'healthy ageing' suggest 'normal' sexual functioning. In fact, Viagra has become yet another site to amplify cultural expectations of gender through notions of male heterosexual 'performance' (Marshall 2002).

Mid-Life Identity

Knowing You Are 'Middle Aged'

Social perceptions of mid-life obviously impact on identity constructions and this is implicit in much of the discussion above. However, there is evidence which suggests that in late or postmodernity the way individuals think about and negotiate mid-life is undergoing significant change. A common theme in much of the relevant literature is one addressing the major cultural trajectories in which the body and bodily change is perceived and that this is intrinsically linked with the way we appraise the ageing process.

An early study by Neugarten (1971) was concerned with how people came to 'know' that they were middle-aged and was based on detailed interviews of several dozen middle-class people. Her data indicated that individuals do subjectively experience this time as having special characteristics that distinguish it from other 'stages' of life. What many interviewees seemed to have internalized was not the chronological passage of time but the social meanings given to being middle age. In regard to perceptions of mid-life, the majority of interviewees in Neugarten's study had come to accept the significance of signs of bodily ageing, alterations in the family structure, changes in the state of career, as all indicating its onset. Perhaps of greatest importance was recognition of being located between two generations. In short, an awareness of a position bridging two generations: of their parents and of their children. This was an awareness, asserted Neugarten, of feeling less involved with their children, while identifying more with their parents.

Later research by Robert Atchley (1988), suggested that middle age (ages 40–55) is the period of life when a person initially becomes aware of the fact that s/he is ageing. Middle age is the time when the person recognizes a reduction in energy and often begins to favour less strenuous activities. Physical breakdown is a terrifying experience for many men since it connects the masculine body with weakness, dependency, and passivity – all the supposedly 'feminine' qualities they have spent a life-time defending themselves against. Thus the decline in sexual desire, illness, and injury can mean a renegotiation of dominant, heterosexual masculine identities.

Works such as that of Kastenbaum (1971) showed perceptions of mid-life were informed by views which suggested it was a fairly clear, stable and predictable 'stage of life'; one where people believed their work career had more or less reached a plateau, and where children had left home to lead their own lives. It appeared to be a time of life when parents or other older people close to the individual die – reminding individuals of a lim-ited time-span and their own mortality. An integral aspect of such recogni-tions are changing time perspectives (Atchley 1988). The older person avoids thought of the future because of the limited time left and instead dwells on the past, their achievements and failures. The middle-aged, so Karp and Yoels concur, become more conscious of the time they have left rather than the time since birth. The deaths of one's friends and associates serve as 'mortality markers', as constant reminders of one's own limited time in this world (Karp and Yoels 1982, 81). Such time perceptions also seemed caught up with some of the principal processes of *modernity*. In particular, mid-life was a product of the emergence of a new and distinctly bounded period between the completion of child-raising and retirement from work.

Other research suggests that some of these attitudes associated with mid-life, as linked to some clear 'stage of life' with fairly deterministic roles and fatalistic viewpoints, are changing. While many conventional roles have become increasingly flexible and no longer subject to the con-forming social pressures associated with past generations, individual choice as to whether or not people assume these roles or not has also come to the fore. A related consideration is the matter of adaptation. Mid-life, for many men and women, would still seem to constitute a re-adjustment and brings a re-appraisal which ushers in profound changes in identity construction and how individuals perceive themselves. Such adaptations are not merely linked to perceptions of biological change and ageing processes, but to the changing experiences of 'significant others', not least of all family members.

One social role which some mid-life people have to deal with is that of being a grandparent. While grandparenting is often portrayed by the media as associated with being old, it is increasingly the case that grand-parenthood is occurring among middle-aged segments of the population.

From the 1970s, studies have indicated around 20 per cent of grandparents assume this role somewhere between the ages of 31 and 46 with another 44 per cent having adopted grandparenthood during the age of 47–54. It is evident, then, that early marriage, earlier child-birth, and longer life expectancy are producing grandparents in their forties. In this regards, Lillian Troll and her associates (1979) maintained that as parents come to anticipate becoming grandparents, seeing it as a natural part of the life course, they find themselves in a social role bridging middle and old age. Some men discover that they are grandfathers while still in the work force, and women increasingly become grandmothers during the period when they have re-entered the workforce after a long absence due to child-raising activities.

Neugarten (1973) found with a sample of grandparents in 70 middle-class families that there were varied meanings associated with the role. The findings related to those who were middle-aged as well as those in older age categories. Comments of these respondents suggest several different responses to grandparenthood.

First, there is what Neugarten and Weinstein refer to as 'biological renewal' and/or 'biological continuity' where grandchildren provide the opportunity to 'feel young again'. Here emotional self-fulfilment is discovered in the chance to be 'a better parent' as if it were the second time around. The grandparent role also increases activity as a 'resource person'; in providing financial aid and wisdom acquired through a lifetime of experience. There are, in addition, 'vicarious accomplishments' which denote the possibility of reliving, through the grandchildren, frustrated ambitions: an opportunity to 'aggrandize the ego'.

Alternatively, there may be 'feelings of remoteness' – a sense that some people have of restricted involvement in the lives of their grandchildren and little in terms of a relationship with them. Even if the grandparent role is not part of the experience of all those in mid-life, for many others this period does frequently involve seeing their own children growing up and leaving home – perhaps to seek higher education or start marriage or cohabitation with someone else.

More recently research throws light on the possibility that a certain ambiguity also informs grandparenthood and this is partly due to absence of clearly defined norms on the one hand, and changes in family structures on the other. Hearn sees this as particularly the case with men where the relative 'invisibility' of grand-fatherhood prevails since the role is rarely talked about and when it is, it is often through allusions, caricatures, or humour (Hearn 1995, 102). This ambiguity in the grandparent role is also compounded by step-grandfathering, an increasing phenomenon with the rates of re-marriage and the growth of re-constituted families, where there are no socially specified roles or norms.

Whether adopting a grandparent role or not, whatever the precise family structure, being an ex-parent is something experienced by many people in mid-life. Those in mid-life are provided with several socializing opportunities which prepare them for the transition to post-parental life. One such cultural expectation is that people will adapt themselves to inevitable change and that the 'empty nest' is indeed inevitable. The anticipation is leaving home constitutes a 'breaking point' and personal and family adjustment is part and parcel of mid-life even if it adds to the 'crisis' of this time of the life course. In the forging of this 'adjustment' gender variables may be important. The adaptation to the 'empty nest' is arguably easier for the male. Employment may help to prepare the father for his children's departure. Work for the male frequently brings a sense of continuity since he is employed while the children are growing up. He is also likely to be working when his children leave home and even when he assumes the grandfather role. The transition for the mother is arguably more difficult. Even if working, the domestic sphere including child-raising, is still viewed as her primary responsibility.

A rather different and perhaps more gloomy picture is emerging for those who have few family contacts during mid-life. For many reaching mid-life today, marriage and family life does not come into the equation. A report by Emma Besbrode (2001) found an increasingly numbers of single people are living a 'monastic' life which leaves them less happy than married couples. In contrast to the popular view that most unattached adults enjoy a carefree way of life dominated by socializing and romance, most singles lead mundane lives in which drinking alcohol, dating and recreation play only a small part. This is particularly the case as they become older, with one in four 'mid-life singles', those aged 35 and above, admitting they had not had a relationship in five years. Only 5 per cent of this age group claimed that they are still able to meet a wide range of partners. Fourty-nine per cent of older singles confessing feeling happier than they did five years earlier, compared to 61 per cent of couples. Nearly one in three said they were less happy, in contrast with just 18 per cent of their peers who were living with a partner.

Coping With Mid-Life

Lambley (1995) believes that coping with mid-life today involves individuals trying to remake a self-identity. This amounts to an attempt, to establish one's personality against social stereotypes and how society at large sees the ageing process. Some people appear to rebel and this is tied up with an attempt to survive psychologically, especially in coping with so-called 'debilitating problems' often associated with depression anxiety. Such a response is a counterpoint to the rebellious nature of the adolescent years, and constitutes a means of dealing with mid-life changes and to cope effectively with new challenges. At the same time, it also amounts to an attempt to challenge the status quo and cherished assumptions about mid-life (Komesaroff et al. 1997, 9).

As life-expectancy increases, mid-life becomes more important. Now there is almost as much time to live after the mid-life period as there was before it. This is comparable to the nineteenth century in which the life expectancy for a man was under 45 years. However, most people reaching mid-life may be aware that the next part of their life may well be more difficult than the first – a view informed by popular conceptions of ageing and decline. Some may choose to change their careers or become active in aspects of life which may be new to them such as enhancing fitness levels or perhaps try to reduce the effects of ageing. They may now have access to resources offered by consumer society such as body creams, face-lifts, spare-part surgery, and other items constituting part of a commercial industry that can claim a turnover of £ millions per year.

The 'New' Mid-Life

The earlier cultural perception of mid-life discussed above, one perhaps forged by processes of *modernity* – medicalized and associated with a 'crisis', suggested that it was a 'stage' in life when the future was predictable but not entirely welcomed. It was frequently understood to be a time of reflection and fatalistic self-assessment related to careers, relationships, and family life which could trigger a job change or deterioration in the relationship with a partner. Such self-assessment was believed to coincide with perceptions associated with the implications of various physical signs of ageing and apprehensions about the quality of life in the years ahead. Above all, there may have been the fear that time was running out and this may have led to the urgent desire to maximize experiences and live life to the full. A key concern here was the mastery of time in mid-life. If the orientation in modernity was precipitated by discourse around a fairly clearly demarked 'stage' of life, the resultant reflection suggested identity awareness, almost akin to a second adolescence.

To be sure, there were always counter-vailing tendencies. Awareness of middle age could be seen in the context of family relations with the younger generation. The middle years, for some, is viewed in explicitly generational terms and, in particular, by way of the limitations of the traditional boundaries of life. Interaction with teenage children, as the point of reference, rather than association with parents, may involve exposure to new values and fashions and stimulate self-awareness and identification with youth rather than old age. Those middle-aged find themselves caught between youthful idealism and feelings of despair and failure – and that the forties and fifties may not be a source of regret for a wasted life but a stimulus for self-realization. They may have grown up in a late/postmodernist culture with its preoccupation with personal growth and change which is closely linked to increasing dependence on what mid-lifers may see as rewarding interpersonal relationships.

Putting the Clock Back

To 'act one's age' is a popular phrase associated with ageing and its consequences. It may be used as an offensive insult towards a middle-aged person who is attempting to look younger or act like a younger person (covering both physical images and communication). For older women this might include such negative appraisals of trying to look attractive as 'mutton dressed up as lamb'. For this reason, people reaching mid-life are justified in stating that they 'feel young' or are 'young at heart' because although perhaps faced with more health issues, they may well have 40 years more ahead of them.

Age is much more than a physical and biological issue, both of which can be treated and dealt with in a number of ways. When a person over 40 is told to 'act their age' they are being advised to accept their ageing physical appearance and be 'mature', 'reasonable', and perhaps even 'old fashioned' in their actions. This amounts to an unconscious attempt by younger people to create a generation gap – one informed by the cultural emphasis on looking young. For this reason, it is understandable that people of this age embrace the need to revisit their past as a way of coping with middle age at a time when they may still feel healthy, energetic, and ambitious – traits often associated with being young, so their emotions are not that of an 'old', 'ill', or an unfit person, even if they look older in appearance.

In the media there is now much talk about finding ways of restoring the vigour of youth, especially in men. Today, it appears to be more acceptable that middle-aged people will try to put the 'biological clock' back if they have the time and money to make the effort. Such an attempt to retain youth is increasingly accepted as legitimate. The media is in constant pursuit of representing middle-aged people in a new light. This age group is now being portrayed in more positive way by role model celebrates such as Cliff Richard and Joan Collins who are seen as 'ageless'. Currently, a whole age cohort is refusing to adopt the middle-age role. This is the so-called generation of baby-boomers – those born in the 1950s and 1960s – who have reached mid-life in postmodernity and a culture of relativism, choice and lifestyle preferences. These are people who know that they have another 30–40 years of life-expectancy ahead of them. They may see a practically endless future rather than the beginning of the end. It is possible that the trend for trying to stay young for as long as possible will continue to grow. People will thus attempt to redefine the meaning of middle and old age. Many more will come to see themselves as perpetually young and take part in a variety of active creative leisure pursuits. Others will simply opt to 'grow old disgracefully'.

Summary

The main point to recognize in a discussion of mid-life is that 40–50-years old or more is not 'old'. Just because there are outside changes (physical appearance), does not mean to say that the 'inside' (personality, emotions and psychology) necessarily changes. There are now opportunities to stay looking youthful in a consumer culture which circumscribes choice related to this stage of life, but one still impacted by consideration of gender and income rewards. Given the diversity in mid-life and disintegrated norms and roles associated with it, the question may have become 'has middle-age been abolished?' The answer is probably 'not yet'. It is likely to be the case that perceptions of mid-life are still accompanied by various permutations, usually negative and forged by cultural trajectories and the processes of medicalization. In fact, in a youth-orientated society, being middle aged still means being older if not yet elderly.

Further Reading

Gannon,L. (1996) *Women and Ageing: Transcending the Myths*, Routledge: London.
Lambley,P. (1995) *The Middle-Aged Rebel: Responding to the Challenges of Midlife*, New York: Element Books.
Komesaroff,A., Rothfield,P., and Daly,J. (1997) (eds) *Reinterpreting Menopause: Cultural and Philosophical Issues*, London: Routledge.

9
Ageing, Old Age, and Death

While this final chapter considers ageing, old age, and death, in many ways it is perhaps far from unsatisfactory to bring these three themes together since they by no means converge. Certainly, while ageing and death is inevitable, a linear process of ageing is not. Neither do ageing or later life necessarily go together, since ageing is a life-long process. Nonetheless, the themes of ageing and imminent death are commonly associated with the later years of life. For that reason, this chapter is at least partly concerned with how popularized notions of ageing and old age are constructed and structured in contemporary Western societies, although it will be noted that as with other aspects of the life course there is both change and continuity to be observed. As much can be said about social perceptions of death. While death retains a certain stigma in Western societies, late/postmodernity brings new perceptions that are in keeping with a distinctive cultural milieu.

The Ageing Process

A popularly held view, as explored in the previous chapter, is that the ageing process takes off in earnest during the mid-life period and that it is invariably linked to decline. This is a misnomer in the sense that ageing begins at the very height of physical and mental fitness, for instance, human brain-cells begin to quite rapidly die off after the age of 20 years and this increases over the years. However, what the overarching biological causes of deterioration are, of which mental capacity remains only one element, is still largely a mystery to the scientific world. Ageing is known to occur as a result of changes in the cells of the body, yet what makes these changes take place is far from clear.

Many medical theories regarding ageing abound although, as Rosenfeld (1985) suggests, they tend to fall into two broad categories (very much simplified here). First, there are those which conjecture that the important factor is 'wear and tear' on the body over time, causing it to break down and age as part of a natural process. This includes the belief that ageing may be due in large part to deterioration in the integratory homeostasis which exists between cells of the same tissue and those of other tissues. Although the body's DNA is known to have a self-repair capability, it is one which declines over time. When this happens we begin to age. Another approach is one which associates ageing with the decline in immunity. Put succinctly, over time the body loses some of its ability to recognize and attack disease-causing agents and may even attack healthy cells, resulting in autoimmune disorders such as rheumatoid arthritis.

A second set of theories relate to notions of a 'biological clock', ticking away. This suggests that, as with other living species, humans have a genetic clock within them that is programmed to determine the manner and time at which they age and die. Ageing therefore begins at a pre-selected point in time, with the genetic clock perhaps setting certain limits beyond which no one is able to live. There are variations on this theme. A number of medical scientists put emphasis on hormones and the way they seem to change as a part of some pre-determined programme. Exemplifying some of the more optimistic re-evaluations of medicine is the growing assumption that ageing and thus 'decline' may be a process that can be reversed, if not modified. Those such as Daniel Rudman and his colleagues (1990) have produced a measure of evidence suggesting that the development of the human growth hormone could hold up the effects of ageing. It follows that life-expectancy could increase and that we may subsequently choose, by the alleged advances of medical science, to live longer with an average life-span perhaps feasibly increasing in the future to around 110 years old. If so, then an older but fitter population might be only years away. Nonetheless, the implication of such a development is not one that has been seriously pondered in as much as the 'advance' of science may be ahead of both cultural expectations and social policy considerations.

That ageing is related to inevitable decline is, it would seem, very much a medical construct. It is one which tends to stress the interaction of various genetic and other biological factors, alongside the social-psychological influences such as the anxiety related to getting older. Enforcing this is the medical concept of 'primary ageing' and 'secondary ageing'. The former is believed to occur over time and has certain distinguishing features: that the skin will become darker and less elastic, the hair turns grey, wrinkles appear, and there is loss of height and weight. This is assumed to bring an inevitable linear, overall decline in strength and vitality, as well as other physical symptoms such as a decrease in the number of nerve cells in the skin, deficiency in sight and hearing, the stiffening of joints, and a greater vulnerability to chronic illnesses like arthritis and diabetes.

There is also what the medical profession commonly designates 'secondary' or 'pre-mature' ageing – generally attributed to environmental factors. Here, by way of illustration, we can note Rosenfeld's findings of the factors which would seem to hold up the ageing process and hence extend life among certain peoples in the world (Rosenfeld 1985). While noting that most people in 'primitive' societies age quickly and die young, Rosenfeld observed that that the greatest longevity is nevertheless among a limited number of communities living in economically depressed mountain tribes. This includes the Vilcabambans of Equador, the Hunzas on the border of China and Pakistan, and the Abkhasians in the south-west of the former Soviet Union, all of which have people claiming to be 120 years of age or older. Whether their life-span is due to genetics is not known. What is clear, however, is such tribes live a slow paced rural life at high altitudes, work and exercise regularly even at old age, and eat a simple diet which is practically vegetarian, sugar-free, and includes large amounts of fruits, vegetables, and yogurt. These peoples consume fewer calories than North Americans and West Europeans. In other 'developing' countries inadequate diet, stress, adverse working or living conditions, or for women experiences of pregnancy and childbirth, can all hasten the ageing process. It is such factors which clearly limit life-expectancy in other areas of the Third World, so that in many such countries 40-years old might be regarded as 'old'.

Social Perceptions of Old Age

While not doubting the impact of environmental considerations on the ageing process and the life-span, ageing has a further social element in that how it is structured and culturally perceived is in accordance with an infinite number of factors. This is particularly so in the context of the later stages of life. In the West, so Cowgill and Holmes suggest, there have been four simultaneous processes operating since the middle of the nineteenth century. The development of modern society transformed the status of the elderly to one that is lowly: the rise of modern health technology contributed to the ageing of the population; modern economic technology has created new occupations and transformed old ones – exacerbating employment opportunities among older workers; urbanization has attracted rural youth to the cities – breaking down the extended family; and mass education and literacy have undermined the mystique of age (Cowgill and Holmes 1972).

Today, 'old age', if it does indeed designate a 'stage' of the life course, is one open to a degree of negotiation in the current cultural milieu since it is difficult to fix a precise time in which old age commences. Nonetheless, negative connotations remain. This tendency is at least partly due to a unique cultural trajectory which places a great deal of emphasis on youth and being young. Hence, ageing may bring frustration, fear, and self-doubt among the elderly which, in turn, will shape self-perceptions and experiences of old age (Hamel 1990). Those of younger years may feel sorry for those entering old age, or prefer to make light about ageing in order to cover their own ingrained fears about the possibility of physical and mental demise.

Since Western society places a high cultural value on youthfulness, of looking and behaving 'young', signs of ageing are not welcomed. There are social implications here and the elderly arguably participate in what Goffman calls 'life as theatre' (Goffman 1967, 31). They are obligated to play an 'elderly role' and 'put on a face', and this may involve a sense of loss of self-esteem as a result of a deteriorating physical condition. Here, women are exposed to a 'double negativity' in that they are female and old, with the picture of the 'old hag' being a common stereotype (Arber and Ginn 1995). Society's standards of female beauty and physical appeal are almost exclusively youthful. Arguably, then, women may be more aware of the ageing process than men because the physical signs of ageing produce graver social consequences for them.

Much of the Western perception of ageing is in contrast with other societies both past and present. As we saw in the early chapters of this volume, in pre-industrial communities the elderly may achieve a high level of status in recognition of past social roles and for the wealth of experience and knowledge that can be passed on to later generations. Their social and political power might be more than significant. For example, in the case of rural China strong affection and respect for the elderly still remains. The elderly continue to maintain considerable control over the social and economic lives of their adult children, while in their latter years they would expect to be supported and cared for by their adult children.

The important variables in Western perception and construction of old age are the interrelated areas of the value placed on youth and maximum production, loss of social role, and dependency. As far as social roles are concerned, Rostow explains that old age is the only stage of life with systematic social losses rather than gains. When one is elderly, the major tasks in life, such as having a career and starting a family, are accomplished. Thus an older person's responsibilities decline, whereas dependency on others because of reduced income or physical and mental infirmities may increase. Roles include those of being retired, widowed, an aged-dependent, or chronically ill person – those hardly socially valued or conferring high status. Unfortunately people are not adequately prepared for the inevitable social loss that old age brings, nor are they taught how to lead a dignified life within the limitations of advanced age (Rosow 1978, 148).

As we will note below, older people may now be assuming more positively appraised roles. Yet, certain negative connotations of old age endure and are perhaps exemplified by cultural attitudes towards the elderly and sexuality. Here we may contrast attitudes in the West with those of a tribal society. Amongst the Vanatinai of Papua New Guinea, elderly people are expected to be sexually active well into old age. Similarly, the Kaliau, also of New Guinea, have no expectation that during old age women will end their sexual activity. Although social disapproval may condone sex outside of marriage, no more scandal would be attached to it than amongst young people. For the Kaliau, because there is no marked boundary between the 'elder' and 'decrepit' person, the way in which an individual is classified depends wholly on the way he presents him/herself. Sexual activity is therefore encouraged for older people as an effective way to maintain a sense of self and personhood. Those becoming dependents solely because of their age are regarded intolerably. Thus, the majority of older individuals endeavour to maintain and demonstrate their status as an active elder and sexual individual.

Contemporary culture in the West is pre-occupied by the subject of sex but finds the thought of sexual relations for the elderly repulsive. Sexually active older men are often depicted as lewd and reprehensible, while sexuality in old women, according to Barash's analysis, is popularly perceived as laughable at best. This may be why there has been very little literature produced on the sexuality of older men and women. What has been written, in terms of research findings, confirms that older males take longer to become sexually aroused and reach orgasm, while the latency period between intercourse takes longer. It is assumed that older women loose their sex drive, with accompanying reduction in physical sensations which may well have begun with the menopause. Nonetheless, the evidence suggests that the reality is that the elderly do not loose the ability or desire to have sexual intercourse (Barash 1983).

Retirement

Disengagement or Discontinuity?

Andrew Blakie maintains that in the case of the UK, the social construction of ageing has passed through three stages in the twentieth century and that these developments are largely connected with retirement and social disengagement. To begin with, the first half of the twentieth century witnessed the emergence of retirement as a mass experience. Second, this form of social disengagement culminated in its mid-century institutionalization through state legislation. Since the late 1960s, an increasing fragmentation has been evident, both as regards the time in which people leave work and in ways they spend their time afterwards in a phase of the life course which is increasing as life-expectancy is extended (Blakie 1999, 59–60).

The simple explanation for the creation of retirement as an institution is that advanced technology reduces the need for everyone to work literally for life, while placing a premium on current skills implies that the older worker has to give way to the younger. By contrast to these developments in the West, in Third World societies that depend on the labour of everyone, male and female alike, and where no pension schemes exist, most people work until they are physically incapable of doing so.

In terms of a sociological framework applied to the social and economic necessity of retirement, the earliest formulated was that commonly understood as 'disengagement theory'. Cumming and Henry's variation of the theoretical paradigm is perhaps the best known, although it presents a rather negative picture of the social position of the elderly. The theory contends that social disengagement for the aged is socially and psychologically functional and a natural part of the ageing process. Thus, ageing has certain fixed repercussions which, in turn, accounts for the reasons why the elderly become marginalized from society (Cumming and Henry 1961). It is a theory which implies that the major social passage in later life is associated with 'loss' whether one of social role, status, or income.

It is clear that the disengagement theory assumes that biological ageing is a straightforward process and a detachment of older people from the workforce is constructive since deteriorating physical and mental powers undermine their economic contribution. Hence, their 'disengagement' would give way to younger people in the occupational sphere. Disengagement is thus a means by which society promotes its own orderly functioning by removing ageing people from 'normal' and productive roles while they are still performing them. There is also the additional advantage that in a rapidly changing society, young workers typically have the most up-to-date skills and training. Disengagement may advantage the elderly as well as society. Hence, it is assumed that for the most part, older people with diminished capabilities invariably welcome the opportunity for more leisure time and the freedom from the pressures of work. There is a psychological dimension too. As people age, according to the disengagement theory, their most basic social psychological need changes from one of active involvement to one of inactive contemplation about the meaning of life in the face of impending death.

Despite modifications, a number of critiques have damagingly undermined the disengagement theory – many of which are connected with broader culture conceptions related to ageing. First, it largely fails to recognize that many elderly people may not wish to disengage from productive roles since it includes loss of social prestige and brings social isolation. Second, in practical terms many of those retiring, mostly lower paid workers, cannot always readily disengage from paid work because they do not have sufficient financial security to do so. Third, there is no compelling evidence that the benefits of disengagement outweigh their cost to society, since it results in the loss of at least some human resources. Indeed, a comprehensive system of engagement would have to take into account the widely different abilities of the elderly. Fourth, retirement means the care of people who might better be able to provide for themselves. This is particularly so in an ageing society where governments are increasingly concerned about how such a large portion of the population can be supported. Finally, it is possible to argue that the elderly's contribution to society is hugely underestimated, especially because they take part in such unpaid work as childcare and participate in charity work in a voluntary capacity.

Another difficulty with the disengagement theory is that retirement is not a simple stage of adaptation but part of a process which has both positive and negative consequences. Atchley identifies various possible phases of retirement. To begin with, there is pre-retirement where, as retirement approaches, the individual begins to prepare for the experience and relevant activities. When retirement occurs the person takes one of three paths: the 'honeymoon' phase that is marked by euphoria since the individual does many of the things s/he 'never had time for before'. This phase requires money and good health. Others will move instantly to 'an immediate retirement routine' that in all probability stabilizes over time and involves scheduled activities at a regulated pace which will likely turn into a more or less permanent lifestyle. Still others will see retirement as a 'rest and relaxation' phase consisting of a very low level of activity. Many may initially adopt this but become restless and subsequently more active (Atchley 1988).

After experiencing one of these three phases during the initial retirement, movement to other phases is probable. Some people edge into a 'disenchantment phase' as they discover retirement does not live up to expectations, but this may be relatively rare. Another possibility is a 're-orientation' phase in which retired persons change their approach to retirement. Perhaps they become increasingly involved with friends and family, after initially pursuing their interests more or less on their own. But eventually the great majority of retired persons enter into the phase of 'routine' in which they know what it is they want and are able to do – a set of stable activities often constituting a particular lifestyle. Finally, they may adopt a – 'termination phase' and go back to the job they left or start a new one because they enjoy working or need to support themselves in old age. Eventually, however, all older people adopt the phase of routine as they settle down to live out their last years.

Recent Trends in Retirement

Another critique of the disengagement theory is that there is now no standard age at which people retire in Western societies – suggesting the complexity of contemporary economic life. Around the world there is little consensus as to when a person should retire and it is the vast differences in the interests and capacities of older people which also make the notion of a fixed retirement age so controversial, while mandatory retirement is also challenged by notions of the right to work and equality of opportunity. Moreover, the reasons for retirement are not always discernibly linked to societal or individual 'needs'. Retirement ages are being reduced in some countries and this may be related to the growth of unemployment, allowing perhaps a greater guarantee of work for younger generations. Certainly, the number of people working in their sixties has continued to decline. According to *Social Trends* (27, 1997), the percentage of men in the UK over 65-years old still in paid employment has diminished from 66 per cent in 1961 to 7 per cent in 1992.

In recent years, the phenomenon of early retirement has become more prevalent and there are various reasons why people might retire before the statutory age. These are largely related to economic factors which cut across the life course as one linear, ordered process. Thus, the occupational structuring of 'retired' older men has been greatly complicated by early retirement, voluntary severance, 'retirement at 50', and a 'no jobs for life' culture in industrial society. Contractual employment agreements might include 'the rules of the job' that stipulate time of retirement and length of service. Early retirement in this respect is essentially a system under which employees are allowed to retire with employer or occupational union usually providing supplemental pension payments to keep it at an adequate level until the retiree becomes old enough to collect a state pension. In so far as the individual has a choice, many factors may be influential including whether or not a person is self-employed, demands of the family, pre-retirement planning, the desire for leisure, or the spouse's plans in respect of family or work. Others reasons include income, health, and finding work too difficult or challenging especially in the light of rapid technological change.

There has been a further development among the retired that is intrinsically linked to the subject of inequalities in later life. In middle-class and professional sectors, there has arisen a new younger 'retired' constituency which, in turn, has proved to be a significant consumer grouping in the organization of pensions, insurances, and purchasing.This consumerist aspect is part of the way that old age and identity is now negotiated, although much depends on economic circumstances as to who participates in the developing 'leisure worlds'. Therefore, while older people may not generally fill roles of great power and influence because of their age, old age does have its compensations and the effect of role loss in the wider community can mean a greater pre-occupation with one's self and private activities. It is not surprising, then, that the social construction of men as 'retired' has in turn produced a wealth of literature, including that specializing in retirement planning. Nonetheless, early retirement can generate its own problems. One, as Jeff Hearn points out, addresses the role and experience of married men in particular and the possibility of problems of them spending more time at home and with their wives. Men in this sense are 'newcomers' in the home and this requires adjustments by both parties (Hearn 1995, 101).

The possible restructuring of retirement is also linked to demographic trends and their potential considerable repercussions. Despite the general consensus about the value of retirement and its apparently positive consequences, there are serious social and economic questions about whether it can continue as present in an ageing society. The economic quandaries have to do with the ability and willingness of society to continue providing social security benefits and health insurance through contributions of the active labour force that would involve additional taxation of those who are earning. While extra taxation would not be politically popular, there is likely to be pressure mounting as the age structure of society becomes older and the elderly a powerful lobby group in their own right, especially through such organizations as Age Concern. Whichever way it develops, older people will likely take up more and more of the state budget.

At the same time, it might be possible to allow older people to remain productive and part of economic life as long as possible – reversing the trend towards early retirement. Thus the age of retirement in the future will probably become increasingly flexible. In all possibility, there will be phased retirement consisting of reduced work schedules, prorated salaries, and varying health and benefit services. Therefore, the retirement pattern is likely to be one that is highly variable, as older people adopt different approaches to dealing with the period of life in which retirement will be common. All this suggests that the aged will be closer to the social, cultural, and economic mainstream of society than ever before.

The Third Age

One repercussion of increasing life-expectancy will be the breakdown of familiar age categorizations, subsequently complicating perceptions of ageing and the identity of older people. Similarly, it will bring changing perceptions of retirement as being the primary 'cut off' point which signifies an induction or rites of passage into 'old age'. There are now several new broad distinctions: between the so-called 'third age' (50–74 years) – a period of life often free from parenting and paid work when a more active, independent life is achieved – and a 'fourth age' – an age of eventual dependency (Laslett 1994). This means we can draw a division between a very large group – the younger elderly (65–75 years) – individuals who will largely enjoy good health and financial security, are typically autonomous, and likely to be living as part of a couple; and the 'older elderly' (75–85 years) who will become increasingly dependent on others because of both health and financial problems. The former is an ever-growing sector – adding to the complicated definition of what constitutes 'mid-life' as distinct from 'the elderly'. All these divergent ways of grouping the elderly nonetheless suggest a move from periods of increased activity and autonomy to one of growing dependency.

Peter Laslett was probably the first to speak of the Third Age as part of a 'New Division of the life course'. First, he conjectured, there comes an era of dependence, socialization, immaturity, and education associated with the early years of life. Second, there is an era of independence, maturity and responsibility, of earning and financial saving. Third, there may be an era of freedom and personal fulfilment. Finally, there is a period of final dependence, decrepitude, and death. The emergence of the Third Age, according to Laslett, coincided with demographic changes where over half of all men and women aged 25 can now expect to reach 70 years. The advent of the Third Age also converged with a point where industrialized societies switched into being an ageing society characterized by high numbers of men in retirement (the figure for women being difficult to commute, and not strictly comparable, because of the prevalence of interrupted paid work) (Laslett 1987).

For the first time there is now a social group whose daily experience does not consist of work or schooling, or in a period of dependency. Therefore, the Third Age is potentially a period of self-realization and perhaps empowerment for an emerging economic and political constituency although, as Blakie notes, cohort effects may be important here in the future. Nonetheless, those reaching the Third Age at this point in time are very different from the age cohorts gone before. They were raised in an age of prosperity and experienced the emergence of the consumer culture – one which has created more disposable income that tends to be spent on leisure products and pursuits whilst commodities are bought to enhance personal styles and lifestyles. For retired people, according to Blakie, 'social identity increasingly relies upon what one buys, how one dresses, what sports one plays, or where one goes on holiday' (Blakie 1999, 59, 72).

The implication of the elderly as a consumer group was, in fact, evident even before a coherent Third Age was identified. As Ekerdt had explored, retirement meant older people leaving the economy in terms of production or services. Yet, they do not disengage as consumers. Those of retirement age can now embrace the consumer ethic and active lifestyles – bringing them into line with mainstream cultural values (Ekerdt 1986). This undoubtedly adds to a more optimistic appraisal of the later years of life. Thus, older people may develop a lifestyle that is almost synonymous with 'positive ageing' and the hedonistic joys of leisured retirement (Counts and Counts 1996, 16). In many respects, then, the later years of life increasingly follow the contours of late/postmodernity, as do the earlier phases of the life course – embracing aspects of consumption, lifestyles constructs, choice, and variety.

The Self in Old Age

While the consumer society undoubtedly ushers in more positive aspects of the later years of life, this does not necessarily compensate for negative social perceptions of ageing – cultural constructs of the older self which invariably impact on how the elderly see themselves. Although the interest in the construction of self and identity throughout the life course has enjoyed something of resurgence in recent years, largely through postmodernist theorizing, the topic still remains somewhat neglected when it comes to the elderly and the impact of actual or perceived ageing on perception of the self. There are, however, a number of important studies that directly or indirectly throw light on how the elderly view themselves.

While aspects of consumption may bring a greater association with mainstream values, lack of geographical and social mobility may still forge separable social age-sets and generational-sets whereby older people have become separated off from those who are younger and closer to the child-raising age. Thus, a number of sociological accounts have argued that the elderly form themselves into a subculture with its own distinctive norms, values, and lifestyles. The emergence of such an age group based around a sense of solidarity comes through frequent interaction with peers, as well as how other people perceive the elderly. The growing size of the aged as a social category, alongside increasing segregation into retirement communities and retirement practices, may well have helped the forging of a distinct subculture.

Rosow, in an early study, found that a low feeling of self-worth and well-being among the aged was widespread, and that this tended to make them something of a low status age-set which had limited interaction with younger generations (Rosow 1974). Such evidence might suggest a more negative perception of self because of the way Western society constructs and frames old age. To some extent, as noted above, this results from statutory retirement which constitutes a major status passage in an individual's life course and perceptions of old age precipitated by popular notions equating the ageing process with inevitable decline. For the most part this status passage brings with it a loss of prestige, privileges, and power, not to mention income. On retiring, the individual departs from his/her familiar environment of employment in which roles, functions, and personal relationships associated with work are typically well-established. This can bring a distinct sense of loss of worth and role since work plays an important part in constructing a master-status and constitutes a principal source of identity. Retirement effectively means, for many people, leaving the public sphere. Thus, for the elderly, the bases of identity and self-worth must come from the private sphere – family, leisure, and the commitment to clubs and associations. Here, some older people may actively seek to meet others, develop a sense of belonging, and reappraise themselves through new challenges which plausibly have positive or negative consequences.

Contributions from gerontology have tended to suggest that most people cope fairly well with the challenges of growing old and their self-perceptions and evaluation are not necessarily negative. Among the research findings are those of Neugarten (1971) who argued there are three smaller subgroups in the elderly population whose sense of self is adversely affected. The first constituency developed a 'disintegrated' or 'disorganized personalities' as a result of finding it extremely difficult to come to terms with old age. Above all, there is a frequent sense of despair to the extent of older people 'giving up' and becoming passive residents of hospitals or nursing homes.

Neugarten found that a second group of people displayed 'passive-dependent personalities'. These have little confidence in their own abilities to cope on a day-to-day basis – sometimes seeking help even if they do not necessarily need it. Their social withdrawal tends to mean that their level of life satisfaction remains relatively low. A third category of people Neugarten designated as 'defended personalities'. Such people live independently but were afraid of growing older. They tried to shield themselves from the reality of old age by fighting to stay youthful and physically fit, but in doing so they frequently set unrealistic standards which, in turn, could bring stress and disappointment.

The majority of Neugarten's subjects, however, fared far better, displaying what she called 'integrated personalities'. Their success lay in retaining their personal dignity, self-confidence, and optimism, while accepting that growing old was inevitable. These personal problems and adjustments are unavoidable at this time and old age may even bring positive experiences. This latter observation is backed up by a more recent European survey of the elderly which found that only one in five were not satisfied with their lives, whilst two out of three reported they were very active or leading fulfilling lives (Walker and Maltby 1997, 23, 122).

Another relevant study is that of Preston and Guidiken (1996) which compared the attitudes of retired and non-retired older people and discovered no significant differences between the two groups in terms of life satisfaction. In a subsequent study, Preston (1996) discovered that the aged felt more positive about themselves than had been previously assumed. There may be important variables, however, since Preston found that those who reported more chronic health disorders and more incapacity due to illness displayed a greater tendency to think of themselves as being 'old' than those who reported no such problems.

An earlier important piece of research related to how the elderly perceive themselves was Kaufman's work, *The Ageless Self* (1978). As the title of the volume suggests, older people do not necessary slip into some 'old age identity' which brings a deterministic change in the perceptions of self. Rather, Kaufman shows that the self is ageless. The older people in her study expressed a personal identity that had maintained continuity over the life-span, regardless of the physical and social changes associated with old age. That is, they defined themselves as being essentially the same person they were when younger: they had simply grown old. Kaufman argues that in old age one is not a different person even if some personality traits become more pronounced. Furthermore, those interviewed often regarded themselves as much younger than they really were. Thus, biological ageing and how people are expected to think and act do not necessarily coincide.

Understanding the subjective experiences of older people has led to a shift in sociological thinking about this age group, as well as a reconsideration of their requirements. The need to encourage a positive appraisal of the self in old age is one advanced by so-called 'activity theory' which brings a greater optimistic assessment of old age and avoids the determinism of disengagement theory. Thus activity theory shifts the focus of analysis from the needs of society in encouraging the elderly to 'disengage', to the needs of the elderly themselves. The basic conjecture is that a high level of activity enhances the personal enjoyment and satisfaction of old age. Because all individuals build their social identities from statuses and roles, disengagement in old age is bound to undermine the satisfaction and meaning many elderly people find in their lives. What older people require is to be encouraged in developing productive and recreational activities, in short, to become socially active.

Activity theory proposes that, to the extent elderly people do disengage from society, they should ideally find new positive roles and responsibilities to replace those which they have left behind. To some extent this is backed up by empirical evidence since studies show that the elderly pursue active lives as much as young ones, and that they follow their own interests, remaining engaged with daily activities and relationships

(Palmore 1979). This approach also highlights social diversity among elderly people by way of class, gender, ethnicity, and marriage status, all of which must be regarded as important considerations in formulating government policy.

The increasing interest in identity in old age has also led to a distinct perspective which has influenced the relevant literature: the so-called 'biographical approach' has become an increasingly popular one with gerontologists, sociologists, and specialist therapists. It is very much a humanist perspective and principally attempts to listen to the accounts and stories of the lives of the elderly. The value in such an approach is to cut across commonsense and medicalized notions of ageing and 'older people' and their taken-for-granted experiences. By contrast, the wealth of differing experiences as related to dimensions of inequality and the relevant of age cohorts are highlighted in a more integrated approach to how older people interpret their past experiences.

Such narratives can be said to be of three forms. First, there is the 'reminiscence story'. Gerontologists have discovered that a characteristic of many elderly people is their desire to constantly relate some key highlights of their life. This appears to be therapeutic, since the telling of life stories is often an important part of the elderly person's adjustment process. Second, the 'oral history'. Here, the life story is related in order to illuminate the times of the elderly such as stories of World Wars or other great historical events. An associated enterprise is the attempt to gather family history, for example, through family photograph albums or diaries. A third option is the 'sociological life history'. In this strategy the life story is told through a series of stages and themes which help us understand the social background of an individual over the life course.

Social Networks of the Elderly

Older people's perceptions of self may be enhanced by primary social networks. Robert Atchley (1988) observes that Rostow's argument concerning society failing to socializing the elderly for participation in a particular role of 'old person' is not a wholly accurate description of role relationships among the aged. He points out that elderly persons usually have few required contacts with the broad community. Instead, they associate on a daily basis primarily with people they know. Typically, they continue to function in their usual roles in the family and network of friends. Thus, most roles older people play are those they have been socialized to for a long time.

Bernard et al.'s research, however, suggests both continuities and change in the family and community life of the elderly. While the elderly among some ethnic minorities, such as older Bangladeshi people, are part of flourishing family networks, whites typically have only one child living close by, with others dispersed. Nonetheless, when white older people were asked to name who is important to them, most identified kin as being the main group with whom reciprocal relations were maintained. Above all, relationships with their own children appeared to be the cornerstone of social integration. Thus, those who are significant to older individuals in terms of interaction are people of their own age, plus their own children. Fewer than one in five interviewed placed themselves within a network which stretched beyond two generations. Another observation concerned the vital role older people play within the helping network and reciprocal nature of these intergenerational ties. Older people continue to see themselves as playing a supportive role to family and friends, notably in areas such as confiding in personal problems and giving advice on health. Bernard et al. conclude that intergenerational support is crucial to the present-day family and community life of older people. They are not being abandoned wholesale by their families, neither are they falling victim to extensive conflict between generations (Bernard et al. 1995).

For those without a good family life and networks social isolation may be an unwelcome predicament for the elderly, but one exacerbated by some recent developments related to an increased life-span. Retirement may mean isolation from friends and workmates, while illness could reduce the opportunity for contact. The death of a spouse may leave the old on their own without the companion they have had for many years. Nearly half of those over 80-years old now find themselves living on their own (Walker and Maltby 1997, 13). This is not to imply total isolation and often the most important regular source of contact for the elderly are adult children and grandchildren – either by living near to them or what might be referred to as 'intimacy at a distance' – communication by phone or letter.

At least one study has found that almost three quarters of widows and widowers cited loneliness as their most serious problem and it is they who must often rebuild their lives at this late stage of life (Lund 1989). As with practically everything to do with old age, social isolation is strongly influenced by factors related to gender (Arber and Ginn 1995). The problem of social isolation, then, falls most heavily on women, who typically outlive their husbands. Over 40 per cent of older women (especially the older elderly) live alone, compared to 16 per cent of older men. Bereaved older males, however, may face their own difficulties. An earlier study of elderly men noted a sharp increase in mortality, sometimes by suicide (although this is not always easy to detect) in the months following the death of their wives – perhaps indicating once again who it is that benefits in practical terms from marriage (Benjamin and Wallis 1963).

Another recent development appears to be the increase in social isolation as a result of marital breakdown and divorce. The Family Policy Studies Centre has predicted that older people continue to be more and more isolated and lonely due to the rise in divorce. The following figures show that a growing proportion of pensioners will be living alone. One consequence is undoubtedly that fewer disabled old people will have a spouse to be their carer and so there may be increasing reliance on middle-aged daughters to fill this role. According to *Social Trends*, the number of divorced people living on their own expected in 2025 will be 20 per cent, six times that of 1990.

The Perseverance of Inequalities in Old Age

Kaufman advances the view that old people maintain a sense of continuity with their previous years in a way that helps them cope with changes in old age. The factors which figure most prominently in influencing the lives of the elderly over the life course include socio-economic status in childhood, family ties, level of education, geographic location, and occupational income and status. Thus being old does not mean adopting a new self-concept. Rather, it means making sense of self and personality as developed throughout the years to the last stage of life and then adapting them to the situation in the best way possible (Kaufman 1978). This suggests that the elderly are not a homogeneous grouping, far from it. In fact, one important trend observable within this age category is that it is increasingly identified by fragmentation and diversity – shaping life-experience in old age and influences the way in which the elderly perceive and evaluate themselves.

Differences of occupational reward, ethnicity, and gender splinter older people as they do younger generations. Those in higher social classes have far more economic security, greater access to top medical care and more options for personal satisfaction which clearly impact opportunities, lifestyles, and meaningful choices. While it is possible to see the elderly as especially vulnerable to poverty, this is not the case for all: older people may have a great deal in common but they do not constitute a uniform group. In short, they could be understood in terms of a major division between the 'haves' and 'have nots'. Yet, such inequality is far from new. As early as the 1960s, Titmus (1962) referred to the 'two nations of old age' and stressed the wide variety of income among the over 65s. The variables Titmus identified as important were related not only to social class but also to gender. Titmus suggested that the 'haves' are the younger elderly – 60–75 year-olds, they are more likely to be middle-class, male, married; the 'have nots' are likely to be those over 75-years old, who are working-class, female, single, the divorced or widowed.

Today in the UK, 15 per cent of the elderly live in conditions of poverty below the poverty line – one of the largest groups in poverty since they rely only on state pensions. The richest sections have resources accumulated at earlier stages of the life course. Hence, occupational status determines conditions in old age as it allows resources such as savings and investments, as do occupational pension. Indeed, for the more affluent, old age is not a period of impoverishment, pessimism, or despair. There is a growing segment of the elderly that is frequently referred to as 'woopies', well-off older persons who enjoy an abundant and fruitful lifestyle from the Third into the Fourth Age. Those who are more affluent can afford good health care and will have spent their lives living and working in a safe and healthy environment, perhaps enjoying a better diet. Hence, they are likely to have a higher standard of health well into old age and experience, for better or worse, a greater life-longevity. Yet there may be a downside for the 'have' elderly. In the West, people at the upper-end of the socio-economic scale tend to live longer than those of lower end. But this may mean an affluent lifestyle, involving a rich diet, heavy smoking, and lack of exercise, which can be all detrimental to a person's health, as well as the experiences of a range of chronic diseases associated with old age.

Clearly, certain earlier experiences are not conducive to choice of lifestyle in old age: crowded living conditions, poor diet, inferior housing, violence, as well as high levels of stress, a family history of restricted life longevity, and lack of healthy lifestyles and exercise all take their toll. Looking at Europe generally, the EU sponsored survey, the *European Observation on Ageing*, has concluded that although the living standards of older people have largely been rising in recent years, there are wide differences across countries. For example, there are low poverty rates in Denmark and Germany and high ones in Spain, Portugal, and the UK. Above all, the inequalities are most stark in the USA (Walker and Maltby 1997, 48).

Table 9.1   Poverty: percentage of expenditure on 'Basics' and 'Non-Basics'

	Basics (food, shelter, heating)	Non-basic (Transport, services, leisure)
Average family	57	52
Married pensioners	48	60
Single woman pensioner	40	43

Source: Age Concern, 1998.

Old Age: Gender and Ethnicity

Gender divisions in old age also have considerable significance and may cut across the variable of class. Women have greater life-expectancy than men and are thus more likely to live alone. Those over pensionable age are the largest group of single-person households (around 11 per cent). It follows that women outnumber men in the elderly population and the discrepancy increases with advancing age. This is a tendency generally referred to as 'the feminization of old age'. Since the 1990s the ratio of men to women in the 60–64 age group has been about 50:50; at ages 65–69 the ratio is 47 males to 53 females; at ages 70–74 there are 44 males to 56 females; and at age 75 and over the ratio is approximately 38 males to 62 females. Women are also more inclined to be subject to higher rates of poverty: 38 per cent of women and 24 per cent of men over 65 years live on the poverty line. Some 77 per cent of carers of the elderly at home are women, and around 66 per cent are over the age of 55.

Throughout Europe, at least, a major source of income for the elderly is a pension. Generally, this is a two-tier system: public and private (usually an occupational pension). The latter is much more easily available to men, once again reinforcing the weaker position of women in old age. The woes for older women do not stop here however. More health problems inflict the older elderly, those past the age of 75 years. Because women typically live longer than men do, it follows that it is they who will spend more years suffering from chronic diseases and the need for support in daily living from other people.

There exists an ethnic dimension to old age as well. With regards to the ethnic minority populations there is a younger age structure largely reflecting the history of immigration in the UK and other Western countries, particularly those migrating in the 1950s and 1960s. Some 25 per cent of the black Caribbean and 47 per cent of the Pakistani and Bangladeshi population in the UK are in the under-15 years age group compared to 21 per cent of whites. Only 3 per cent of the ethnic minority population are aged 65 and over, compared to 17 per cent of whites. However, the proportion of ethnic minority elderly people will increase in the future, as the ethnic minority population itself ages. Better-off whites typically enjoy a host of advantages denied to older members of ethnic minorities. For some ethnic groups, ageing is compounded by what might be referred to as the 'triple jeopardy' of being old, black and poor, to which can be added aspects of gender inequality.

Other than these demographic trends, the relationship between age and ethnicity remains an under-researched area. Certainly, there are often major differences in the 'ageing experience' between ethnic groups, for example, in self-identity, morale, life-satisfaction, and standards of living.

Thus, Blakemore and Boneham (1993) suggests that there is the danger of generalizing about ethnic groups, such as the insistence that Asian extended families are more likely to have caring family networks responsible for the elderly. Nonetheless, they maintain that the situation of the elderly in ethnic groups can be divided into three categories. First, the 'Self-Reliant Pioneer' – older people in minority ethnic groups who are influenced more by their roles and position in their own communities than by mainstream norms and expectations. The position of old people in the country of origin will be replicated as far as possible, for example, in terms of status, and extended family ties.

A second category is, the 'Gradually Adjusting Migrant' who makes certain adaptations to the 'role' of old age in common with mainstream society. This suggests a partial social integration. Third, there is the 'Passive Victim' – those who are part of a minority that feel discriminated against because they are both old and members of an ethnic community. It is a group likely to experience vast differences of health, environment, and income in comparison to the white population. They are more likely to be black rather than members of white ethnic groups.

The 'Very Old'

We have noted the negativity surrounding perceptions of ageing, especially that being elderly does not confer enhanced social status by virtue of age as in many non-industrial societies. A survey commissioned by Age Concern in 1992 revealed that four out of five young adults in the UK feared old age, with two-thirds citing either loss of independence or poor health in old age as a predominant concern. This is partly because of the acute problems associated with 'real' old age. For those 75-years old and over, in contrast to other stages of life, old age is likely to be a less pleasant period, for there is a higher probability of loneliness, boredom, and loss of self-esteem. Moreover, physical and mental infirmities and the reality of being tired, ill, and less able to cope with problems – all set in a framework of the recognition of impending death – can and does produce severe problems of adjustment and depression for the elderly.

It may well be that the major development regarding older people over the last three decades, is not just the emergence of the Third Age, but that the evasion of old age can apparently be accomplished through a range of youth-preserving techniques and lifestyles, so that it might be difficult to gauge when 'real' old age sets in. Blakie, however, notes the difficulty in transferring from the Third to the Fourth Age. In terms of self-perception it may be negative and involve infantization, stigmatization, and institution-alization (Blakie 1999, 194–6). Indeed, Blakie maintains that Western society is facing a cultural problem in relation to the very old. To talk of the 'end of old age' is to go too far. Yet, he suggests that we have arrived at a postmodern impasse where neither lifelong socialization to a series of socially approved goals or individualized departures from the script offer coherent guidelines how as a society we confront the end of life. Neither is there is a positive image of later life which can prepare us for decline and death (Blakie 1999, 210–11).

Institutionalization

Another example of how old age is differentially dealt with can found in formal health-care systems. Social services in the UK as elsewhere are subdivided into services for children, services for adults, and services for the elderly. Old age is not given the same status as earlier adulthood. To some extent this is a result of infantization, that is, the perception of the elderly as inevitably returning to a child-like state. This is a process built into the medical model of ageing. In old age 'post-adults' are perceived as returning to a subordinate child-like position, while in the health-care system patients are discriminated against by being denied operations and transplants that would prolong their lives in favour of transplants for the young. Over several decades in the UK, the national health resources directed towards the elderly have failed to rise in proportion to their number. Moreover, geriatric patients are not treated as a priority, while geriatric nursing has a relatively low status.

'Deep' old age may also lead to institutionalization which marks an essential part of the medicalization of later life. Infantization is likely to be enhanced in this setting where 'adult' (nursing staff) – 'infant' (elderly inmates) relationship will have a detrimental effect. Hockey and James note that this treatment by the nursing staff may lead to patient resistance and even a resort to childlike tactics in response by way of attempting to

Table 9.2 The context of residential care (those over 65) (UK)

	1980	1992
Local authority homes	102,890	71,369
Voluntary homes	25,449	31,483
Private homes	28,854	132,063
Total	157,193	234,915

Source: *Social Trends*, 27, 1997.

undermine the power of the nursing staff and to re-establish self-esteem and empowerment (Hockey and James 1993, 131, 172–3).

Institutionalization, however, is not the experience of the majority of the elderly. Surveys by Townsend among others in the UK have shown older people to be actively involved with their relatives and friends. Even among the bedridden over half are looked after outside of hospitals (Townsend 1979). In fact, only 5 per cent of all old people are in residential institutions – about the same figure as the early 1900s. However, the fact that over 70 per cent do not live with their children shows the endurance of the nuclear family as a social institution. Moreover, the institutionalization of the elderly is not to suggest the ageism of younger generations but the possibility that the elderly, like other age groups, may prefer the company of their own generation.

The ultimate expression of ageism is perhaps violence. Fairly recently research has noticed the phenomenon of 'granny battering' – or abuse of the elderly inside and outside of institutions for the elderly. Such abuse takes many forms, from passive neglect to actively inflicted suffering, and includes verbal, emotional, financial, and physical harm. Research suggests that between 3 and 4 per cent of elderly people (mainly women) suffer serious maltreatment each year and three times as many sustain abuse at some point, although it is difficult to determine how widespread it is and the figures may be far from reliable (Whittaker 1997). However, it is probable that as the proportion of elderly people rises, so does the incidence of abuse (Holmstrom 1994).

Often the causes of abuse lies in the stress of caring – financially and emotionally – for ageing parents perhaps at a time that children are also being cared for. This care-giving responsibility is especially pronounced among adult women who not only look after parents and children but hold down jobs as well. There are other considerations too. Abuse appears to be most common where the stresses are greatest: in families with a very old person suffering from serious health problems which bring overwhelming demands and tensions (Yates 1986).

Death and Dying

While it may be inappropriate to discuss death in the same breath as ageing, late/postmodernity has produced a unique culture that tends to bring together these themes – coupling them alongside generalized notions related to life-expectancy. Death is viewed as the climax of the ageing process. Many people expect to live to old age and at some time will likely anticipate and plan for it. What they may give far less consideration to, however, is their death. For most people the event may seem a long way off. Indeed, in the death-denying societies of the West the limit of life-expectancy is forever being pushed back and perhaps thoughts of death pushed ever more to the back of the mind. It may be true that older people anticipate their own deaths with legal and financial planning, yet death is something that many do not like to think about.

Changing perceptions of death in Western societies have also been accompanied by the changing causes of death. Over the last century and a half improved sanitary conditions in particular, and environmental conditions in general, have not only prolonged life but brought a drastic reduction in death caused by infections and parasites. In 1900 the leading causes of death were pneumonia, tuberculosis, diarrohea, cholera and related diseases. None of these are listed among the five leading causes of death in developed countries at the current time. Today, almost 70 per cent of all deaths are a result of heart disease, cancer, and strokes. By contrast, many of the causes of death are related to the so-called 'diseases of affluence' resulting from stress, fatty 'fast food' diets, alcohol consumption, smoking, and obesity. To illustrate these developments we may note the *Historical Statistics of the United States* (1983) which showed diseases of the heart and cancer malignancies as by far the major causes of death compared to 1900 where pneumonia, influenza, and tuberculosis were the predominant killers. The 'diseases of affluence', then, have become the new 'risks'.

Control over many causes of mortality particularly among the young largely explains why old age is linked to death. Fewer children die at birth, and accidents and disease now take a smaller toll among adults. Except during times of war or catastrophe, people came to view premature death as extraordinary. By 1995, 85 per cent of the population in Western societies died after the age of 55. Thus death and old age have become fused. Although most retired people can look forward to decades of life, growing old cannot now be separated from eventual physical decline and ultimate death. This is all in marked contrast to the past where, in 1900, some one-third of all deaths in Europe occurred before the age of 5, another third took place before the age of 55, and the remaining third died in what was then defined as old age.

The Social Significance of Death

Whatever the cause of death, how societies perceive and deal with the event varies as much as the way they construct other significant events of life. Hence, there are infinite variations by which death has been perceived and attributed meaning throughout human history and differs considerably between cultures even today. The cultural prism through which Western societies view death is in many respects quite unique and can be compared to developing countries where death is a familiarity and is, in short, a part of life. Where life-expectancy is low and infant mortality is high in most under-developing countries, death is a common aspect of daily existence especially where resources are scarce.

Throughout most of human history, confronting death has been commonplace. It was rarely assumed that a newborn child would necessarily live for very long, a fact that frequently led parents to delay naming a child until it had survived for a year or two. For those who lived through infancy, illness prompted by poor nutrition, accidents, and natural disasters such as drought or famine, combined to make life very uncertain. In times of great need, death was often deliberate, the result of a strategy to protect the community by sacrificing a group's less productive members, namely infanticide and geronticide. If death was routine, it was also readily accepted and this is historically evidenced by Medieval Christianity which assured the European populace that death fitted into the divine plan for the human race.

Irrespective of the degree of familiarity with death, its occurrence has a social relevance, although there are considerable cultural variations as to its significance. Halbwachs (1930), a student of Durkheim, was one of the first to study the social relevance of death and he stressed the fact that it must be comprehended and appraised within the environment of wider social relationships. This is certainly so in 'traditional' societies where the broader social context and extended kinship networks are important. To illustrate this point Halbwachs distinguished between 'physical death' and 'social death'. The former refers to the medical definition of death: simply, the human body ceases to biologically function. The latter, denotes the social consequence of death. The physical person may have gone, but the social significance remains. This is starkly seen in the example of Malay where death is a 'process' – a series of ceremonies marking the slow transition from the 'living world' to the after-life. Due to a very hot climate the deceased is buried as soon as possible. This represents the physical death. A few days later the body is exhumed and a funeral ceremony takes place in which friends and relatives say a final 'goodbye' to the dead. This constitutes social death.

In a sense, the deceased is still part of continuing social relations for an appreciable period of time. The dead are not easily forgotten since they were, and remain for a short while, an integral and significant element of the lives of those left behind, as well as probably once fulfilling various important social roles. Frequently this means that relatives and, in the case of small-scale pre-industrial societies entire communities, have to deal with psychological problems left in the wake of the death of a social member. This is why most cultures have elaborate funeral ceremonies and an accompanying period of mourning which symbolize the fact that society slowly withdraws from the dead over a time of transition until the memory of that person diminishes and the implications of the loss of an individual gradually recedes.

Western Perceptions of Death

According to Freud (1938), all societies have a subconscious fear of death. The corpse, in particular, is a thing of taboo: we have a dread of touching that which is in such an 'unclean' condition. Western society, however, appears to have a heightened aversion to death. In the midst of plenty in the consumer culture of late/postmodernity death is hidden and excluded from everyday experience. For a society preoccupied with health and human potential, death is a subject infrequently discussed. At the same time, however, there is what may be referred to as 'celluloid death'. In other words, death is often presented to a mass audience in popular fiction, magazines, the cinema, simulated computer games or, alternatively, the 'real' death seen in news clips. It is thus frequently 'invented' death or death in another part of the world that prevails as contemporary images and does not really touch us beyond media portrayals.

At the same time, in Western societies the death of the individual is also of less and less of social significance in the sense that Halbwachs understood: death is largely anonymous. Aries notes how once in Europe the dead were often buried together in unmarked graves. Later burial was in individual plots with information provided on the tombstone as to whom was buried there and the years in which they lived. These plots were in church graveyards with the church itself being an important part of social life. The need to indicate who was buried where was initiated to remind the living, whereas in the past it would have been common knowledge to the people of the village who were well aware of the generations that went before them (Aries 1973). This indicated the importance of wider kinship and social relationships, as well as the low level of geographical mobility. Today, the dead are generally disposed of by cremation. Their ashes are interned in the gardens of crematoriums which are frequently to be found on the outskirts of towns and cities – signifying that death is very much out of sight, out of mind.

Beginning with Barney Glasner and Anselm Strauss's seminal work, *Awareness of Dying* (1965), sociologists and psychologists have become increasingly interested in studying the process of death and dying in a contemporary setting. Death has been and remains a fearful and frightening event for most human beings. Glasner and Strauss suggested that when death occurs slowly, the dying patient is forced to cope with death by overcoming the apprehension of loss of self and the fear of death.

In modern industrial society, as Aries (1973) and others have shown, death is feared all the more because it makes life seem meaningless in a largely secular culture where beliefs in the after-life are on the decline.

Where anxiety of death is perhaps most in evident in the Western cultural setting, is in responses to the death of a child. In a culture where we have come to see longevity as our right, the death of a child is often viewed as unimaginable. For the most part, even more distant friends and associates, not to mention the parents and immediate relatives, are ill-prepared to express their own emotions. Embarrassment or fear of saying something inappropriate may mean people disassociating themselves from the death or distancing themselves from close relatives. The resulting isolation of the family may therefore add to the grief that is experienced.

The Medicalization of Death

In contemporary societies the process of dying has been removed from everyday experience and taken into specialized institutions (hospitals or nursing homes) to be supervised by professional personnel and managed by specialized technologies. Other institutions such as the hospice have long catered for the needs of the terminally ill and dying. In the hospital or similar institution the dying are isolated from the rest of society. This reverses the social processes evident in the past: society may retire from the individual before they die, rather than afterwards which is the pattern in pre-industrial societies. Thus older adults may approach the end of their own lives and that of their age peers with more fear and distress than the elderly in societies where people directly observe death and where dying is more readily discussed. There are, admittedly, alternatives to dying in hospital and programmes have been designed for the care of the terminally ill, but these are relatively recent innovations in today's society.

Since old age and death, as with birth, are increasingly within the context of the institutional setting, it is clear that the medical profession has now come to have an almost complete hegemony in overseeing the great milestones of life. Illich (1969), in his work *Medical Nemesis*, lamented this development, arguing that the nineteenth century saw a shift from death as the domain of the church, to the domain of medicine. The doctor took the place of the priest at the bedside, religion was usurped by science. Death, according to Illich, had also lost its 'human' dimension. We are no longer surrounded in our last days by the people we know and love. Perhaps we are obliged to take pain-killing drugs and have little idea what is happening to us. While medicine eases the process of death, it denies it as part of the human experience of life.

In the UK, 25 per cent of men are more likely to die in their own homes compared to women (19 per cent) and women are almost twice as likely to die in 'communal institutions', which includes nursing and residential homes. This is partly a product of the greater life-longevity of women. Unfortunately, there is little research into the experiences of dying in communal institutions, where the majority of women over 85 will see out their lives. However, among the observations made by Field et al. (1997) is that it is women's self-identity that is put at greater risk than men's once they become dependent upon the care of others within the institutional setting.

Western societies are increasingly death-defying. This defying aspect may not only include the application of medication in aiding us to live longer, but the development of 'spare part' surgery. Thus important moral questions, in some cases, are raised about extending life – perhaps unnecessarily. At the same time, medically speaking, we give a low priority to the elderly and the dying. This apparent contradiction is atleast partly evident in the debate surrounding euthanasia. At the moment euthanasia is illegal in the great majority of Western countries. Should it become legal, the processes would undoubtedly be overviewed by the medical profession. Such a development may still be a long way off. It is legal in Holland, a country with a very high level of medical care. Queensland, an Australian territory, legalized euthanasia for six months, but subsequently reversed the decision. Several states in the USA have presented (unsuccessful) challenges to constitutional law against euthanasia. Thus, the culture of choice is not, at present, extended to the voluntary ending of life or what is alternatively referred to as 'assisted suicide' – freely chosen by the individual.

Those who call for a legalization of euthanasia argue that it is a fundamental human right to die when one wishes to and to prevent human suffering and a condition of life which has little or no quality. This was exemplified by the case of Diane Pretty, a terminally ill woman in the UK who fought a legal challenge to establish a 'right' to assisted-suicide, but lost her appeal to the House of Lords in 2001. Her argument, and others like her, was that the experience of life was so unbearable under the weight of terminal illness that death would be a welcomed relief. The rhetoric surrounding such cases indicates that those who oppose to euthanasia do so on two broad grounds; moral and utilitarian. The moral view is largely taken by religious groups who believe that it is morally wrong to take life under any circumstances. These constituencies often refer to the 'right to life' and see euthanasia as an issue related to abortion – that the unborn as well as the elderly and disabled have a right to life. Others argue that voluntary euthanasia is the 'thin end of the wedge' and would eventually lead to compulsory euthanasia for those with terminal medical conditions or who could not be easily looked after. And, moreover, that 'official' euthanasia would become the norm under the power of the medical profession, thus further extending the medicalization of the life course.

Mourning and After-Life Beliefs

It has been briefly suggested above that Western perceptions of death have impacted upon both processes of mourning and after-life beliefs. Here, there is a noteworthy comparison with other cultures, especially in pre-industrial societies where funerals are of considerable importance. This final rite of passage in the life course amounts to a ceremony that has both a psychological and social function in providing a ritual which expresses solidarity and a set of beliefs about the next life. There may be religious significance and taboo status attached to this transition from one social status to another, from the living to the dead. It is perhaps death which constitutes the most profound 'life crisis' – generating an uncertainty and demanding significant psychological adjustment for those who are left to come to terms with it.

In the secular societies of the West, where a religious perception of the world is in demise, 'supernatural' explanations for the causes of death likewise decline. One of the consequences is that in a culture where a religious worldview has experienced demise, satisfactory answers as to why death occurs cannot always be provided at a meaningful level. At the same time, funerals and mourning, which often give expression to religious sentiment, are often inadequate, rushed events. Thus, Tony Walter (1994), paints a depressing picture of the way in which we deal with death in Western societies. Funerals are often brief, staid, unemotional affairs that leave little time for mourning. We are also unsure of our after-life beliefs. There has been, Walter suggests, an 'eclipse of eternity'. For that reason, the alternative funeral, like the alternative wedding is in vogue – often providing the meaning and significance woefully missing from the standard funeral and, more often than not, void of its religious trappings. Hence, the funeral, as with so much else in a culture of choice, is open to personal preferences and self-expression.

This is all in stark contrast to pre-industrial societies, many of which appear to deal more effectively with the psychological problems generated by death. Malinowski's (1954) work with the people of the Trobrian Islands showed that religion was particularly significant during certain times, in particular, situations of individual emotional stress that threat-ened collective solidarity and sentiment. For Malinowski, anxiety and tension tended to disrupt social life. Contexts which produced these emotions included crises such as birth, puberty, marriage, and death. He noticed that in all pre-industrial societies life crises are surrounded with religious ritual. Death was the most disruptive of these events since it severed strong personal attachments and thwarted people's future plans. This is why Malinowsky regarded the ability to deal with the problems associated with death as probably the main source of religious belief. Thus through funeral ceremonies belief in immortality can be expressed, in a sense denying the fact of death itself and thus comforting the bereaved. Indeed, bereavement signifies a particular type of discontinuity. Death means the cessation of someone's life and the end of the relationships that the deceased shared with others. Moreover, it brings a unique form of psychological challenge since death is final.

Individuals must deal with their grief and society must allow expressions of mourning. Yet, mourning is clearly expressed contrastingly in different cultural contexts. For instance, English people are not prone to wearing their emotions 'on their sleeves' and are expected to bear suffering with 'a stiff upper lip'. This emotional reserve leads to a unique way of dealing with grief, perhaps resulting from the desire not to break down in front of children. Much may be derived from a desire to protect the child from pain or the belief that the young are incapable of experiencing grief. Such reserve is not necessarily to be welcomed. However it is interpreted, according to Gorer (1965), the holding back of grief, the forbidding of its public manifestation, the obligation to suffer alone and secretly, have further aggravated the trauma stemming from the loss of a dear one.

It may now be possible to speak of a postmodern approach to mourning. In short, there is a culture of grief which accepts that containing emotion works for some people, while expressing feeling is relevant for others. This is an approach which refuses to judge whether forgetting or remembering the dead is the healthier. Rather ironically, suggests Walter, people do not know how to use their newfound freedom of expressing grief. There are all sorts of dilemmas. For instance, individuals may choose to grieve in private but it is not always clear to others that they know that this is the case (Walter 1999a, 141).

In much the same way as there are changing attitudes to mourning, after-life beliefs tell us something about recent cultural changes and shifting values in contemporary societies. *The European Values Survey* of 1981 and 1990 asked respondents whether they believed in life after death, and found those answering 'yes' constituted around 40 per cent of the sample: this figure changing little over the decades. However, surveys also contained more specific questions about what the after-life was supposed to actually entail. For example, it showed that whereas belief in heaven remained fairly buoyant (at around 30–50 per cent), belief in hell had definitely gone out of fashion (at around 15–25 per cent).

The European Values Survey (EVS) data indicated that those who believe in an after-life tend to be religious according to other measurements.

This is almost certainly the biggest single reason why the USA and Europe are so far out of line with each other on after-life beliefs: Europe is, by and large, a much more secular continent than North America. The other factor very clearly associated with after-life belief is gender: up to twice as many women as men say they believe in some kind of after-life (Davies 1997).

Belief in an after-life may, possibly, also be related to stages in the life course. In the 1970s, Witzel (1975) conducted research in which he found far higher levels of belief in an after-life among those on their deathbeds than a control group of seriously but not fatally ill patients. In so far as older people typically have higher levels of belief in a life after death, it is not clear whether this is because they have lived longer and are nearer death, or because they were brought up in a more religious era.

Douglas Davies (1997) has identified five options of a possible after-life which respondents find fairly easy to choose between. In his study of 1603 individuals he found the following distribution of beliefs: That nothing happens, we come to the end of life (29 per cent); our soul passes on to another world (43 per cent); our bodies await a resurrection (8 per cent); we come back as something or someone else (12 per cent); trust in God, all is in his hands (22 per cent).

In Davies' survey 12 per cent of respondents appeared to believe in rein-carnation, a belief traditionally alien to Western culture. Other research has put such belief as high as 20 per cent when respondents answered 'yes' to the question 'Do you believe in reincarnation?'. In this case the pollsters presented those asked with the option of replying 'yes', 'no', or 'don't know' (Gallop and Proctor 1982, 137–8). Walter and Waterhouse (1998) found in their survey that those in the UK who answered the question 'yes' to whether they believe in reincarnation far outnumber those who belong to such religions as Hinduism, Sikhism, and Buddhism which formally teach reincarnation or rebirth. Reincarnation therefore is not in most Western societies part of a well-established and communally held folk-religion. This means that belief in reincarnation is not something that has been formally codified by the respondent's own culture and religion. The ideas are scarcely developed and rarely seem to originate clearly in any world religion. Walter and Waterhouse also argue that after-life beliefs are becoming semi-detached from other religious beliefs and almost entirely detached from morality, hence there is no overriding fear of hell in retribu-tion for actions in this life.

Walter maintains that despite secularization, belief in an after-life remains buoyant. But for many people this belief is a tentative one, and the content of the after-life remains vague. For a fair number of young adults, it may be the case that they are refusing to rule out an after-life, though they would not go so far as to say they positively believe one actually exists. It is a generation which finds itself in the culture of relativism that is associated with postmodernity, one which does not trust religion but also no longer has faith in science and thus keeps an open mind on life after death (Walter 1999b).

Summary

This chapter has explored various themes related to ageing and old age. It has described demographic patterns of ageing in Western societies, noting that life-expectancy is increasing and that the proportion of the aged is growing significantly. There has not been the scope, however, to explore the fact that the ageing of human society on a global basis is rapidly becoming one of the most distinctive features of the contemporary world. The fact that older people will exist in greater numbers than ever before means not only significant changes in the age composition of many societies, but a corresponding changing in values, attitudes, and perceptions, as well as social policies affecting them.

The picture drawn of old age has been a mixed one. It is one associated with decline but, at the same time increasingly seen as a period of fresh opportunities. Today's elderly have attained higher levels of education and economic position, are larger in number than in the past, and therefore are becoming a major social and political force. It is also true that in terms of everyday experience, interaction with elderly people will become more and more commonplace in coming decades and this familiarity may feasibly lessen discrimination and make others aware of what the future has in store for them.

It may well be that as the proportion of women and men in old age increases, we can expect the culture of late/postmodernity to become more comfortable with the reality of death. In recent years people have discernibly discussed death more openly and the trend is to see dying as preferable to painful and prolonged suffering. There still remains another factor linked to the fear of ageing however. This is the decline in the belief of an after-life which reinforces the difficulty in coming to terms with our own morality and inevitable death. As Cole notes, to negotiate the later stage of life 'successfully' is to fail to deliberately accommodate death and dying as anything other than sudden and painless death. This may, he suggests, lead to a kind of transcendent, yet world-accommodating form of spirituality that will reflect our beliefs about old age and death (Cole 1993, 239). Thus the fear of death remains but spiritualities surrounding death, as well as after-life beliefs, may be transformed, signifying the ambiguities and uncertainties of the emergent culture. How we approach death, then, as the close of life, displays many of the changes and continuities evident throughout the contemporary life course at the beginning of the twenty-first century.

Further Reading

Arber,S. and Ginn,J. (eds) (1995) *Connecting Gender and Ageing: A Sociological Approach*, Buckingham: Open University Press.

Blakemore,K. and Boneham,M. (1993) *Age, Race and Ethnicity. A Comparative Approach*, Buckingham: Open University Press.

Counts,D.A. and Counts,D.R. (1996) *Over the Next Hill?*, Peterborough, ONT: Broadview Press.

Hearn,J. (1995) 'Imaging the Aging of Men', in M.Featherstone and M.Wernick (eds), *Images of Age*, New York: Routledge.

Walter,T. (1994) *The Revival of Death*, London: Routledge.

Glossary of Terms

Age Cohort: A constituency of people who simultaneously reached their formative years during a distinct historical period.

Ageing: A process which has natural, environmental, and social elements.

Ageism: Discrimination against a person or persons on the grounds of their age.

Age-Set: Those who have passed through the 'stages' of the life course at the same time.

Biological Life-Cycle: The linear development of natural human processes, especially those related to ageing and reproduction.

'Classical' Sociology: The sociological tradition that largely accounted and described the emergence of modernity. Much of such work has been inspired by the work of Emile Durkheim, Karl Marx, and Max Weber.

Capitalism: That economic system identified by mass machine production, waged labour, a 'free' market and increasing monopoly of the ownership and control of the means of production.

Commodification: The process by which an object will be subject to consumerism and allotted a money value.

Discontinuities: Interruption or displacement during a 'stage' or phase of the life course due to such factors as economic fluctuation, lack of opportunity, or injury.

Ethnicity: A term denoting the traditions, values and other distinguishing features of the culture of a community based on nationality, regionalism, or 'race'.

Enculturated: Natural and biological processes which are subject to cultural perceptions.

Engendered: A reference to institutions and processes that are impacted by the social construct of gender differences.

Feminism: The political movement advancing the cause and interest of women, as applied to an understanding of the social world.

Folk Devils: A term denoting the popularized view of certain communities as belligerent 'outsiders'.

Fordism, post-: A flexible, non-standard form of economic production that is particularly aimed at niche-marketing and consumer choice.

Globalization: Those cultural and economic processes which may impact in different parts of the world, irrespective of their local origin.

Infantization: The perception of the elderly as inevitably returning to a child-like state, perhaps bringing about a self-fulfilling prophecy.

Institutionalization: The negative effects of institutions mostly given over to the care and welfare of a sizeable number of people.

Late-Modernity: A more advanced stage of modernity characterized by globalization, sophisticated technology, science and rationalism, individualism, political rights, strategies of self-actualization, reflexivity, and consumption.

215

Life Course: The social element of a life span which may have fairly clear 'stages' of life and regulation, but may also be marked by variety and discontinuity.

Life-Cycle: A deterministic model of the life-span that follows biological 'stages' of human development, along with regulated and predictable social processes.

Lifestyle: A mode of living reflecting culture, values, status, income reward, and commodity choice.

Life-Span: The expected life longevity of human beings as determined by natural, environmental, and social processes.

Marginalization: Processes related to the social exclusion of individuals or social groups.

McDonaldization: A term denoting the monopoly, standardization, and globalization of a product, culture, or institutional arrangement.

Medicalization: The increasing dominance of the medical profession in various areas of social life, a dominance reflecting the interests of a professional group.

Modernity: A term denoting social arrangements characterized by plurality, industrialization, differentiation, achieved status, secularity, and frequently the dominance of capitalism.

Moral Panics: An amplified fear that cherished social values are under threat by 'outsiders'. Amplification is accentuated by media sensationalism.

Patriarchy: Expressions of the male-dominated society.

Post-Industrial: Denoting a social and economic order largely based on service and finance rather than employment in industry, alongside a consumer economy.

Postmodernity: A disputed term given to denote an economic and cultural order that has supplanted the key aspects of modernity or mark an accentuation of a number of its characteristic trends.

Race: The term commonly used to differentiate between people on the grounds of skin colour or other physical attributes.

Reflexive: The capacity of human beings to reflect upon their actions, be aware of self-identity, and subsequently determine future action.

Risk Society: A social order that is identified by a high degree of unpredictability and far-reaching global processes.

Rite of Passage: Ceremonies marking the transfer of individuals or age-set from one stage of life to another.

Self: The individual's conscious appraisal of his/her social worth, status and identity – often forged by how others see them.

Self-fulfilling Prophecy: Behaviour as influenced by the internalization of how other people negatively perceive the value and status of an individual.

Social Constructionism: The process by which society comes to shape and perceive the 'nature' of individuals, communities, or natural phenomenon.

Stereotypes: The generalization of the perceived (largely negative) attributes of individuals or groups.

'Traditional' society: A generic term used to denote pre-industrial societies ranging from tribal to settled agricultural communities identified by slow change, simple economic production, and political under-development.

Youth: That stage of the life course conventionally seen as a stage between childhood and adulthood, one created in modernity through consumerism and educational developments.

References

Abrams,M. (1959) *The Teenage Consumer*, London: Routledge & Kegan Paul.
Albee,G. (1982) 'The Politics of Nature and Nurture', *American Journal of Community Psychology*, 10: 1–36.
Alexander,C. (2000) *The Asian Gang: Ethnicity, Identity, Masculinity*, Oxford: Berg.
Allat,P. Keil,T. et al. (eds) (1987) *Women and the Life Cycle: Transitions and Turning Points. Explorations in Sociology*, Basingstoke: MacMillan.
Arai,S. and Pedlar,A. (2003) 'Moving Beyond Individualism in Leisure Theory: A Critical Analysis of Concepts of Community and Social Engagement', *Leisure Studies*, 22 (July): 185–202.
Arber,S. and Ginn,J. (eds) (1995) *Connecting Gender and Ageing: A Sociological Approach*, Buckingham: Open University Press.
Aries,P. (1965) *Centuries of Childhood*, London: Cape.
Aries,P. (1973) *Western Attitudes Towards Death: From the Middle Ages to the Present*, Baltimore, MD: John Hopkins Press.
Ashton,D. and Field,D. (1976) *Young Workers*, London: Routledge & Kegan Paul.
Assiter,A. (1996) 'Enlightened Women: Modernist Feminism in a Postmodern Age', London: Routledge.
Atchley,R. (1988) *The Sociology of Retirement*, Cambridge, MA: Shenkman.
Atkinson,J. (1985) 'The Changing Corporation', in D.Clutterbuck (ed.), *New Patterns of Work*, Aldershot: Gower.
Attias-Donfurt,C. and Arber,S. (2000) 'Equity and Solidarity Across the Generations', in C.Attias-Donfurt and S.Arber (eds), *The Myth of Generational Conflict*, London: Routledge.
Ball,S., Bowe,R., and Gerwitz,S. (1994) 'Market Forces and Parental Choice', in S.Tomlinson (ed.), *Educational Reform and Its Consequences*, London: IPPR/Rivers Omran Press.
Banks,F., Daugherty,R., and Wiliams,M. (1992) *Continuing the Education Debate*, London: Cassell.
Baos,G. (1996) *The Cult of Childhood*, London: Warburg Institute.
Barash,D. (1983) *Aging: An Exploration*, Seattle,WA: University of Washington Press.
Baudrillard,J. (1983) *Selected Writings*, Cambridge: Cambridge Polity Press.
Bauman,Z. (1992) 'Is There a Postmodern Sociology?', *Theory and Society*, 2–3.
Beck,U. (1992) *Risk Society: Towards a New Modernity*, London: Sage.
Beechy,V. (1983) 'Women in Production', in A.Kuhn and A.Wolpse (eds) *Feminism and Materialism*, London: Routledge & Kegan Paul.
Beidelman, T. (1966) 'The Ox and Nuer Sacrifice', *Man*, Series 1 (4): 453–67.
Benjamin,B. and Wallis,C. (1963) 'The Mortality of Widowers', *The Lancet*, 2: 454–6.
Bernard,M., Phillips,J., Phillipson,C., and Ogg,J. (1995) 'Family and Community Life of Older People', in S.Arber and J.Attias-Donfurt (eds) *Connecting Gender and Ageing: A Sociological Approach*, Buckingham: University Press.
Bernstein,B. (1961) 'A Socio-Linguistic Development: A Theory of Social Learning', in Halsey et al. (eds), *Education, Economy and Society*, New York: The Free Press.
Bernstein,B. (1975) 'On the Classification and Framing of Education Knowledge', *Class Codes and Control*, vol. 13, London: Routledge & Kegan Paul.
Besbrode,E. (2001) *Sunday Telegraph*, 4/3.
Blakemore,K. and Boneham,M. (1993) *Age, Race and Ethnicity. A Comparative Approach*, Buckingham: Open University Press.
Blankenhorn,K. (1995) *Fatherless America*, Seattle, WA: University of Washington Press.
Blakie,A. (1999) *Ageing and Popular Culture*, Cambridge: Cambridge University Press.

Boulton,M. (1983) *On Being a Mother,* London: Tavistock.

Bowlby,J. (1961) *Child Care and the Growth of Love,* Harmondsworth: Penguin.

Bradley,H. (1996) *Fractured Identities: Changing Patterns of Inequality,* Cambridge: Polity.

Branem,J. and Nilsen,A. (2002) 'Young People's Time Perspectives. From Youth to Adulthood', *Sociology,* 36 (3): 513–57.

Bryman, A. (1995) *Disney and His Worlds,* London: Routledge.

Busfield,J. and Paddon,M. (1977) *Thinking About Children: Sociology and Fertility in Post-War England,* Cambridge: Cambridge University Press.

Cancian,F. (1987) *Love in America: Gender and Self-Development,* Cambridge: Cambridge University Press.

Cashmore, E. (1985) 'Rewriting the Script', *New Society,* 4 December: 7–8.

Castells,M. (1989) *The Information City,* Oxford: Blackwell.

Chester,R. (1985) 'The Rise of the Neo-Conventional Family', *New Society,* 9 (May): 14–17.

Clark,J. and Critcher,C. (1985) *The Devil Makes Work: Leisure in Contemporary Britain,* London: MacMillan.

Cohen,P. (1986) 'Subcultural Conflict and Working Class Community', in S.Hall et al. (eds), *Culture, Media, Logica,* London: Hutchinson.

Cohen,S. (1971) *Images of Deviance,* Harmonds worth: Penguin.

Cole,T. (1993) *Jouney of Life: A Cultural History of Aging in America,* Cambridge: Cambridge University Press.

Cote,E. and Allahar,A. (1996) *Generation on Hold: Coming of Age in the Late Twentieth Century,* New York: New York University Press.

Counts,D.A. and Counts,D.R. (1996) *Over the Next Hill?,* Peterborough, ONT: Broadview Press.

Cowgill,D. and Holmes,L. (ed.) (1972) *Ageing and Modernization,* New York: Appleton-Century-Crofts.

Crawford,D., Jackson,E. and Gpdbey,G. (1991) 'A Hierarchical Model of Leisure Constraints', *Leisure Sciences,* 13: 309–19.

Crompton,R. (ed.) (1999) *Restructuring Gender,* Oxford: Oxford University Press.

Crooks, S., Pakulski,J., and Waters,M. (1992) *Postmodernization,* London: Sage.

Cumming,E. and Henry,W. (1961) *Growing Old: The Process of Disengagement,* New York: Basic Books.

Daly,J. (1997) 'Facing Change', in Komesaroff,P. et al. (eds), *Reinterpreting Menopause: Cultural and Philosophical Issues,* London: Routledge.

Davies,D. (1997) 'Contemporary Belief in Life After Death', in P.Jupp and T.Rogers (eds), *Interpreting Death: Christian Theology and Pastoral Practice,* London: Cassell.

Deem,R. (ed.) (1980) *Schooling for Women's Work,* London: Routledge.

Delcroix,C. (2000) 'The Transmission of Life Stories from Ethnic Minority Fathers to Their Children', in S. Arber and J. Ginn (eds) (1995) *Connecting Gender and Ageing: A Sociological Approach,* Buckingham: Open University Press.

Dennis,N. and Erdos, G. (1993) *Families without Fatherhood,* London: Institute of Economic Affairs.

Dobash,S. and Dobash,S. (1980) *Violence Against Wives,* London: Open Books.

Douglas,J. (1964) *The Home and the School,* London: MacGibbon & Kee.

Douglas,M. (1966) *Purity and Danger,* London: Routledge.

Du Bois-Reymond,M. (1998) ' "I Don't Want to Commit Myself Yet": Young People's Life Concepts', *Journal of Youth Studies,* 1 (1): 63–79.

Duelli-Klein,R. (1989) *Infertility: Women Speak Out About Their Experiences of Reproductive Medicine,* London: Pandora.

Durkheim,E. (1970) *Suicide,* London: Routledge & Kegan Paul.

Eisenstadt,S. (1956) *From Generation to Generation,* Basingstoke: Collier-Macmillan.

Ekerdt,D. (1986) 'The Busy Ethic: Moral Continuity Between Work and Retirement', *Gerontologist,* 26: 239–44.

Epstein,S. (2003) 'Sexualizing Governance and Medicalizing Identities', *Sexualities,* 6 (2): 131–71.

Erikson,E. (1959) *Identity and the Life-Cycle*, London: Norton

Evans,M. (2003) *Love: An UnRomantic Discussion*, Oxford: Blackwell.

Eyde,D. and Lintner,V. (eds) (1996) *Contemporary Europe*, Hemel Hempstead: Prentice Hall.

Fagin,L. and Little,M. (1984) *The Forsaken Families*, Harmondsworth: Penguin.

Featherstone,M. (1982) 'The Body in Consumer Culture', *Theory, Culture and Society*, 1: 18–33.

Featherstone,M. (1991) *Consumer Culture and Postmodernism*, London: Sage.

Featherstone,M. and Hepworth,M. (1991) 'The Mask of Ageing and the Postmodern Life Course', in M.Featherstone, M.Hepworth, and B.Turner (eds) *The Body Process and Cultural Theory*, London: Sage.

Featherstone,M. and Wernick,M. (1995) (eds) *Images of Ageing*, London: Routledge.

Field,D., Hockey,J., and Small,N. (1997) *Death, Gender and Ethnicity*, London: Routlege

Follette, La, M. (1996) *A Guide to Family Law*, London: Butterworth.

Friedan,B. (1993) *The Foundation of Age*, New York: Simon & Schuster.

Freud,S. (1938) *Totem and Taboo*, Harmondsworth: Penguin.

Funken,K. and Cooper,P. (eds) (1995) *Old and New Poverty: The Challenge for Reform*, Buckinghamshire: Open University Press.

Furlong,A. and Cartmel.F. (1997) 'Capitalism Without Classes', in A.Giddens (ed.) *Sociology. Introductory Readings*, Cambridge: Polity.

Gallop,G. and Proctor,W. (1982) *Adventures in Immortality*, New York: McGraw Hill.

Gamoran,A. (1992) 'The Variable Effects of High-School Tracking', *American Sociological Review*, 57 (6): 812–28.

Gannon,L. (1996) *Women and Ageing: Transcending the Myths*, London: Routledge.

Gennep,A. Van (1908) *Les Rites of Passage*, London: Routledge.

Ghail,M. (1995) *The Making of Men: Masculinities, Sexualities and Schooling*, Buckingham: Open University Press.

Giddens,A. (1991) *Self-Identity. Self and Society in the Late Modern Age*, Cambridge: Polity.

Giddens,A. (1992) *The Transformation of Intimacy, Sexuality, Love and Eroticism*, Cambridge: Cambridge University Press.

Gielle,J. (1988) 'Gender and Sex Roles' in N.Smelser (ed.), *The Handbook of Sociology*, Newbury Park, CA: Sage.

Gielle,J. and Elder,G. (1998) *Methods of Life Course Research: Qualitative and Quantitive Approaches*, Thousand Island, CA: Sage.

Giroux,H. (1997) *Channel Surfing. Race Talk and the Destruction of Today's Youth*, Basingstoke: Macmillan.

Glanser,B. and Strauss,A. (1965) *Awareness of Dying*, Chicago: Aldine.

Glendinning,F. and Millar,J. (eds) (1987) *Women and Poverty in Britain*, Brighton: Wheatsheaf.

Gluckman,M. (1963) *Essays in the Ritual of Social Relations*, Manchester: Manchester University Press.

Goetting,A. (1981) 'Divorce Outcome Research', *Journal of Family Issues*, 2 (3): 350–78.

Goffman,E. (1967) *The Presentation and Self in Everyday Life*, Harmondsworth: Penguin.

Goldberg,S. and Lewis,M. (1972) 'Play Behaviour in the Infant: Early Sex Differences', in J.Bardwick (ed.), *Readings on the Psychology of Women*, New York: Harper & Row.

Goode,W. (1961) 'Family Disorganisation', in R.Merton and R.Nesbit (ed.), *Contemporary Social Problems*, New York: Harcourt Brace.

Goode,W. (1982) *The Family*, Englewood Cliffs, NJ: Prentice-Hall.

Gorer,G. (1965) *Death, Grief, and Mourning in Contemporary Britain*, London: Cresset.

Green,E., Hebron,S., and Woodward,D. (1990) *Women's Leisure. What Leisure?*, London: Macmillan.

Griffin,C. (1985a) 'Turning the Tables: Feminist Analysis of Youth Unemployment', *Youth and Policy*, 14: 6–11.

Griffin,C. (1985b) 'Adolescent Girls: Transition from Girlfriends to Boyfriends?', in C. Griffin (ed.), *'Typical Girls'. Young Women From School to the Job Market*, London: Routledge & Kegan Paul.

Gwartney-Gibbs,P., Stockard,J., and Bohmer,S. (1987) 'Learning Courtship Aggression: The Influence of Parents, Peers and Personal Experiences', *Family Relations*, 36 (3): 276–82.

Haggard, L. and Williams,D. (1991) *Self-Identity Benefits of Leisure Activities'*, in B.Driver et al. (eds), *Benefits of Leisure*, Stage College, PA: Venturer Publishing.

Halbwachs,F. (1930) *Les Causes de Suicide*, Paris: Alcan.

Hall,G. (1920) *Senescence: The Last Half of Life*, New York: Appleton.

Hall,S. and Jefferson,T. (1975) *Resistance Through Rituals: Youth Subcultures in Post-War Britain*, London: Hutchinson.

Hamel,R. (1990) 'Raging Against Aging', *American Demographics*, 12 (3): 42–5.

Hayman, S. (2001) *Moving On: Breaking Up Without Breaking Down*, New York: Vermillion.

Hearn,J. (1995) 'Imaging the Aging of Men', in M.Featherstone and M.Wernick (eds), *Images of Age*, New York: Routledge.

Heidensohn,F. (1985) *Women and Crime*, London: Macmillan.

Henwood,F. and Miles,I. (1987) 'Unemployment and the Sexual Division of Labour', in D. Fryer and P.Ullah (eds), *Unemployed People*, Buckingham: Open University Press.

Hetherongton,M. (1991) 'Coping with Family Transitions: Winners, Losers and Survivors', in M.Woodhead, P.Light, and R.Carr, (eds), *Growing Up in a Changing Society*, London: Routledge.

Hey,V. (1997) 'Even Sociologists Fall in Love: An Exploration in the Sociology of Emotions', *Sociology*, 27 (2): 37–53.

Hill, J. (1977) *The Social and Psychological Impact of Unemployment*, London: Tavistock.

Hislop, J. and Arber, S. (2003) 'Sleepers Wake! The Gendered Nature of Sleep Disruption Among Mid-life Women', *Sociology*, 37 (4): 695–711.

Hockey,J. and James,A. (1993) *Growing Up and Growing Old. Ageing and Dependency in the Life Course*, London: Sage.

Holmstrom,D. (1994) 'Abuse of Elderly, Even by Adult Children, Gets More Attention and Official Concern', *Christian Science Monitor*, 28 (July): 1.

Holloway,S. and Valentine,G. (2000) 'Spatiality and the New Social Studies of Childhood, *Sociology*, 34 (4): 763–83.

Hwang, C. (1989) 'The Changing Role of Swedish Fathers', in M.Lamb (ed.), *The Father's Role: Cross-Cultural Perspectives*, Hillsdale, NJ: Erlbaum.

Illich,I. (1969) *Medical Nemesis*, London: Calder & Boyars.

Jackson,R. and Nesbitt,E. (1993) *Hindu Children in Britain*, Stoke-on-Trent: Trentham Books.

Jagger,E. (2001) 'Marketing Molly and Melville: Dating in a Postmodern, Consumer Society', *Sociology*, 35 (1): 39–57.

Jenks,C. (1996) *Childhood*, London: Routledge.

Jones,T. (1993) *Britain's Ethnic Minorities*, London: Policy Studies Institute.

Kalish,R. (1979) 'The New Ageism and the Failure Models: A Polemic', *The Gerontologist*, 19 (4), August: 398–402.

Karp,D. and Yoel,C. (1982) *Experiencing the Life Cycle. A Social Psychology of Ageing*, Springfield, IL: Charles C. Thomas.

Kastenbaum,R. (1971) 'Age: Getting There', *Psychology Today*, 5: 53–4, 82–3.

Katz,S. (1995) 'Imagining the Life-Span. From Pre-modern Miracles to Post-Modern Fantasies', in M.Featherstone and A.Wernick (eds), *Images of Ageing: Cultural Representations of Later Life*, New York: Routledge.

Kaufman,S. (1978) *The Ageless Self*, Madison, WI: University of Wisconsin Press.

Kindon,D. (2001) *Too Much of a Good Thing*, Harvard, MA: Harvard University Press.

Kohli,M. (1988) 'The World We Forgot: A Historical View of the Life Course', in V.Marshal (ed.), *Later Life: The Social Psychology of Ageing*, London: Sage.

Kohn,M. and Schooler,C. (1982) 'Job Conditions and Personality', *American Journal of Sociology*, 87 (6): 1275–83.

Komesaroff,A. Rothfield,P., and Daly,J. (1997) (eds), *Reinterpreting Menopause: Cultural and Philosophical Issues*, London: Routledge.

Kuhn,M. (1960) 'Self Attitudes by Age, Sex, and Professional Training', *Sociological Quarterly*, 1: 39–65.

Laing,R. (1976) *The Politics of the Family*, Harmondsworth: Penguin.

Lamb,M. (1987) (ed.) 'Introduction', *The Father's Role: Cross-Cultural Perspectives*, Hillsdale, NJ: Erlbaum.

Lambley,P. (1995) *The Middle-Aged Rebel: Responding to the Challenges of Midlife*, New York: Element Books.

Laslett,P. (1987) 'The Emergence of the Third Age', *Ageing and Society*, 7: 113–60.

Laslett,P. (1994) *Fresh Map of Life: Emergence of the Third Age*, Basingstoke: Macmillan.

Latouche (1996)

Laurance,J. (1986) 'Unemployment: Health Hazards', *New Society*, 21st March: 23–6.

Lees,S. (1986) *Losing Out: Sexuality and Adolescent Girls in London*, London: Hutchinson.

Lees,S. (1993) *Sugar and Spice: Sexuality and Adolescent Girls*, London: Penguin.

Leonard,D. (1980) *Sex and Generation: A Study of Courtship and Weddings*, London: Tavistock.

Levinson,D., Darrow.C, Klein,C.,Levinson,M., and Braxton,B. (1978) *The Seasons of a Man's Life*, New York: Alfred A.Knopf.

Lewontin,R.(1992) *Biology as Ideology: The Doctrine of DNA*, New York: Harper.

Lund,D. (1989) 'Conclusions About Bereavement in Later Life and Implications for Interventions and Future Research', in D.Lund (ed.), *Older Bereaved Spouses: Research With Practical Implications*, London: Taylor-Francis-Hemisphere.

Lynott,P. and Logue,P. (1993) 'The "Hurried Child": The Myth of the Lost Childhood on Contemporary American Society', *Sociological Forum*, 8 (3): 471–91.

Lyon,D. (2000) *Jesus in Disneyland: Religion in Postmodern Times*, London: Polity.

Lyotard,J. (1984) *The Postmodern Condition: A Report*, Minneapolis, MN: Minnesota University Press.,

Macionis,J. and Plummer,K. (1997) *Sociology: A Global Introduction*, London: Prentice Hall.

Malinowski,B. (1954) *Magic, Science and Religion*, London: Souvenir Press.

Martens.L. (2000) *Exclusion and Inclusion: The Gender Composition of British and Dutch Work Forces*, Aldershot: Avebury.

Marshall,B. (2002) ' "Hard Science": Gendered Constructions of Sexual Dysfunction in the "Viagra Age" ', *Sexualities*, 5 (2): 131–58.

Mauss, De,L. (ed.) (1976) *The History of Childhood*, London: Souvenir Press.

Mayall,B. (2002) *Towards a Sociology for Childhood*, Oxford: Oxford University Press.

McRobbie,A. (1978a) *Jackie, an Ideology of Adolescent Femininity*, Birmingham University: Centre for Contemporary Cultural Studies.

McRobbie,A. and Garber,J. (1976) 'Girls and Subcultures', in S.Hall and T.Jefferson (eds), *Resistance Through Rituals*, London: Hutchinson.

Mead,H. (1931) *Mind, Self and Society*, Berekley, CA: University of California Press.

Mead,M. (1928) *The Coming of Age in Samoa*, New York: Morrow.

Merton,R. (1969) *Social Theory and Structure*, New York: Free Press.

Mills,C.W. (1951) *White Collar: The American Middle-Classes*, New York: Open University Press.

Mills,R. (2000) 'Perspectives of Childhood' in J.Mills and R.Mills (eds), *Childhood Studies: A Reader in Perspectives of Childhood*, Routledge: London

Mooney, J. (1994) *The Hidden Figures: Domestic Violence in North London*, Middlesex: Middlesex University.

Morgan,D. (1986) 'Gender', in R.Burgess (ed.), *Social Theory and the Family*, London: Routledge & Keegan Paul.

Nauright,J. & Chandler,T. (1997) *Making Men: Rugby and Masculine Identity*, London: Frank Cass.

Neugarten,B. (1965) *Norms, Age Constraints, and Adult Socialization*, Glenview,IL: Scott: Foreman.

Neugarten,B. (1971) 'Grow Older With Me. The Best is Yet to Be', *Psychology Today*, 5 (2): 45–8.

Newgarten,B. (1973) 'Personality and Aging' in J.Birren and K.Warner Schael (eds), Handbook of the Psychology of Aging, New York: Uan Nostrand Reinhold.

Oakley,A. (1980) *Women Confined: Towards a Sociology of Childbirth*, London: Robertson.

Pahl,R. (1984) *Divisions of Labour*, Oxford: Blackwell.

Palmore,E. (1979) 'Predictors of Successful Ageing', *The Gerontologist*, 19 (5), October: 427–31.

Parker,S. (1973) *The Future of Work and Leisure*, London: Longman.

Parsons,T. (1959) 'The Social Structure of the Family', in R.Anshen (ed.), *The Family: Its Function and Destiny*, New York: Harper & Row.

Phoenix,A. (1991) *Motherhood, Meanings, Practices and Ideologies*, London: Sage Publications.

Pilcher, J. (1995) *Age and Generation in Modern Britain,* Oxford: Oxford University Press.

Polhemus,T. (ed.) (1978) *Social Aspects of the Human Body,* Harmondsworth: Penguin.

Pollert, A. (1988) 'Dismantling Flexibility', *Capital and Class,* 34: 23–44.

Pollock,L. (1983) *Forgotten Children: Parent–Child Relationships from 1950 to 1900,* Cambridge: Cambridge University Press.

Popenoe,D. (1988) *Disturbing the Nest: Family Change and Decline in Modern Societies,* New York: Aldine.

Postman,N. (1982) *The Disappearance of Childhood,* London: New York: Aldine

Preston,C. (1996) 'Subjectively Perceived Agedness and Retirement', *Journal of Gerontology,* 23: 201–4.

Preston,C. and Gudiken,K. (1996) 'A Measure of Self-Perception Among Older People', *Journal of Gerontology,* 212: 63–7.

Pryce,J. (1979) *Endless Pressure,* Harmondsworth: Penguin.

Punch,S. (1993) Children in the Majority World: Miniture Adults or Tribal Children?, *Sociology,* 37(2): 227–95.

Radcliffe-Brown,A. Religion and Society', in *idem, Structure and Function in Primitive Society* (1952), London: Cohen & West.

Rapoport,R. and Rapoport,R. (1975) *Leisure and the Life-Cycle,* London: Routledge.

Reay,D., Davies,J., David,M., and Ball,S. (2001) 'Choices of Degree or Degrees of Choice? Class "Race" and the Higher Education of Choice Process', *Sociology,* 35 (4): 855–74.

Redhead,S. (1993) *Subcultures to Clubcultures: An Introduction to Popular Cultural Studies,* Oxford: Blackwell.

Rex,J. (1970) *Race Relations in Sociological Theory,* London: Widenfeld & Nicolson.

Rex,J. and Thomlinson,S. (1979) *Colonial Immigration in a British City,* London: Routledge & Kegan Paul.

Richardson,D. (1993) *Women, Mothering and Childrearing,* London: McMillan.

Ritzer,G. (1983) *The McDonaldization of Society,* Thousand Oaks, CA: Pine Forge Press.

Roberts,K.(1978) *Contemporary Society and the Growth of Leisure,* New York: Longman.

Roberts,K. (1993) 'Career Trajectories and the Mirage of Increased Social Mobility', in I.Bates and G.Riseborough (eds), *Youth and Inequality,* Buckingham: Open University Press.

Roberts,K., Noble,M., and Duggan,J. (1989) *Youth Unemployment: An Old Problem or a New Life-style, Employment and Unemployment?,* Milton Keynes: Open University Press.

Rosenfeld,A. (1985) 'Stretching the Span', *Wilson Quarterly,* 9: 96–107.

Rosow,I. (1974) *Socialization of the Aged,* New York: Free Press.

Rousseau,J. (1991) *Emile Or On Education,* London: Penguin.

Rowland,R. (1993) *Living Laboratories: Women and Reproductive Technologies,* Indiana: Indiana University Press.

Rubery,J., Smith,M. & Fagan,C. (1999) *Women's Employment in Europe: Trends and Prospects,* London: Routledge.

Rubin,L. (1976) *Worlds of Pain: Life in the Working-Class Family,* New York: Basic Books.

Rudman,D., Feller,A., and Hoskote,S. et al. (1990) 'Effects of Human Growth Hormone in Men Over 60 Years Old.' *New England Journal of Medicine,* 323: 1–6.

Rutter,M. (1979) 'Maternal Deprivation 1972–78: New Findings, New Concepts, New Approaches', *Annals, Academy of Medicine,* 8 (3): 312–23.

Sawchuch,A. (1995) 'From Gloom to Boom', in M.Featherstone and M.Wernick (ed.), *Images of Ageing,* London: Routledge, pp. 173–87.

Scott,J. (1996) *Poverty and Wealth,* London: Longman.

Seider, S. (1989) *Rediscovering Masculinity,* London: Routledge.

Selwyn,J. (2000) 'Infancy', in M.Boushel, M.Fawcett and J.Selwyn (eds), *Childhood: Principles and Reality,* Oxford: Blackwell.

Shanir,B. (1992) 'Commitment and Leisure, *Sociological Perspective,* 31: 238–58.

Sharpe,S.(1994) 'Great Expectations', *Everywoman,* December.

Shorter (1985) *The Making of the Modern Family,* New York: Fonturer Collins.

Sinfield,R. (1981) *What Unemployment Means,* London: Martin Robertson.

Skellington.R. & Morris,P. (1996) *'Race' in Britain Today,* London: Sage.

Smart,C. and Neale,B. (2001) 'Constructing Post-Divorce Childhoods' in A.Giddens (ed.), *Sociology. Introductory Readings,* Cambridge: Polity.

Smith,A. (1991) *National Identity*, London: Penguin.
Smith,D. and Tomlinson,S. (1989) *The School Effect: A Study of Multi-racial Comprehensives*, London: Policy Studies Institute.
Spates,J. (1983) 'The Sociology of Values', in R.Turner (ed.), *Annual Review of Sociology*, 9, Palo Alto, CA: Annual Reviews.
Spender,D. (1982) *Women of Ideas and What Man Has Done to Them: From Aphra Behn to Adrienne Rich*, London: Routledge.
Stacey,J. (1996) *In the Name of the Family: Rethinking Family Values in the Postmodern Age*, Boston, MA: Beacon Press.
Stanworth,M. (1983) *Gender and Schooling: A Study of Sexual Divisions in the Classroom*, London: Huntchinson.
Stanworth, M. (1987) *Reproductive Technologies; Gender, Motherhood and Medicine*
Stone,L. (1977) *The Family, Sex and Marriage in England 1500–1800*, New York: Harper & Row.
Storr,M. (1999) 'Postmodern BiSexuality', *Sexualities*, 2 (3): 309–63.
Strauss,M. and Gelles,R. (1986) 'Societal Change and Change in Family Violence From 1975 to 1985 as Revealed in Two National Surveys', *Journal of Marriage and the Family*, 48 (4): 465–79.
Stryker,S. (1987) 'Identity Theory: Developments and Extensions', in L.Yardley and T.Honess (eds), *Self and Identity*, Chichester: John Wiley & Sons.
Tew,M. (1990) *Safer Childbirth? A Critical History of Maternity Care*, London: Chapman & Hall.
Thew,N. (2000) 'Race, Class and Gender', in J.Mills and R.Mills (eds), *Childhood Studies: A Reader in Perspectives of Childhood*, Routledge: London.
Thomson,R. Bell,R., Holland,J., Henderson,S., McGrellis,S., and Sharpe,S. (2002) 'Critical Moments: Choice, Chance and Opportunity in Young People's Narratives of Transition', *Sociology*, 36 (2): 335–54.
Titmus,S. (1962) *The Two Nations of Old Age*, Basingstoke: Macmillan.
Tomlinson,J. (1999) *Gobalization and Culture*, Oxford: Polity Press.
Townsend,P. (1979) *Poverty in the UK*, Harmondsworth: Penguin.
Townsend,P. (1987) *Poverty and Labour in London*, London: Low Pay Unit.
Townsend,P. and Walker,N. (1983) (eds), *Inequalities in Health: The Black Report*, Harmondsworth: Penguin.
Troll,B. (1979) *Looking Ahead*, Englewood Cliffs: Prentice Hall.
Tunstall,J. (1966) *Old and Alone: A Sociological Study of Old People*, London: Routledge & Kegal Paul.
Uhlenberg,P. (1969) 'A Study of Cohort Life Cycles', *Population Studies*, 23: 407–20.
Vincent,J. (1996) *Inequality and Old Age*, London: UCL Press.
Waites,M. (2003) 'Equality at Last? Homosexuality, Heterosexuality and the Age of Consent in the United Kingdom', *Sociology*, 37 (4): 637–55.
Walker,A. and Maltby,T. (1997) *Ageing Europe*, Buckingham: Open University Press.
Wallace,M. (1990) *Black Macho and the Myth of the Superwoman*, London: Verso.
Walter,T. (1994) *The Revival of Death*, London: Routledge
Walter,T. (1995) *The Eclipse of Eternity: Religion and Death in the Modern Era*, Basingstoke: Macmillan.
Walter,T. (1999a) *On Bereavement: The Culture of Grief*, Buckingham: Open University Press.
Walter,T. (1999b) 'Popular Afterlife Beliefs in the Modern West', in P.Badham and C.Becker (eds), *Death and Eternal Life in the World Religions*, London: Paragon.
Walter,T. and Waterhouse,H. (1998) *The Meaning of Reincarnation in Contemporary England*, Unpublished research paper.
Ward,J. (1976) *Social Reality for the Adolescent Girl*, Swansea: University College of Swansea, Faculty of Education.
Warr,P. Banks,M., and Ullah,P. (1985) 'The Experience of Unemployment Among Black and White Urban Teenagers', *British Journal of Psychology*, 76: 45–55.
Waters,M. (1995) *Globalization*, New York: Routledge.
Weber,M. (1978) *Economy and Society: An Outline of Interpretive Sociology*, G.Roth and C.Wittich (eds) Berkeley, CA: University of California Press.
Weeks,J. (1985) *Sexuality*, London: Routledge.
Weeks,J. (1990) 'The Value of Difference', in J.Rutherford (ed.), *Identity*, London: Lawrence & Wishart.

Weston,K. (1991) *Families We Choose: Lesbians, Gays, Kinship*, New York: Columbia University Press.

Westwood,S. and Bhachu,P. (1988) (eds), *Enterprising Women: Ethnicity, Economy and Gender Relations*, London: Routledge.

Whiting,J., Kluckhohn,C., and Anthonu,A. (1958) 'The Function of Male Initiation Ceremonies at Puberty', in C.MacCoby et al. (eds), *Readings in Social Psychology*, New York: Henry Holt.

Whittaker,J. (1997) *Caring for Troubled Children: Residential Treatment in a Community*, New York: Aldine de Gryter.

Willis,P. (1977) *Learning to Labour*, Farnborough: Saxon House.

Winn,M. (1983) *Children Without Childhood*, New York: Pantheon Books.

Witzel,L. (1975) 'Behaviour of the Dying Patient', *British Medical Journal*, 2 (12), April: 73–90.

Wyatt, G. (1997) Stolen *Women: Reclaiming Our Sexuality, Taking Back Our Lives*, New York: Wiley.

Wyness,M. (2000) *Contesting Childhood*, London: Falmer

Wysocki,D. (1998) 'Let Your Fingers Do the Talking: Sex on an Adult Chat-line', *Sexualities*, 1 (4): 425–52.

Yates,R. (1986) 'Self-Managed Work Teams: Innovation in Progress', *Business and Economics Quarterly*, Fall–Winter: 2–6.

Yeatman,A. (1994) *Postmodern Revisioning of the Political*, London: Routledge.

Young,M. and Willmott,P. (1957) *Family and Kinship in East London*, Harmondsworth: Penguin.

Young,M. and Willmott,P. (1962) *Family and Class in a London Suburb*, London: New English Library.

Young,M. and Willmott,P. (1973) *The Symmetrical Family*, London: Routledge & Kegan Paul.

Index